Applied UNIX® Programming
Volume I

Bharat Kurani

P T R Prentice Hall
Englewood Cliffs, New Jersey 07632

Library of Congress - Catalog in Publication Data
Kurani, Bharat.
    Applied UNIX programming / Bharat Kurani,
        p.   cm.
    Includes index.
    ISBN 0-13-304338-X (v. 1)
      1. UNIX (Computer file)   2. Computer software--Development.
    I.Title.
    QA76.76.o63K86 1993
    005.13'3--dc20   94-861
                                     CIP

Editorial/production supervision: *Ann Sullivan*
Cover design: *Aren Graphics*
Buyer: *Alexis R. Heydt*
Acquisitions editor: *Mike Meehan*
Editorial assistant: *Nancy Boylan*

©1994 by P T R Prentice Hall
Prentice-Hall, Inc.
A Paramount Communications Company
Englewood Cliffs, New Jersey 07632

In Chapter 1, parts of the section on the History of Open Systems is from "The Evolution of Open Systems", a white paper prepared by 88open Consortium, Ltd., San Jose, California, January 1992. Also the section on Standards Organization is derived from "The World of Standards" an Open Systems Reference Guide, Edition 2, published by 88open Consortium, Ltd., 1991. Information is reproduced with permission of 88open Consortium, Ltd.

The information in italics contained in Chapter 2 is copyrighted information of the Institute of Electrical and Electronics Engineers, Inc., extracted from IEEE 1003.1-1998. This information was written within the context of this document in its entirety. The IEEE takes no responsibility or liability for and will assume no liability for any damages resulting in the reader's misinterpretation of said information resulting from the placement and context in this publication. Information is reproduced with the permission of the IEEE.

The section on Automated X Testing in Chapter 3 is derived from an article by Alex Azulay in "X Journal", May 1993 issue with the permission of Alex Azulay of Mercury Interactive Corporation.

The publisher offers discounts on this book when ordered in bulk quantities. For more information, contact: Corporate Sales Department, PTR Prentice Hall, 113 Sylvan Avenue, Englewood Cliffs, NJ 07632; Phone: 201-592-2863; FAX: 201-592-2249

Printed in the United States of America
10 9 8 7 6 5 4 3 2 1

0-13-304338-X

Prentice-Hall International (UK) Limited, *London*
Prentice-Hall of Australia Pty. Limited, *Sydney*
Prentice-Hall Canada Inc., *Toronto*
Prentice-Hall Hispanoamericana, S.A., *Mexico*
Prentice-Hall of India Private Limited, *New Delhi*
Prentice-Hall of Japan, Inc., *Tokyo*
Simon & Schuster Asia Pte. Ltd., *Singapore*
Editora Prentice-Hall do Brasil, Ltda., *Rio de Janeiro*

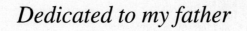

Dedicated to my father

Contents

C H A P T E R 2 UNIX Model and Terminology   28

CHAPTER 6 The C++ Language

Preface

Introduction

The introduction of ANSI C, C++, POSIX, ABI, and CDE standards for the UNIX® environment in recent years has opened up a new arena of software design and coding techniques. This also has changed how one implements the operating system, compilers, programming languages, libraries, and the like, and writes applications adhering to these standards. The goal is not only to achieve interoperability of software across different UNIX platforms, but across many international languages as well, thus reducing software development and porting costs.

Many good books, technical papers, and magazine articles have been written on operating systems, compilers, programming languages, software design, coding, testing, X window programming, and the like. All these have been effectively used by software professionals to write excellent programs. Today, applications are written by students of many disciplines who may or may not be familiar with the entire software production process. The objective of APPLIED UNIX PROGRAMMING, Volume 1, is to provide the software development process, software internationalization, and C and C++ programming language features in a single book within the frame work of new standards to write portable applications. This also eliminates the need to refer to many books.

This book covers open systems evolution, the UNIX model and terminology, software development, software internationalization, software localization, and C and C++ programming languages with numerous application examples. In each section, theory is followed by an application program with the source code listing and output. The program source also contains comments explaining the theory implementation. This makes it a good practical reference.

This book can be used as a college text for undergraduate or graduate level software engineering and programming courses. It covers various new software globalization concepts, as well as C and C++ programming language features. Every section is followed by program source code with program output, which helps students to quickly grasp the subject matter.

Chapter 3, on software design and testing, offers a complete practical approach to writing a software application. A small organization or a start-up venture may find it a very useful guide. It also includes new internationalization and localization quality specification definitions, crucial to providing user interfaces in different languages. The software tester will find the sections on automated X testing beneficial. International software vendors and language translators will find chapters on software internationalization very helpful. The reader of this book should be conversant with UNIX commands, shell, and environment. Familiarity with the data structures and algorithm is not required but advisable.

Structure of the Book

This textbook is divided into six chapters

Chapter 1, Open Systems, contains a discussion on open systems evolution and various standards bodies and their activities. The history of open systems (usually associated with the UNIX operating system) gives a snapshot of the past, present, and future. Important standards organizations are discussed to allow the reader to participate in the refinement of current implementation and contribute to future development of open interface standards.

Chapter 2, UNIX Model and Terminology, covers the UNIX system structure. The UNIX glossary as specified by the IEEE 1003.1 POSIX committee is presented here. This chapter also contains libraries, important header files, and error description. Signal generation and delivery process are also explained. This will help the UNIX novice to understand the UNIX model.

Chapter 3, Software Design and Testing, details the entire software development process. The process is explained with an xdtool (X application to search dictionary words and display the descriptions) example, including the program source code listing. It contains the software specification form (SSF), software design form (SDF), software coding form (SCF), software testing form (STF), software release form (SRF), and software user form (SUF). Also, corresponding documents are presented for the xdtool application. The items listed in all these forms can be easily applied to many applications with some variations by software designer, coder, tester, and documentation writers to track the development of the software by filling in the required data for a given application.

Chapter 4, Internationalization, describes the programming interface to the UNIX System V software globalization and localization features. The intended audience is application programmers and language translators. Practical examples in languages such as French, German, Italian, Swedish, Chinese, Taiwanese Chinese, Korean, and Japanese, with the source code listing and translated message file are presented. Both X/Open® catgets and the Sun Microsystems® gettext message catalog scheme are covered.

Chapter 5, The C Language, covers basic theory and new enhanced features with examples of program code and program output. It includes a discussion on the static and dynamic library development process. Pointer assignment rules to assign a pointer to a memory address are also presented. The application developer will find this discussion of new features very helpful.

Chapter 6, The C++ Language, offers a new approach to writing large, complex programs. The object-oriented programming concepts of objects, encapsulation, polymorphism, and inheritance are covered. This chapter provides 90+ program source code listings with program output. It includes recent templates, references, and operator overloading features.

Examples in the Book

This is an example-oriented book. In every section, theory is followed by tested program source code and output. Figures have been used for explanation where applicable. There are about 200+ program source code listings with output. Every program also contains comments explaining theory. The program source code is also available on a floppy disk included with the book. This will allow the reader to play with the programs while learning. The example programs are based on the basics of a variety of subjects, such as algebra, chemistry, computer science, engineering, geometry, mathematics, and physics. Chapter 4s translated European and Asian files are also included. All the source code has been written from scratch by the author.

All the programs have been tested on a variety of platforms such as Sparc® running Solaris® 1.1, Sparc running Solaris 2.3, and Intel® 486 running Univel® 4.2. Programs using UNIX System V Release 4 features will not work on UNIX System V Release 3. The programs were also compiled and tested against GNU C and the C++ release 2.4.5 compiler.

Acknowledgments

First, I would like to thank my wife, Usha, for providing continuous support in finishing this project and helping me with choosing the title page name and designing the cover page.

I am very grateful to Ginger Ferguson of SunSoft® for proofreading and reviewing my chapters. From time to time she provided me with very good suggestions to enhance the quality of the book. She tested programs from Chapter 4 and made them better. She also translated the English text of the program source of Chapter 4 into Swedish and Spanish.

I would like to thank Michael Meehan, executive editor of Prentice Hall, for supporting this project and providing technical reviews to improve the contents of the book.

Many thanks to the technical reviewers: Don Merusi; his comments: "An appealing professional and reference text, idea of standards, openness, and portability is carried to the ultimate in Chapter 4... a comprehensive book that discusses software testing, an extremely important part of software production," Jack Beidler (Computer Science Department, University of Scranton, PA); his comments: "The audience is any software developer who is working in a UNIX environment and understands the importance of reuse.... The C++ templates and operator overloading examples nicely illustrate object-oriented features."

Thanks to SunSoft's Gary Hethcoat for German, Melissa Biggs for Italian, Marine Metais for French, Ik Kim for Korean, Shinobu Matsuzuka for Japanese, and Roland Wang for Chinese translations of English text of the program source code in Chapter 4. And finally I would like to thank Cindy Hall for copyediting, and reviewing some chapters, as well as providing desktop publishing support.

The author would like to sincerely thank the Usenet community for quick replies to technical issues. The author can be contacted for any comments or suggestions at bck@netcom.com.

Open Systems

1.1 Introduction

This is an age of information processing that calls for the exchange of data at the speed of light in a usable format at any level, but in the real world it is limited by the entity processing data. In the computing domain the entity is both hardware and software. At the hardware level there exists a variety of computer systems running on different CPUs or microprocessors. At the software level there is a variety of operating systems and associated calls running on computer systems. The large combinations of hardware and software are a bottleneck for the seamless flow of data; there are probably few computer users who have not encountered hardware compatibility or software portability problems. The easiest way to tackle the problem is to address the exchange of data at the software level with certain guidelines and rules. This allows natural growth of computer systems with higher speeds and computing power. Open systems are those in which one can choose from any component—hardware or software from a variety of vendors—without changing or making obsolete any other part of the system. Three commonly accepted components defining a open systems are:

- **Adherence to standards**
- **Vendor independence**
- **Compatible software**

The degree of openness is first measured by compliance with industry standards. Second, by relying on an openly available standard, multiple vendors can produce competitive, yet compatible, products. Third, the software must be certified to be compatible across multiple variant systems at the user's level. One can then construct a multivendor network of compatible and interoperable computers, as in Figure 1-1.

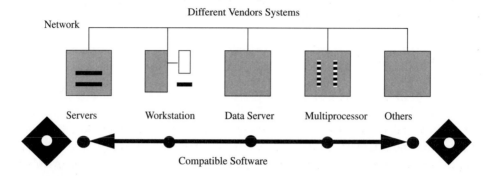

Figure 1-1
Multivendor network of compatible and inter operable computers

This chapter looks into the definition of open systems, a brief history of the evolution of open systems and their future, and the various standards organizations.

1.2   Definition of Open Interface Standards

Open interface standards are defined as a set of freely available, well-documented computer and communication interface principles.

1.3   Definition of Open Systems

Open systems are multivendor computer and communications environments based on agreed upon, freely available interface standards. The interface standards should not be controlled by a single vendor.

1.4   True Open Systems

Systems based on UNIX operating systems adhering to related interface standards are true open systems because the standards are freely available and not controlled by a single entity.

1.5   Pseudo Open Systems

Apart from UNIX and other operating systems, there are some major success-ful operating systems in the computer industry,

- MS-DOS, MS-Windows by Microsoft Corporation
- Apple A/UX by Apple Computer Inc.
- VMS by Digital Equipment Corporation

Systems based on the these operating systems fall under pseudo open sys-tems, for although they *do* adhere to single interface standards and provide source, object, and binary compatibility, the interface standards are controlled by single entity or organization.

1.6   Open Systems Versus PC Clone Technology

If one compares the open systems based on UNIX operating systems and the PC clone technology running DOS or OS/2 operating systems, the open sys-tems have the technological edge over the PC clone technology.

The open systems are based on internationally agreedupon standards. They allow innovation in differing architectures, operating systems or variants, buses, or drives. The systems vendors can effectively design their own machines anyway they want—they can move the operating system around a bit, add dual processing, or increase the speed. The end user gets the best of both worlds—a choice of software vendors with the same technology and a full range of systems, all with aggressively innovative technology.

In the case of PC clone technology, the computer vendors dissect the most pop-ular selling machines and literally create another machine with the same chipset, hardware, and operating system. This replication process is necessary to guarantee that the machine runs the same off-the-shelf software that is being run on the leading brand. The machine is usually the best selling brand name (take the example of the IBM PC and clones); the only difference is price. This has produced an advantage of increased choice of hardware in the market with low prices and of off-the-shelf software, but it has also limited the range of choice and innovation for end users. Since the original successful DOS version of operation was based on 16 bits the subsequent DOS versions had to stick with 16 bits for backward compatibility reasons. This inhibited the full exploitation of the Intel 32-bit 386 and 486 and the 64-bit Pentium microprocessor power. The introduction of Windows NT operating system by Microsoft is an example of trying to break from 16 to 32-bit technology.

1.7   Advantages of Open Systems

1. Systems built using open interface standards provide portability of software across standard computer platforms from the same computer manufacturer.

2. Systems built using open interface standards from different system manufacturers provide interoperability of software between different systems.

3. The cost of developing software for open systems is reduced. The development costs are lower because the development staff need skills in only one computing environment, and also because moving an application from one open system to another is very easy.

4. The cost of maintaining the software is greatly reduced. Maintenance overhead is dramatically cut because there will be only one source code version of the product, however many hardware platforms can be supported.

5. The cost of software documentation is reduced since there is only one version of the product.

6. The cost of selling open systems software is low, for the product can be sold off the shelf, providing a larger market share and also eliminating site visits to install software.

7. For open systems that are binary compatible, the cost of selling software can be dramatically reduced, because the porting costs are totally eliminated and product sales volume goes up. The MS-DOS, MS-WINDOWS, and Apple software have been overwhelmingly successful because of binary upward and backward compatibility.

8. Open systems have particularly advantages for independent software vendors (ISVs) and value-added resellers (VARs)

- Reduced support costs for multiple environments; in particular, multiple chip architectures can be supported by a single set of source code
- Cost of training and recruiting appropriate skilled staff is reduced, providing a greater return on investments
- Access to a wide market
- Lower prices for the software product

1.8 History of Open Systems

The exact time, date, and the place of inception of open systems is unknown, lost in the day to day beginnings of computer history. It certainly was not a single moment in time. However, the first demand for open systems must have arisen early in the 1950s when an agency of the federal government, such as the Bureau of Census or Los Alamos National Laboratory, tried to work with two different manufacturer's computers at the same time. The machines may have been a Remington-Rand UNIVAC 1 and an IBM 703 or any other equally incompatible combination. Each machine cost several million dollars to purchase and several million more to write software for and to support. Machine language had to be hand-coded and punched onto paper tape twice; separate tape readers, printers, and operators were required. Sharing tapes or punched card decks among different machines was out of question.

During this era, the programmers and managers began to realize that this doubling of effort and equipment was not just a necessary part of the technology, but rather was a costly waste of time, energy and money. The only choice that existed was to buy systems from one system manufacturer. The change from one vendor to another involved tens of millions of dollars committed to an unproven entity. The dream of an open system had begun. Table 1-1 shows the evolution of open systems.

1.8.1 1955–1965: The First Multivendor Standards

In the 1950s and early 1960s, the performance of computing machines increased by leaps and bounds, and computer design focused on segregating the various functions of the system input, compute engine, and output. Simultaneously, software designers achieved the same independence with the introduction of higher-level languages. Software code could be separately processed into machine language. From frustration with the drudgery of individual machine code of the early 1950s, came the ability to write in a more understandable, although rigidly controlled language that could potentially be used on machines from different manufacturer.

Table 1-1 Evolution of Open Systems

	Late 1960s	Early 1970s	Late 1970s	Early 1980s	Late 1980s	Early 1990s
Multivendor binary compatibility		IBM System/370		IBM PC/XT/AT clones	Sun Sparc clones 88open BCS	IBM/Apple/ Motorola alliance
UNIX standards	Original AT&T UNIX	Berkeley	System III	System V	POSIX SVR4	OSF/1 SVR4 MP
Connectivity standards	IBM 2780/3780 emulation	HASP (Multileaving RJE) DECNet	IBM 3270 emulation IBM SNA TCP/IP	OSI Reference Model Ethernet	Sun NFS X.11 FDDI	OSF DCE
User interface standards				DOS Command Interpreter	OSF/Motif Sun OPEN LOOK	Microsoft Windows 3.0/3.1 CDE
Certification and verification					POSIX X/Open XPG COSE	SVVS ITS

FORTRAN, first released by IBM in 1957, was widely copied by other vendors, becoming the first product to span different vendors and systems. As each vendor sought to outdo the other, multiple, slightly different versions of FORTRAN proliferated from different computer vendors. In an attempt to bring order to chaos, the American Standards Association (later the American National Standards Institute, or ANSI) established a FORTRAN committee in 1962, producing the first FORTRAN standards in 1966. For the first time, substantially identical source code could be recompiled and run on different machines with only minor modifications. A new advance in open systems had been made.

Multivendor compatibility brought a new measure of choice into the market. Software created for one machine could now, at least in theory, run on different machines with only the cost of recompiling and testing the software. While each vendor still kept their own proprietary extensions in their product, necessitating software changes to make this compatibility work, it was a great leap forward. Unfortunately, although the custom application could move relatively easily, the banks of existing data were not so portable, and elaborate schemes had to be concocted in order to move the lifeblood of the organization—the information itself—between systems from different vendors. Still, the concept of source-level compatible software was introduced.

1.8.2   1965–1975: The First Pseudo Open Systems

An early version of a later stage in open systems made its debut in the late 1960s with the first third-party hardware for the market-dominant IBM System/370 mainframes. Remote job entry (RJE) stations from third-party vendors that were compatible with IBM/2780, 3780, and HASP workstations allowed batch jobs to be submitted to IBM mainframes from non-IBM equipment. Other vendors introduced compatible terminals and disk drives. In the early 1970s, a major data center could run IBM's MVS, VM, or DOS/VSE operating systems entirely on IBM-compatible, non-IBM hardware, Amdahl processors, 3270-compatible Memorex terminals, STC disk drives, and IBM 3705-compatible Comten front-end processors. Customers, with the help of small, innovative suppliers, had for the first time wrenched a measure of independence from a domineering vendor. It would happen many items again over the next 20 years, most spectacularly in the PC revolution. It was the first instance of the clone approach to open systems, and it offered users a real choice at most levels of their computing needs.

An unexpected effect of this first clone market was the creation of a legion of smaller suppliers with strong technical capability. Previously, when the supplier had to be able to provide entire solutions to customers on their own, the cost of entry to the market was prohibitive for all but the largest companies. With the dawn of the plug-compatible era, smaller companies had an opportunity to participate. The inevitable result was a far larger group of competitors in the market than ever before. Like all competitors, this new group demanded ever increasing opportunities to compete, supporting the nascent march toward standards and market access.

Plug compatibility was a great leap forward, and the companies that made it work are among the largest contributors to today's computer industry. By cloning the IBM/370, several companies and IBM were able to expand a market, deliver very high priced products in a controlled competitive environment, and give users a choice of vendor. Strings remained attached, however. The architecture, designs, features, capabilities, and ultimately the price structure were under the control of the dominant player IBM. The participating suppliers could not offer truly differentiated products without jeopardizing what users were demanding above all else: complete compatibility was essential to eliminate the problem of reinvesting in software programs, service, user education, and data transfer. These costs were simply prohibitive in considering moving from one supplier to another.

1.8.3 1975–1985: Multivendor Interoperability

Whereas the early 1970s saw the first instance of multivendor binary compatibility, the mid to late 1970s saw the first steps toward interoperability. It was at this time that DEC, HP, Data General, Prime, and Wang introduced departmental minis that could use IBM de facto standard protocols (2780, 3780, HASP, 3270) to exchange data with the mainframe and each other. In 1974, in an attempt to gain control of newly emerging computer networks, IBM introduced the first network architecture, Systems Network Architecture (SNA), allowing interactive file and data-base access among IBM systems—and only IBM systems. Other vendors followed suit with their own proprietary networks: Digital and DECnet in 1975 and HP with HP-Distributed Systems Network in 1977. However, departments in major accounts using the mini-makers systems needed to communicate with corporate IBM mainframes. The need to solve this problem provided the mini-makers with an incentive, and vendors soon cracked the SNA code to allow their minis to be part of an IBM network as well.

Once again, a technological innovation shared among a select group of participants created a choice for users. Now, combining source-level recompilation, data transfer, and increasingly similar hardware architectures, a user could realistically consider moving among suppliers. At the same time, the costs of all these transitions was still heavy, and the typical response was to add new systems around the old ones, rather than replace the core. The ball and chain of binary compatibility was not loosened by interoperability. Further more, the basis of the new interoperability was in the hands of the dominant vendor, and all those who wished to participate in its market had to compete based on their ability to zig when IBM zigged, and zag when it zagged. Freedom of choice was still illusory.

While the early FORTRAN standards by ANSI became the first noncompany-driven standard, they were still derived from IBM origins. In contrast, the International Standards Organization's (ISO) Open Systems Interconnect (OSI) Reference Model for communications in data networks did not have specific product origins. The first workable versions of the now famous seven-layer model emerged in the late 1970s, providing standards for connecting computer data networks. For the first time, vendors could promote compliance with common, international standards, rather than either their own or an IBM-proprietary protocol. ISO would take may years to flesh out the seven layers of the OSI model, but its open-door process, along with those of other standards bodies such as ANSI and the Institute for Electrical and Electronics Engineers (IEEE), would help shift market demand from proprietary networking schemes to industry-standard ones. Compatibility with existing "legacy systems" still controlled the market with a clone open systems approach, but another step in the evolution of open systems had been reached—interoperability.

Interoperability as a form of open systems did indeed free the buyer from having to work with a particular vendor. Now not only could programs be moved through recompilation of source code, but the data themselves could be moved. A true measure of freedom had arrived, although it would take many years to come to the point where it was an easy transition. In fact, that point has still not entirely been reached today. Interoperability still requires the user to learn a completely new system and to recompile and retest all application code, a substantial expense. It has made the competing system more expensive—a form of financial handcuffs unacceptable in a world dedicated to user choice and a level competitive playing field.

1.8.3.1 The Rise of UNIX

Toward the end of the 1970s, the first commercial implementations of AT&T's UNIX operating systems appeared as an adjunct to the rise of a mid-range market. The genie in UNIX was that the operating system itself had become portable to machines of different architectures (or processor instructions sets). Written in a high-level language C, UNIX could itself be recompiled to run (much like FORTRAN programs) on a different machines while making only small adjustments in the code. This allowed the operating environment for applications to look much the same on any number of systems in the market. Applications could be ported among different vendor's systems much more easily than among those with proprietary or different operating systems, such as IBM MVS, DEC VMS, and HP MPE. Users in scientific and engineering fields, where UNIX was first adopted, were the first to experience the freedom that UNIX provided from re-coding entire applications when moving them among platforms with different architectures.

Another side effect of the advent of UNIX and AT&T's willingness to license the product to anyone who wanted it was yet another reduction in the cost of entering the market, No longer did a company need to invest millions of dollars in creating an operating system from scratch. Nor for that matter, was the company left on its own to create compilers and other application software. By incorporating UNIX, a company could bring a new product to market much more cheaply and quickly. The cost of entry had tumbled again, and, just as day follows night and economics sometimes works, a host of new, aggressive competitors entered the market. Users found they had even more choice. In the early days it was a low-quality, underpowered choice, but nevertheless it was a good beginning. By the late 1980s and early 1990s, UNIX could offer equal quality and power to any of the original offerings at a fraction of the cost.

With the UNIX revolution, the spiraling evolution of open systems continued, this time revisiting the source code compatibility area. The addition of a common operating environment to the source code compatibility of higher-level languages gave users the ability to choose between system vendors with even less cost in transferring software and data. Further more, the development of a set of file and data transfer protocols, including such now well known protocols as TCP/IP and NFS, ensured interoperability between these architecturally different, but source-compatible systems. A true subculture of open systems was beginning to develop, populated by users, software suppliers, and vendors who were convinced that multivendor compatibility would drive costs down, thereby creating unprecedented demand in the market.

Yet, while the foundations were laid, several obstacles still lay in the way. First, the power of the new open systems was simply not up to the capabilities of the mainframe systems. New applications had to be found, applications that would sustain their own market until a true challenge to the high priced systems could be made. Second, the legacy systems did not interoperate well with the new open environment. While TCP/IP became ubiquitous in the UNIX world, it remained largely nonexistent in the legacy world, with IBM fighting to protect its world from encroachment by the new systems. Adding to the obstacles was the lack of legacy applications software that had been ported to the new environment to accept all the accumulated data. Finally, each new system was still a different system, with only paper compatibility. Each had its own proprietary additions or interpretations of the UNIX standard. Even when there was a commitment to a single standard, there was no way to prove that the commitment had been carried out. Many of the costs of recompiling, retesting, and modifying software remained.

1.8.3.2 Rise of the Desktop PC

While System/370-compatible mainframes had brought a minimal form of open systems to powerful, central data centers, the IBM PC and its clones brought the concept, and a limited piece of the reality, of choice to the masses. Begun in 1977 with the creation of the first Apple computer in a fabled garage and solidified by the introduction of the IBM PC in 1981, the face of the information age was changed forever. The most obvious result, often overlooked because it is so obvious was that the basic price of a powerful computing engine came within the reach of even the most miserly individual, creating a huge community of users, each of which made separate decisions to buy. No longer were the decisions made by a select few in MIS departments for employees who would follow exactly the rules laid down by the needs of the computing application. Instead, low cost computers and their inherent flexibility meant that each participant was a decision maker, choosing which product to use and what to use it for. These decision makers were also far less willing to deal with technical issues. Their buying choices were heavily influenced by ease of use and suitability of the application to their daily tasks. Chief among these criteria was the need for similar look and feel (lower training time) and absolutely no compatibility issues.

Second, the PC introduced multivendor, clone style, binary compatibility and a billion-dollar market for shrink-wrapped software to the masses. With such a large market, the price floors could not be contained and competition reigned. The control dynamics of the previous era of clone binary compatibility—the IBM/370—could not be repeated. Hundreds of vendors participated, minimizing the architectural control of the founders. Still, the same decisions resulted: the masses chose systems that allowed them choice over better product while requiring an absolute compatibility between systems so as not to incur the costs of recompiling, retesting, data transfer, and user education when moving from vendor to vendor. The PCs solved this by restricting themselves to a single architectural design including the operating system, the hardware design, and the microprocessor chip itself. Thus, the age of the clone open systems had arrived.

Cloning was a mixed blessing for users because it provided choice with strings. Its reliance on copycat technology protected those in other markets from significant competition. PCs could not become large systems, in spite of all the claims to the contrary. Clones were essentially not scalable to the full range of system needs of major organizations, and thus compatibility among all elements of the computing organization was not available. Further more, because of the software compatibility relied wholly on the hardware and operating system not changing, innovation and creative design were minimized, leaving users once again without choice in a technological sense. Finally, cloning allowed certain vendors— in this case the chip maker and the operating system vendor to control the flow of the market. These two companies became the necessary ingredients, allowing them to control pricing, the rate of technical innovation, and, as a result, the entire spectrum of choices that were made by users. Clones were not the ideal open systems.

1.8.4   1985–1994: Multivendor RISC Compatibility

By the late 1980s, different version of open systems were available to serve different clientele, and the components of today's computing environment were in place. Data-center computing, networking, and communications, and finally individual computers had proliferated throughout the world, but each with a different open systems paradigm. Open systems had reached such a level of conscious development that organizations to develop the standards that would underlie them were created. The first such organizations were

IEEE's POSIX committees, X/Open, and ultimately, in late 1980s, UNIX International and the Open Software Foundation.

At the same time, the technology wheel was turning once again. The power of commercially available microprocessors took a long leap forward with the introduction of a new technique called <u>reduced instruction set computing</u>, or RISC. With this new technology, poised to replace existing systems from desktops to mainframes, the key issue of open systems, compatibility, has come to a head.

1.8.5 1994 and Beyond: ANDF, Architecture Neutral Distribution Format

An ideal solution is to eliminate the dependence of software on variations in chip design. RISC technology takes us part of the way by reducing the number of instructions that the microprocessor must interpret. Since the bottom 70 or so instructions are the same throughout the industry, reducing the number above that minimizes the differences. With today's RISC technology, less than 50% of the remaining instructions need to address compatibility issues. As performance capabilities of the chip increase, it is entirely reasonable to assume that the chip itself will begin to provide trap and emulate capabilities to handle instructions that might come from foreign binary software.

A second approach that shows promise is the <u>architecture neutral distribution format</u> (ANDF) technology being worked on by the Open Software Foundation. ANDF essentially allows software applications code to be distributed without regard to the underlying microprocessor instruction set by relying on an ANDF installer that must be put on every machine.

1.9   The Future of Open Systems

The problem with software and system standards in the past was twofold. First, the standards were set at the source level. Although this provided substantial compatibility, the process of compiling on a particular machine and linking with system resources inevitably introduced differences. Unless the entire system was essentially identical—chip, hardware design, operating system, compiler—the resulting software was not transferable to other systems in binary or shrinkwrapped form. Second, even when de facto binary standards existed by the proof case of a clone leader like the IBM PC, there was no guarantee in place to test the compatibility. To address the issue of compatibility, as well as to create market presence, each new entrant has created alliances. Some of these are Power Open Association representing the Apple/IBM/ Motorola alliance and the Power Chip, Sparc International representing the Sun and SPARC companies, ACE representing the Mips community, 88open Consortium representing Motorola 88000 processor, and PRO Member Consortium representing Hewlett-Packard PA RISC architecture.

In mid June of 1993, six major UNIX system suppliers introduced the Common Desktop Environment (CDE) part of the Common Open Software Environment (COSE). It incorporates aspects of HP's Visual User Environment (VUE); IBM's Common User Access mode and Workplace Shell; the Open Software Foundations Motif toolkit and Window Manager; SunSoft's ToolTalk software with an incorporated HP Encapsulator and OPEN LOOK and DeskSet productivity tools; and USL's UNIX SVR4.2 desktop manager components and scalable systems technologies.

For compatibility the alliances have introduced two innovative test suites: (1) system testing for operating systems interface standards and (2) software testing through application compatibility tests. The hierarchy of open systems is shown in Figure 1-2.

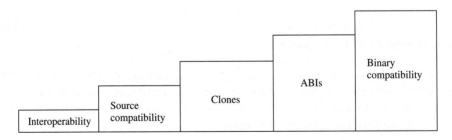

Figure 1-2
Hierarchy of open systems

Meanwhile, open systems will continue to evolve. When the day arrives that a user can change vendors or add a vendor to an existing installation without either having to pay an additional penalty for compatibility or being limited to a particular set of vendors or equipment, we will have reached the epitome of open systems. With certified, multivendor, binary compatibility, open system has broken down all the barriers but one, the instruction set of the chip itself. It was once believed that there would eventually be one chip that would become the single standard. However, this would anoint a single vendor king of the world, an uncomfortable, nonopen situation for users and vendors alike, and limit innovation.

1.10   The World of Standards

For a user to buy open systems, there should be crystal-clear, unambiguous specifications for the way the system work. There are roughly three categories of standards as discussed next.

1.10.1 International Standards

Standards set by the International Standards Organization (ISO) for Open Systems Interconnect (OSI) fall into this category. Such standards are agreed upon in an open international forum and provide the strongest possible definition of open systems. ISO's main job is to coordinate the development and formal approval of standards produced by the various national standards bodies. International standards provide a solid standardized base, defining operating system interfaces, communications protocols, and programming languages. ISO is best known for its contributions to open systems standards in communications.

1.10.2 National Standards

Each country operates its own standards bodies to set standards for industry, for controlling the localization and quality of software. National standards bodies clarify the gray area not clear in international standards. National bodies make mandatory certain optional features of an international standard or forbid the use of other options. Some of the organizations are:

AENOR, Asociación Española de Normalizació y Cretifcación in Spain
AFNOR, Association Française de Normalisation in France
ANSI, American National Standards Institute in the USA
AOW, Asia-Oceania Workshop in Japan
BSI, British Standard Institute in the UK

CSA, Canadian Standards Association in Canada
DIN, Deutsches Institut für Normung in Germany
IEEE, Institute of Electrical and Electronics Engineers in the USA
SAA, Standards Association of Australia

1.10.3 Industry Standards

Standards provided by industrial companies fall into this category. The Application Binary Interface (ABI) standard from UNIX System Laboratories (USL) provides industrial standards for UNIX System V Release 4. The generic ABI standards are common to all the system vendors, the processor-specific ABI standards are CPU and architecture-dependent, provided by each industrial CPU or microprocessor manufacturer.

1.11   Standards Organizations

This section discusses the histories and purposes of some of the important standards organizations.

1.11.1 ANSI

The American National Standards Institute (ANSI) was founded in 1918. It is a private, nonprofit membership organization responsible for coordinating the United States voluntary consensus standards system and approving American National Standards.

ANSI information technology standards provide nationally agreed-upon solutions to a wide range of information technology problems. These standards were developed primarily under the guidance of voluntary nonprofit organizations, such as the Computer and Business Equipment Manufacturers Association (CBEMA) and the Institute of Electrical and Electronics Engineers (IEEE). These groups voluntarily submit standards to ANSI for approval.

ANSI standards are widely used on a voluntary basis. Many have also been adopted as Federal Information Processing Standards (FIPS) for government procurement or for mandatory use by the Department of Defense (DoD).

ANSI also adopts standards developed by the International Organization for Standardization (ISO). These standards are produced by the ISO/IEC Joint Technical Committee 1 (JTC 1). ANSI administers the secretariat of JTC 1 and four of its subcommittees: open systems, interconnection, telecommunications, flexible magnetic media, and text and office system.

ANSI represents the United States as a member of ISO. It participates in ISO's entire technical program, holds the secretariats of 280 technical committees and subgroups, and is represented on ISO governing bodies.

Contact Information

American National Standards Institute (ANSI)
Customer Service
11 West 42nd Street
New York, NY 10036
USA
Phone: +1 (212) 642-4900

1.11.2 IEEE

The Institute of Electrical and Electronics Engineers (IEEE) was founded in 1884 by practitioners of the new electrical engineering discipline. It is the world's largest technical professional organization with more than 320,000 members in over 130 countries. Its mission is to enhance the quality of life for all people through the constructive theory and application of electrical engineering and computer science technologies. To that end, the IEEE is responsible for publishing over 20% of the world's available literature on electrotechnology.

IEEE is also recognized as a world leader in the development and dissemination of industry standards. IEEE standards provide relevant information that serves to facilitate processes, simplify communications, safeguard against hazards, and promote quality. Drafted and developed by dedicated, expert volunteers acting in their respective fields of interest, IEEE standards are subjected to a strict consensus approval process that ensures their technical integrity.

With a product line consisting of more than 600 active standards and approximately 80 new standards published annually, the IEEE is a world leader in standards development. IEEE standards span the spectrum of electrotechnology, from electric power engineering to the computer sciences. They offer relevant information relating to units and measurements, testing and rating methods, design specifications, safety codes, and more.

In addition to its publishing activities. the IEEE sponsors a seminar program that instructs users in the application of IEEE standards. It also sponsors the IEEE Standards Press, a publishing program that provides relevant information pertaining to standards and their use.

Contact Information

IEEE
Publishing Sales
445 Hoes Lane, P.O Box 1331
Piscataway, NJ 08855-1331
USA
Phone: +1 (908) 981-0060

1.11.3 ISO

The International Organization for Standardization (ISO) is a worldwide federation of standards bodies with over 90 members. ISO's mission is to promote standardization and related activities throughout the world to facilitate the international exchange of goods and services and to develop cooperation in the sphere of intellectual, scientific, technological, and economic activity.

ISO's technical work is carried out in a hierarchy of some 2,600 technical committees, subcommittees, and working groups in which more than 20,000 experts from all parts of the world participate. To date, ISO has published over 7,700 standards.

ISO standards are voluntary; they are interindustry agreements in nonregulated spheres of economic activity. National voluntary standards are often direct adoptions of ISO standards, even though such adoptions are also voluntary. Voluntary standards may also be used in regulated spheres of economic activity at the discretion of the regulator involved.

ISO cooperates with other international and regional organizations. In the field of information technology, ISO and the International Electrotechnical Commission (IEC) have established a joint technical committee, ISO/IEC JTC 1 (JTC 1). This committee, through its subcommittees, prepares standards for Open Systems Interconnection (OSI). It also prepares standards for magnetic and optical media, software engineering, electronic data interchange, application portability, programming languages, computer graphics, microprocessor systems, interfaces, security techniques, and multimedia/hypermedia.

Contact Information

International Organization for Standardization (ISO)
Central Secretariat
1, Rue de Varembé
CH-1211 Geneva 20
Switzerland
Phone: +41 22 749 0111.

1.11.4 NIST

The National Institute of Standards and Technology (NIST) was established by the U.S. Congress to assist industry in the development of the technology needed to improve product quality, to modernize manufacturing processes, to ensure product reliability, and to facilitate rapid commercialization of products based on new scientific discoveries.

A principal agency of the Commerce Department's Technology Administration, NIST has as it goals to aid U.S. industry through research and services, to contribute to aid U.S. industry through research and services, to contribute to the public health and safety, and to support the U.S scientific and engineering research communities.

NIST coordinates the development of technical and data standards and conformance tests for the Computer-aided Acquisition and Logistic Support (CALS) standardization effort. CALS is a Department of Defense (DoD) and industry strategy to transition from paper-intensive, nonintegrated weapon design, manufacturing, and support processes to a highly automated and integrated mode of operation.

The National Computer System Laboratory (NCSL) is one of NIST's major science and engineering research components. NCSL's programs seek to overcome barriers to the efficient use of computer systems, to provide cost-effective exchange of information and to protect valuable information resources in computer systems. NCSL's technical work is carried out in five divisions: Information Systems Engineering Division, Systems and Software Technology Division, Computer Security Division, Advanced Systems Division, and Systems and Network Architecture Division.

Contact Information

National Institute of Standards and Technology (NIST)
Gaithersburg, MD 20899
USA
Phone: +1 (301) 975-2000

1.11.5 OSF

The Open Software Foundation (OSF) was founded as a not-for-profit research and development organization to develop open systems software that would allow hardware and software from different vendors to work together. Today OSF has more than 300 members, including hardware and software vendors, end users, and university and research organizations, working cooperatively to further the development and adoption of open systems.

OSF provides enabling technologies, which are software that allows system and software suppliers, as well as programmers in end user organizations, to build on a common software platform. OSF's open computing environment includes the OSF/1 operating system, the OSF/Motif graphical user interface, the OSF Distributed Computing Environment (DCE), the OSF Distributed Management Environment (DME), and the OSF Architecture-Neutral Distribution Format (ANDF). These technologies comply with relevant industry standards and specifications, such as IEEE Std. 1003.1 (POSIX) and the X/Open Portability Guide (XPG), to provide interoperability among diverse systems.

Contact Information

Open Software Foundation (OSF)
OSF Direct
11 Cambridge Center
Cambridge, MA 02142
USA
Email: direct@osf.org
Phone: +1 (617) 621-7300

1.11.6 UI

UNIX International is a nonprofit organization responsible for directing the evolution of the open systems environment based on UNIX System V. UNIX International is open to all parties interested in the evolution of UNIX System V and open systems.

The organization ensures that the future enhancements and releases of System V contain the features demanded by a changing marketplace, while conforming to the specifications formulated by industry standards organizations such as X/Open. UNIX International also works to ensure that System V maintains forward compatibility for the installed base of more than 16 million UNIX system users worldwide, protecting their existing investment in software and training.

Through its one-member, one-vote system, UI has created a new model of worldwide cooperation in the information technology industry. UI provides the structure for the entire UNIX system community to directly participate in defining the direction of UNIX System V. These requirements are delivered to UNIX System Laboratories (USL), which produces and licenses the operating system code.

UI and USL have forged a successful partnership and responded to the demands of end users by providing a source and binary-compatible open system that conforms to all applicable industry standards. At the same time, UI and USL work closely with UI member companies. These technology partnerships assure that development of System V is attuned to market demands.

Contact Information

UNIX International, Inc.
Worldwide Headquarters
Waterview Corporate Centre
20 Waterview Boulevard
Parisppany, NJ 07054
USA
Phone: +1 (201) 263-8400

1.11.7 The UNICODE Consortium

The Unicode Consortium is a nonprofit organization founded in January 1991 to promote the use of Unicode as a character standard. Its first accomplishment was to formally set the specifications for Unicode version 1.0. The Unicode Consortium now provides technical information and news about Unicode, and works to maintain the Unicode standard, expanding and refining it as necessary.

The Unicode Consortium started out as an informal collaboration between engineering teams at Apple and Xerox, who produced the original design of Unicode. They were joined by representatives of several additional computer hardware and software companies concerned with handling international text files. These corporations are now part of the Unicode Technical Committee, the managing group within the Unicode Consortium that actively maintains the Unicode Standard.

The Unicode Consortium offers two types of memberships: regular membership and affiliate membership. Regular members are typically corporations and institutions that sit on the Unicode Technical Committee. Affiliate members are typically individuals interested in technical information or news releases about Unicode. They receive mailings from the consortium and are invited to give suggestions about Unicode matters to the technical committee.

Contact Information

The Unicode Consortium
1965 Charleston, Rd.

Mountain View, CA 94043
USA
Phone: +1 (415) 961-4189

1.11.8 UniForum

UniForum, the International Association of Open Systems Professionals, is a nonprofit, vendor-independent association dedicated to promoting environments running UNIX and open systems. It is a worldwide organization that serves as a forum for users, developers, and vendors to exchange information about open systems, the UNIX operating system, software, and applications. Currently, UniForum has more than 6,500 members worldwide and 31 affiliate groups in the United States and around the world.

UniForum hosts an international trade show and conference that is dedicated to UNIX system products and services. UniForum co-hosts the annual Executive UniForum Symposium with Patricia Seybold's Office Computing Group and X/Open Company Ltd. in Santa Barbara every spring. The symposium is targeted for MIS executives who want to better understand the importance of UNIX and open systems in the commercial computing environment. UniForum also jointly sponsors OpenForum, a European trade show and conference.

In addition, UniForum conducts research studies on the open systems market and provides technical services and publications, including the annual UniForum Products Directory, the biweekly UniNews newsletter, and the UniForum Monthly magazine. UniForum is also active in formal standards bodies, including IEEE's POSIX working groups and ISO/IEC SC22/WG15 and WG20 internationalization committees.

Contact Information

UniForum Association
2901 Tasman Drive, Suite 201
Santa Clara, CA 95054
USA
Phone: +1 (408) 986-8840

1.11.9 X Consortium

The X Consortium is a vendor consortium that was formed to support the further development of the X Window System (X Windows). Headquartered at the Massachusetts Institute of Technology (MIT) Laboratory for Computer Science, the X Consortium focuses on providing continued technical leadership for X software in a way that is consistent with MIT's role as a source of innovation.

The X Consortium provides formal specifications for standard X Window System (X Windows) components and releases periodic software and documentation updates. The X Consortium also sponsors an annual technical conference. These activities are supported by a full-time technical staff at MIT.

Members of the X Consortium appoint one or more technical officers to act as liaisons for consortium activities. These liaison officers review design specifications, help select architecture team members, and provide general technical advice.

Contact Information

MIT X Consortium
545 Technology Square
Cambridge, Massachusetts 02139
USA

1.11.10 X/Open

X/Open Company Ltd., founded in 1984, is a worldwide, independent, open systems organization dedicated to developing an open, multivendor Common Applications Environment (CAE) based on formal de jure standards and widely supported de facto standards. Figure 1-3 shows the X/Open CAE environment. X/Open's mission is to increase the value of computing through the practical implementation of open systems.

X/Open brings together information technology user organizations, system vendors and independent software vendors within Associate Member Councils. This council structure provides for direct input from all segments of the market and results in a practical definition of open system specifications to which products are developed and technology is evaluated for procurement. The formal specifications are contained in a set of detailed publications called the X/Open Portability Guide (XPG). The current edition of the guide is Issue 4, also referred to as XPG4.

It awards the X/Open brand trademark to products that comply with the X/Open definition, both formal and industry standards are included to make the CAE as comprehensive as possible. The relationship between POSIX, XPG, and SVID (System V Interface Definition; Specification from UNIX provider UNIX System Laboratories for various level of UNIX; it supports source code portability) is shown in Figure 1-4. X/Open in July 1993 introduced its first COSE/CDE specifications for review.

Contact Information

X/Open Company Ltd.
1010 El Camino Real, Suite 230
Menlo Park, CA 94025
USA
Phone: +1 (415) 323-7992

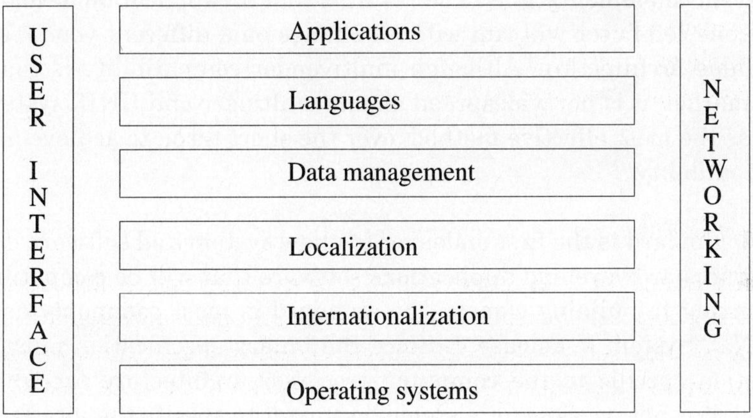

U S E R I N T E R F A C E	Applications	N E T W O R K I N G
	Languages	
	Data management	
	Localization	
	Internationalization	
	Operating systems	

Figure 1-3
The X/Open CAE

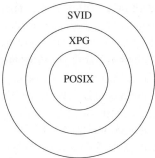

Figure 1-4
Relationship among POSIX, XPG and SVID

1.12   System V ABI Standard

An application binary interface (ABI) defines a set of interfaces that allows compiled software to be ported in binary form across different vendors' systems that share a common processor architecture. Each computer is designed to offer the same programmatic interface to its operating system but allows for different implementations. The result is that an application developed and built on one computer will run without change on a different vendor's system of the same architecture. Although multivendor compatibility is common in the PC market, it is not widespread among multiuser and UNIX systems. ABI is seen as the most effective method, over the short term, to achieve multivendor compatibility.

The ABI standard is the first endeavor to allow system and software designers to construct hardware and applications software that will be compatible without resorting to building clones. The standard is most commonly associated with UNIX System V, release 4. Since the binary specification must include information specific to the computer processor architecture for which it is intended, it is not possible for a single document to specify the interface for all possible System V implementations. ABI is a family of specifications, as opposed to a single one.

The System V ABI essentially consists of two parts: generic ABI standards (gABI) and processor-specific ABI standards (psABI).

1.12.1 Generic ABI Standards

The generic part of the specification describes the set of interfaces that remains constant across all different processor implementations. The generic ABI consists of existing standards for operating systems, user interfaces, programming languages, and networking. Some important standards are:

IEEE POSIX P1003 standard operating system specification
X/Open Portability Guide (XPG), Issue 4
System V Interface Definition (SVID), Third Edition
ANSI X3/11 C Language specification
X Window System graphical user interface specification

1.12.2 Processor-specific ABI Standards

A processor-specific part of the specification describes the set of specifications that are specific to a particular processor architecture. The processor addresses issues of dynamic linking, low-level interface definitions as described in the architecture manual for the target system's processor.

The union of generic and processor specific ABI sets for a single hardware architecture provides a complete interface specification for compiled application programs on systems that share a common hardware architecture.

1.13   Conclusion

For four decades computer systems and software have become more and more open through end user demand, competition among vendors, and vendor cooperation through industry consortia. Through open systems, system price-performance improvements have accelerated. Power has shifted from vendors to customers and from central MIS to end users; users have gained more options and greater independence from specific vendors. The trend to total open systems will continue. Hardware and software will become more compatible, interoperable, and interchangeable as they are adapted to an increasingly open environment. The recent COSE/CDE agreement is first step in that direction.

UNIX Model and Terminology

2.1   Introduction

The UNIX System V operating system adheres to open interface standards to applications and this makes UNIX System V an open system. Sometime the usage of the term open systems is synonymous to UNIX systems. This chapter explores UNIX system structure and the general terms commonly used. The glossary should guide the new student through UNIX jargon, and for experienced programmer it may act as a reference. Additional primitive system data types in the UNIX environment are covered. The section on signals covers signal names with a generic description, signal generation and delivery, signal actions, and signal effects on other functions. The error numbers with their generic meaning are covered at the end of the chapter.

2.2   UNIX System Structure

UNIX System V is a powerful general purpose operating system offering rich functionality, flexibility, and multitasking features. The UNIX System V in its simplest form can be viewed as layer of systems software that sits between the hardware and applications, as in Figure 2-1. The UNIX operating system provides an interactive user with a powerful and flexible command language interpreter known as the shell. Today the graphical user interface (GUI) offers even more powerful user interfaces.

The kernel is the core of the UNIX operating system. The kernel manages the system resources, disk drives, tape drives, cd-rom, printers and other peripherals. Although the internal workings of UNIX kernels on different hardware vary, all systems offer a standard interface to applications. Figure 2-2 shows

the architecture of the UNIX system

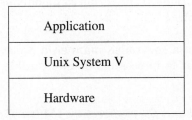

Figure 2-1
UNIX System V in simplest form

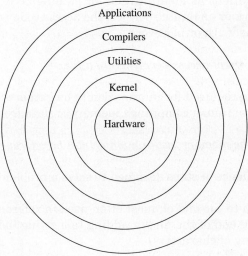

Figure 2-2
UNIX system architecture

The shell and other system utilities sit on the top of the kernel. The software development tools such as compliers, linkers, and assemblers. are one layer above the system utilities. The applications are at the topmost layer. The UNIX operating system or kernel is written in a high-level language C. The use of C and the modular design of the system make it a very portable operating system. Some salient features of the UNIX operating system are that it allows multitasking, fault-tolerant transaction processing, and high security. They are powerful gateways connecting to other open systems and to proprietary systems of all kinds.

2.3   UNIX Glossary

The following are definitions of the terms commonly used in the UNIX operating system environment.

abort: To terminate, in a controlled manner, a processing activity in a computer system because it is impossible or undesirable for the activity to proceed.

absolute pathname: *For a file or directory, the list of directories from the root directory through the tree structure to the desired file name or directory name, each name in the series separated by a slash character (/).*

access code: A unique combination of characters, usually letters or numbers, used in communications as identification for gaining access to a remote computer. On a network or an on-line service, the access code is generally referred to as user name, user ID, or password.

access mode: *A form of access permitted to a file.*

access time: Time required for information to be gathered from some remote source, such as data from a computer's memory or data from a hard disk.

address space: *The memory location which can be referenced by a process.*

algorithm: A sequence of steps designed to solve a problem.

append: To attach to the end of; most often used in reference to writing a file (adding data to the end of the file) or adding to a string (adding characters to the end of the string of characters).

application: A software program specifically designed for particular users needs or the specific use of a software program. Graphics applications are usually designed to enable the user to manipulate data or images or to create images from data or from a library of shapes. The graphical applications external interfaces are often referred as graphical user interface (GUI).

application developer: The person who creates an application for a particular user need.

application programmer's interface (API): A set of calling conventions defining how a service is invoked through a software package. The functions usually reside in libraries.

appropriate privileges: *An implementation-defined means of associating privileges with a process with regard to the function calls and function call options defined that need special privileges. There may be zero or more such means.*

architecture: The specific components of a computer system and the way they interact with one another.

archive: A collection of several files bundled into one file by a program (such as ar, tar, cpio) for shipment or archiving. A collection of several object files into a library known as a library archive.

ASCII: American Standard Code for Information exchange; a standard set of 128 characters (including letters, numbers, punctuation marks, and control commands) used to code information for data processing and data communications.

aspect ratio: In computer graphics, the ratio of a pixel's height to its width.

asynchronous: Without regular time relationship; unexpected and unpredictable with respect to the execution of a program's instructions. In a network environment, a form of data transmission in which information is sent one character at a time, with variable time intervals between characters; generally used in communicating via modem.

background process group: *Any process group that is a member of a session which has established a connection with a controlling terminal that is not in the foreground process group.*

baud rate: The rate at which information is transmitted between devices; for example, between a terminal and the computer. Usually measured in terms of number of bits per second (bps) transmitted.

big endian: A format for storage or transmission of binary data in which the most significant bit (or byte) comes first.

bit: Short for binary digit. Indicates the smallest unit of information stored in a digital memory. Binary digits indicate two possible values: on and off. A single bit is represented in memory as 0 (off) and 1 (on).

bitmap: The array of values in the frame buffer for a given picture, particularly in the case of monochrome (single-bit) displays. The term pixmap is often used for the array of pixel values in the raster in more complex gray scale or color monitors, which have more than one bit for each pixel in raster display.

block special file: *A file that refers to a device. A block special file is normally distinguished from a character special file by providing access to the device in a manner such that the hardware characteristics of the device are not visible.*

boot: To load the system software (operating system) into memory and start running.

boot server: A server system that provides client systems on the network with the programs and information that they need to start up.

bridge: A device that connects two or more physical networks and forwards packets between them.

buffer: A storage device that holds data to be eventually transmitted to another device. From a systems point of view, a temporary work area or storage area set up within the system memory. Buffers are often used by programs, such as editors, that access and alter text or data frequently.

byte: A grouping of adjacent binary digits (bits) operated on by the computer as a unit.

C Standard: *The abbreviated name for the ANSI/X3.159-198x Programming Language C Standard.*

cache: A buffer of high speed memory filled at medium speed from the main memory, often with instructions and programs. A cache increases effective memory transfer rates and processor speed.

character: *A sequence of one or more bytes representing a single graphic symbol.*

character special file: *A file that refers to a device. One specific type of character special file is a terminal device file. Other character special files have no structure defined and their use is implementation-defined.*

child process: *A process created by another usually parent process.*

class: A grouping of data having similar characteristics.

client: In the client-server model for file systems, the client is a machine that remotely accesses resources of a computer server, such as compute power and larger memory capacity. In the client-server model for window systems, the client is an application that accesses windowing services from a server process. In this model, the client and the server can run on the same machine or on separate machines.

clock tick: The number of intervals per second, defined by {CLK_TCK}, used to express the value in type clock_t.

COFF: Common Object File Format; COFF refers to the format of the output executable file produced by the assembler and the link editor for UNIX System V Release 3.

command: An instruction to the computer. A command typically is a character string typed at a keyboard and is interpreted by the computer as a demand for a particular action.

controlling process: The session leader that established the connection to the controlling terminal. Should the terminal subsequently cease to be a controlling terminal for this session, the session leader shall cease to be the controlling process.

controlling terminal: A terminal that is associated with a session. Each session may have at most one controlling terminal associated with it, and a controlling terminal is associated with exactly one session. Certain input sequences from the controlling terminal cause signals to be sent to all processes in the process group associated with the controlling terminal.

cron: The UNIX clock daemon that executes commands at specified dates and times.

current working directory: A directory, associated with a process, that is used in pathname resolution for pathnames that do not begin with a slash (/).

daemon: A process that runs in the background, handling commands delivered for remote command execution.

descriptor: A data structure that uniquely identifies a hardware device or software function.

device: *A computer peripheral or an object that appears to the application as such.*

directory: *A file that contains directory entries. No two directory entries in the same directory shall have the same name.*

directory entry: *An object that associates a filename with a file. Several directory entries can associate a name with the same file.*

disk: A round platter, or set of platters, of a magnetized medium organized into concentric tracks and sectors for storing data such as files.

display device: The hardware device that displays windows, text, icons, and graphical pictures. Typically, a display device is a frame buffer and monitor.

dot: *The filename consisting of a single dot character.*

dot-dot: *The filename consisting solely of two dot characters (..).*

driver: A software subsystem that controls either a hardware device (device driver) or another software subsystem.

dynamic linking: It involves the binding of shared objects, usually in a shared dynamic library, into the address space of a process at runtime only.

effective group ID: *An attribute of a process that is used in determining various permissions, including file access permissions. This value is subject to change during the process lifetime, as described in setgid() and exec().*

effective user ID: *An attribute of a process that is used in determining various permissions, including file access permissions. This value is subject to change during process lifetime, as described in setuid() and exec().*

ELF: Extensible Linking Format; ELF is the new object file format in System V Release 4, which supersedes the previous COFF format. The format consists of the ELF header, an optional program header, a section header table, and various sections, which contain instructions, data, symbol tables, string tables, relocation information, and debugging information.

empty directory: *A directory that contains, at most, directory entries for dot and dot-dot.*

empty string (or null string): A character array whose first element is the null character.

environment: The conditions under which a user works while using the UNIX system. A user's environment includes those things that personalize the user's login and how the user is allowed to interact in specific ways with UNIX and the computer.

Epoch: The time 0 hours, 0 minutes, 0 seconds, January 1, 1970, Coordinated Universal Time.

feature test macro: A #defined symbol used to determine whether a particular set of features will be included from a header.

field separator: The character used to separate one field from the next; a string of one or more spaces is the usual field separator.

FIFO special file (or FIFO): A type of file. Data written to such a file are read on a first-in, first-out basis. Other characteristics of FIFOs are described under open(), read(), write(), and lseek().

file: An object that can be written to, or read from, or both. A file has certain attributes, including access permissions and type. File types include regular file, character special file, block special file, FIFO special file, and directory. Other types of files may be defined by the implementations.

file descriptor: A per-process, unique, nonnegative integer used to identify an open file for the purpose of file access.

file group class: A process in the file group class of a file if the process is not in the file owner class and if the effective group ID or one of the supplementary group IDs of the process matches the group ID associated with the file. Other members of the class may be implementation defined.

file mode: An object containing the file permission bits and other characteristics of a file.

filename: A name consisting of 1 to {NAMD_MAX} bytes used to name a file. The characters composing the name may be selected from the set of all character values excluding the slash character and the null character. The filenames dot and dot-dot have special meaning. A filename is sometimes referred to as a *pathname component.*

file offset: *The byte position in the file where the next I/O operation begins. Each open file description associated with a regular file, block special file, or directory has a file offset. A character special file that does not refer to a terminal device may have a file offset. There is no file offset for a pipe or FIFO.*

file other class: *A process is in the file other class of a file if the process is not in the file owner class or file group class.*

file owner class: *A process is in the file owner class of a file if the effective user ID of the process matches the user ID of the file.*

file permission bits: *Information about a file that is used, along with other information, to determine if a process has read, write, or execute/search permission to a file. The bits are divided into three parts: owner, group, and other. Each part is used with the corresponding file class of processes. These bits are contained in the file mode, as described in <sys/stat.h>. The detail usage of the file permission bits in access decisions is described in file access permissions.*

file serial number: *A per-file system unique identifier for a file. File serial numbers are unique throughout a file system.*

file system: *A collection of files and certain of their attributes. It provides a name space for file serial numbers referring to those files.*

foreground process group: *Each session that has established a connection with a controlling terminal has exactly one process group of the session as the foreground process group of that controlling terminal. The foreground process group has certain privileges when accessing its controlling terminal that are denied to background process groups.*

foreground process group ID: *The process group ID of the foreground process group.*

group: A collection of users who are referred to by a common name. Determines a user's access to files.

group ID: *Each system user is a member of at least one group. A group is identified by a group ID, a nonnegative integer that can be contained in an object of type gid_t. When the identity of a group is associated with a process, a group ID value is referred to as a real group ID, an effective group ID, one of the* *(optional) supplementary group IDs, or a (optional) save set-group ID.*

header file: In programming, a file of information, identified at the beginning of the program, that contains the definitions of data types and variables used by the functions in the program.

hidden file: A special type of file, such as .login, that does not show up in normal file listings.

home directory: The directory assigned to the user by the system administrator; usually the same as the login directory. Additional directories the user creates stem from the home directory.

image: A picture or graphic representation of an object.

inode: An entry in a predesignated area of a disk that describes where a file is located on that disk, the file's size, when it was last used, and other identification information.

input: Information fed to a command, a program, a terminal, a person, or the like.

input device: A hardware device that enables the user to communicate with the graphics system. Examples of input devices are keyboard, mouse, track ball, light pen, and joystick.

internet: A collection of networks interconnected by a set of routers that enables them to function as a single, large virtual network.

job control: A facility that allows users to selectively stop (suspend) the execution of processes and continue (resume) their execution at a later point. The user typically employs this facility via the interactive interface jointly supplied by the terminal I/O driver and a command interpreter. Conforming implementations may optionally support job control facilities; the presence of this option is indicated to the application at compile time or run time by the definition of the {_POSIX_JOB_CONTROL} symbol.

kernel: The core of the operating system software. The kernel manages the hardware (for example, processor cycles and memory) and supplies fundamental services such as filing that hardware does not provide.

kill: To terminate a process before it reaches its natural conclusion or life cycle.

link: An entry in a directory file that links a user assigned name for a file to the system's identification number for that file.

link count: The number of directory entries that refer to a particular file.

little endian: A format for storage or transmission of binary data in which the least significant byte (bit) comes first.

locale: A way to specify what information is relevant to a particular location. If locale is set to a language, this would in turn affect how the input/output is formatted and displayed. Locale is queried and set through the setlocale library function.

mode: A collection of attributes that specifies a file's type and its access permissions.

modem: Short for modulator/demodulator. A device that enables a machine or terminal to establish a connection and transfer data through telephone lines.

mount: The process of accessing a directory from a disk attached to a machine making the mount request or remote disk on a network.

mouse: An input device connected to the computer that determines the location of the pointer and thus determines the active window in a window system.

multitasking: Enables more than one user to access the same program at the same time. It also pertains to concurrent execution of two or more tasks by a computer.

multithreading: A technique that enables multiprocessing applications to run more efficiently by breaking sequences of instructions (threads) into multiple sequences that can be executed from the kernel simultaneously.

nibble: Half of a byte.

node: An addressable point on a network. A node can connect a computing system, a terminal, or various other peripheral devices to the network.

null character: An invisible character with an internal code of 0 that occupies no space if printed. Not to be confused with blank, which is invisible but occupies a space.

null string: A character array whose first element is a null character.

open file: A file that is currently associated with a file descriptor.

open file description: A record of how a process or group of processes is accessing a file. Each file descriptor shall refer to exactly one open file description, but an open file description may be referred to by more than one file descriptor. File offset, file status, and file access modes are attributes of an open file description.

orphaned process group: A process group in which the parent of every member is either itself a member of the group or is not a member of the group's session.

owner: The person who created a file.

parent directory: When discussing a directory, the directory containing the directory entry for the directory under discussion. When discussing other types of files, a directory containing a directory entry for the file under discussion. This concept does not apply to dot and dot-dot.

parent process: A process in a multitasking environment which is the parent process of a forked child process.

parent process ID: A new process is created by a currently active process. The parent process ID of a process is the process ID of its creator for the lifetime of the creator. After the creator's lifetime has ended, the parent process ID is the process ID of an implementation-defined system process.

pathname: A string that is used to identify a file. It consists of, at most, {PATH_MAX} bytes, including the terminating null character. It has an optional beginning slash, followed by zero or more filenames separated by slashes. If the pathname refers to a directory, it may also have one or more trailing slashes. Multiple successive slashes are considered the same as one slash. A pathname that begins with two successive slashes may be interpreted in an implementation-defined manner, although more than two leading slashes shall be treated as a single slash. The interpretation of the pathname is described under pathname resolution.

path prefix: *A pathname, with an optional ending slash, that refers to a directory.*

permissions: The attribute of a file or directory that specifies who has read, write, or execution access.

pipe: *An object accessed by one of the pair of file descriptors created by the pipe() function. Once created, the file descriptors can be used to manipulate it, and it behaves identically to a FIFO special file when accessed in this way. It has no name in the file hierarchy.*

portable filename character set: *For a filename to be portable across conforming implementation of IEEE Std 1003.1-1988, it shall consist only of the following characters*

A B C D E F G H I J K L M N O P Q R S T U V W X Y Z
a b c d e f g h i j k l m n o p q r s t u v w x y z
0 1 2 3 4 5 6 7 8 9 . _ -

The last three characters are the period, underscore, and hyphen characters, respectively. The hyphen shall not be used as the first character of a portable filename. Upper- and lowercase letters shall retain their unique identities between conforming implementations. In case of a portable pathname, the slash character may also be used.

process: *An address space and single thread of control that executes within that address space and its required system resources. A process is created by another process issuing the fork() function. The process that issues fork() is known as the parent process, and the new process created by the fork() is the child process.*

process group: *Each process in the system is a member of a process group that is identified by a process group ID. This grouping permits the signaling of related processes. A newly created process joins the process group of its creator.*

process group ID: *Each process group in the system is uniquely identified during its lifetime by a positive integer that can be contained in a pid_t called a process group ID. A process group ID may not be reused by the system until the process group lifetime ends.*

process group leader: *A process whose process ID is the same as its process group ID.*

process group lifetime: *A period of time that begins when a process group is created and ends when the last remaining process in the group leaves the group, either due to process termination or calling the setsid() or setpgid() functions.*

process ID: *Each process in the system is uniquely identified during its lifetime by a positive integer that can be contained in pid_t called a process ID. A process ID may not be reused by the system until the process lifetime ends. In addition, if there exists a process group whose process group ID is equal to that process ID, the process ID may not be reused by the system until the process group lifetime ends. A process that is not a system process shall not have a process ID of 1.*

process lifetime: *After a process is created with a fork() function, it is considered active. Its thread of control and address space exist until it terminates. It then enters an inactive state where certain resources may be returned to the system, although some resources, such as the process ID, are still in use. When another process executes a wait() or waitpid() function for an inactive process, the remaining resources are returned to the system. The last resource to be returned to the system is the process ID. At this time, the lifetime of the process ends.*

read-only file system: *A file system that has implementation defined characteristics restricting modifications.*

real group ID: *The attribute of a process that, at the time of process creation identifies the group of the user who created the process. See group ID. This value is subject to change during the process lifetime, as described in setuid().*

real user ID: *The attribute of a process that, at the time of process creation, identifies the user who created the process. See user ID. This value is subject to change during the process lifetime, as described in setuid().*

regular file: *A file that is a randomly accessible sequence of bytes, with no further structure imposed by the system.*

relative pathname: *A series of directory names separated by the slash (/) character that locates a file or directory with respect to the working directory.*

root directory: *A directory, associated with a process, that is used in pathname resolution for pathnames that begin with a slash.*

router: A system responsible for making decisions about which of several paths network traffic will follow.

saved set-group-ID: *When the saved set-user-ID option is implemented, an attribute of a process that allows some flexibility in the assignment of the effective group ID attribute, as described in setgid().*

saved set-user-ID: *When the saved set-user-ID option is implemented, an attribute of a process that allows some flexibility in the assignment of the effective user-ID attribute, as described in setuid() and exec().*

seconds since the Epoch: *A value to be interpreted as the number of seconds between a specified time and the Epoch. A Coordinated Universal Time name [specified in terms of seconds (tm_sec), minutes (tm_min), hours (tm_hour), (tm_year)] is related to a time represented as seconds since the Epoch according to the expression below.*

If year < 1970 or the value is negative, the relationship is undefined. If year >= 1970 and the value is nonnegative, the value is related to a Coordinated Universal Time name according to the expression

$$tm\_sec + tm\_min*60 + tm\_hour*3600 + tm\_yday*86\,400$$
$$+ (tm\_year - 70)*31536000 + ((tm\_year - 69)/4)*86\,400$$

segmentation fault: A process that attempted to access an area of memory that is restricted or does not exist.

server: In the client/server model for file systems, the server is a machine with compute resources and large memory capacity. Client machines can remotely access and make use of these resources. In the client/server model for window systems, the server is a process that provides windowing services to an application or client process. In this model, the client and the server can run on the same machine or on separate machines.

session: *Each process group is a member of a session. A process is considered to be a member of the session of which its process group is a member. A newly created process joins the session of the creator. A process can alter its session membership; see setsid(). Implementations which support setpgid() can have multiple process groups in the same session.*

session leader: *A process that has created a session; see setsid().*

session lifetime: *The period between when a session is created and the end of lifetime of all the process groups which remain as members of the session.*

shared objects: Type of objects that make up an archive library, which then can be bound into the address space of process at runtime.

shell: A programmable command interpreter. The shell provides direct communication between the user and the operating system.

signal: *A mechanism by which a process may be notified of or affected by an event occurring in the system. Examples of such events include hardware exceptions and specific actions by processes. The term signal is also used to refer to the event itself.*

slash: *The literal character /. This character is also known as solidus in ISO 8859/1.*

supplementary group ID: *A process has up to {NGROUPS_MAX} supplementary group IDs used in determining file access permissions, in addition to the effective group ID. The supplementary group IDs of a process are set to the supplementary group IDs of the parent process when the process is created. Whether a process's effective group ID is included in or omitted from its list of supplementary group IDs is unspecified.*

symbolic link: A symbolic link is a file that reference another file and allows files and directories to be linked across file systems.

system: *A computer that enables a user to run computer programs.*

system process: *An object, other than a process executing an application, that is defined by the system and has a process ID.*

terminal: *A character special file that obeys the defined specifications.*

thread: In programming, a process that is part of a larger process or program.

user ID: *Each system user is identified by a nonnegative integer known as a user ID that can be contained in an object of type uid_t. When the identity of a user is associated with a process, a user ID value is referred to as a real user ID, an effective user ID, or an (optional) save set-user ID.*

UTC: Universal Coordinated Time; UTC is the new standard for the UNIX system's internal clock. UTC replaces Greenwich Mean Time (GMT).

working directory (or current working directory): *A directory, associated with a process, that is used in pathname resolution for pathnames that do not begin with a slash.*

2.4   Primitive System Data Types

Some data types used by the various system functions are not defined by any standard, but are defined by the implementation. These types are then defined in the header <sys/types.h>, which contains definitions for at least the types shown in Table 2-1.

Table 2-1 Primitive System Data Types

Defined Type	Description
dev_t	Used for device numbers
gid_t	Used for group IDs
ino_t	Used for file serial numbers
mode_t	Used for some file attributes, for example file type, file access permissions
nlink_t	Used for link counts
off_t	Used for file sizes
size_t	As defined in C Standard
ssize_t	Used by functions that return a count of bytes (memory space).
pid_t	Used for process IDs and process group IDs
uid_t	Used for user IDs

All of the types listed in Table 2-1 shall be arithmetic types; pid_t shall be a signed arithmetic type.

Additional implementation defined type definitions may be given in this header. These definitions shall have names ending with _t. Such symbols do not require feature test macros to be visible when <sys/types.h> is included.

2.5   Environment Description

An array of strings called the environment is made available when a process begins. This array is pointed to by the external variable environ, which is defined as

extern char **environ ;

These strings have the form "name=value"; names shall not contain character =. There are no meanings associated with the order of the strings in the environment. If more than one string in a process's environment has the same name, the consequences are undefined. The following names may be defined and have the indicated meaning if they are defined:

HOME: *The name of the user's initial working directory from the user database.*

LANG: *The name of the predefined setting for locale.*

LC_COLLATE: *The name of the locale for collation information.*

LC_CTYPE: *The name of the locale for character classification.*

LC_MONETARY: *The name of locale containing monetary-related numeric editing information.*

LC_NUMERIC: *The name of the locale containing numeric editing (that is., radix character) information.*

LC_TIME: *The name of the locale for date / time formatting information.*

LOGNAME: *The name of user's login account, corresponding to the login name in the user database.*

PATH: *The sequence of path prefixes that certain functions apply in searching for an executable file known only by a filename (a pathname that does not contain slash). The prefixes are seperated by a colon (:). When a no-zero length prefix is applied to this filename, a slash is inserted between the prefix and the filename. A zero-length prefix is a special prefix that indicates the current working directory. It appears as two adjacent colons (::), as an initial colon preceding the rest of the list, or as a trailing colon following the rest of the list. The list is searched from beginning to end until an executable program by the specified name is found. If the pathname being sought contains a slash, the search* *through the path prefixes is not performed.*

TERM: *The terminal type for which output is to be performed. This informa-tion is used by commands and application programs wishing to exploit special capabilities specific to a terminal.*

TZ: *Time zone information*

Environment variable names used or created by an application should consist solely of characters from the portable filename character set. Other characters may be permitted by an implementation; applications shall tolerate the pres-ence of such names. Upper- and lowercase letters retain their unique identities and are not folded together. System-defined environment variable names should begin with a capital letter or underscore, and be composed of only capi-tal letters, underscores and numbers.

The values that the environment variables may be assigned are not registered except that they are considered to end with a null byte, and the total space used to store the environment and the arguments to the process is limited to {ARG_-MAX} bytes.

Other name=value pairs may be placed in the environment by manipulating the environ variable or by using envp arguments when creating a process.

2.6   Libraries

A library in the UNIX operating system context is a collection of functions. The function prototypes are declared in the header file. These functions act as building blocks for any application program. Table 2-2 lists important librar-ies that are included as part of most of the UNIX system. The static libraries have suffix .a, for example, libsys.a, and the dynamic libraries have suffix .so, followed by a version number, for example, libsys.so.3. The library name may be different on a given system then from that listed in Table 2-2.

Table 2-2 Common UNIX Libraries

Library	Description
libsys	System calls or functions
libc	General-purpose utility functions

Table 2-2 Common UNIX Libraries (continued)

Library	Description
libm	Mathematical functions
libcurses	Curses library functions
libbsd	Berkely socket library functions
libnsl	Network services library functions
libintl	International library
libX11	X window graphic functions
libXt	X window intrinsics functions
libXm	Motif widget library functions
libXaw	Athena widget library functions

2.7   Header Files

Each library function is declared in a header file of type filename.h, whose contents are made available by the #include preprocessing directive. The header file declares a set of related functions. It also declares any necessary types and additional macros needed to facilitate their use. The programmer can define its own header file containing different reusable constants, structures and other definitions. The #include<filename.h> directive is usually at the beginning of the file:

```
/* sample program */
#include <stdio.h>
#include <signal.h>
...

main()
{
   statements
}
```

Some header files with brief descriptions are listed next.

assert.h: Defines the assert macro and refers to another macro NDEBUG.

cpio.h: Contains cpio archive values and structures.

ctype.h: Declares several functions useful for testing and mapping characters.

dirent.h: Declares functions related to directory information and manipulation.

errno.h: Defines several macros, all relating to the reporting of error conditions.

fcntl.h: Declares macros for file manipulation and defines fcntl() function. The fcntl() is a portable function and should be used instead of ioctl().

float.h: Defines macros for floating-point numbers and values that provide information about an implementation's floating-point arithmetic.

ftw.h: Contains file tree traversal ftw() specific functions and definitions.

grp.h: Defines functions for retrieving group-related information.

ioctl.h: Declares macros for file manipulation and defines ioctl() function.

langinfo.h: Contains the contansts used to identify items of langinfo data.

limits.h: Defines several macros that expand to various limits and parameters.

locale.h: Defines locale specific structure and LC_ macros.

math.h: Declares mathematical functions and related macros.

nl_types.h: Contains definitions for nl_catd and nl_item and defines related constants.

pwd.h: Provides a definition for struct passwd and related macros.

search.h: Defines a type definition ENTRY for structure entry and search functions.

setjmp.h: Defines the functions setjmp() and siglongjmp().

signal.h: Defines signal related functions and several macros for handling various signals.

stdarg.h: Defines macros for advancing through a list of arguments whose number and types are not known to the called function when it is translated.

stddef.h: Defines standard-type definitions and null pointer constant NULL.

stdio.h: Defines functions for performing input and output.

stdlib.h: Declares several functions of general utility and defines related macros.

string.h: Defines string-handling functions and related macros.

sys/ipc.h: Contains interprocess communication access structure and related constants.

sys/msg.h: Defines message queue structures and related constants.

sys/sem.h: Defines the semaphore constants and structures.

sys/shm.h: Defines shared memory symbolic constants and structure.

sys/stat.h: Defines the structure of the data returned by the functions stat() and fstat().

sys/times.h: Defines the structure tms, which is returned by times() and includes at least the following members.

sys/types.h: Defines primitive data types.

sys/utsname.h: Defines structure utsname.

sys/wait.h: Defines process wait specific functions and related functions.

termios.h: Defines terminal-related functions, structures and macros.

time.h: Defines functions for manipulating time and related macros.

ulimit.h: Defines the symbolic constants used in the ulimit() function.

unistd.h: Defines file access permissions and POSIX macros.

utime.h: Declares the structure utimbuf, access and modification times structure.

varargs.h: Defines variable-length argument list macros.

2.8   Numerical Limits

The following subsections list magnitude limitations imposed by a specific implementation. The braces notation {LIMIT} is used to indicate these values, but the braces are not part of the name.

2.8.1   C Language Limits

The limits shown in Table 2-3 are defined in the C Standard.

Table 2-3 C Language Limits

Constant	Description	Value
CHAR_BIT	Number of bits for smallest object that is not a bit field	8
SCHAR_MIN	Minimum value for an object of type signed char	-127
SCHAR_MAX	Maximum value for an object of type signed char	+127
UCHAR_MAX	Maximum value for an object of type unsigned char	255
CHAR_MIN	Minimum value for an object of type char	*
CHAR_MAX	Maximum value for an object of type char	*
MB_LEN_MAX	Maximum number of bytes in a multibyte character	1
SHRT_MIN	Minimum value for an object of type short int	-32767
SHRT_MAX	Maximum value for an object of type short int	+32767
USHRT_MAX	Maximum value for an object of type unsigned short int	65535
INT_MIN	Minimum value for an object of type int	-32767
INT_MAX	Maximum value for an object of type int	+32767
UINT_MAX	Maximum value for an object of type unsigned int	65535
LONG_MIN	Minimum value for an object type long int	-2147483647
LONG_MAX	Maximum value for an object type long int	+2147483647
ULONG_MAX	Maximum value for an object type unsigned long int	4294967295

* If the char is treated as signed integer in an expression, the value of CHAR_MIN is the same as that of SCHAR_MIN and the value of CHAR_MAX shall be the same as that of SCHAR_MAX. Otherwise, the value of CHAR_MIN shall be 0 and the value of CHAR_MAX shall be the same as that of UCHAR_-MAX.

2.8.2 Minimum Values

The symbols in Table 2-4 shall be defined in <limits.h> with the values shown. These are symbolic names for the most restrictive value for certain features on a system conforming to this standard. A POSIX conforming implementation shall provide values at least this large. A portable application shall not require a larger value for correct operation.

Table 2-4 Minimum Values

Name	Description	Value
_POSIX_ARG_MAX	Length of the arguments for one of the exec functions in bytes, including environment data	4096
_POSIX_CHILD_MAX	Number of simultaneous processes per real user ID	6
_POSIX_LINK_MAX	Value of a file's link count	8
_POSIX_MAX_CANON	Number of bytes in a terminal canonical input queue	255
_POSIX_MAX_INPUT	Number of bytes for which space will be available in a terminal input queue	255
_POSIX_NAME_MAX	Number of bytes in a filename	14
_POSIX_NGROUPS_MAX	Number of simultaneous supplementary group IDs per process	0
_POSIX_OPEN_MAX	Number of files that one process can have open at one time	16
_POSIX_PATH_MAX	Number of bytes in a pathname	255
_POSIX_PIPE_BUF	Number of bytes that can be written atomically when writing to a pipe	512

2.8.3   Run-time Increasable Values

*The magnitude limitations in Table 2-5 shall be fixed by specific implementa-
tions. A Strictly conforming POSIX Application shall assume that the value
supplied by <limits.h> in a specific implementation is the minimum that pertains whenever the Strictly Conforming POSIX Application is run under that
implementation. A specific instance of a specific implementation may increase
the value relative to that supplied by <limits.h> for that implementation. The
actual value supported by a specific instance shall be provided by the sysconf()
function.*

Table 2-5 Run-time Increasable Values

Name	Description	Value
NGROUPS_MAX	Maximum number of simultaneous sup-plementary group IDs per process	_POSIX_NGROUPS_MAX

2.8.4   Run-time Invariant Values

*A definition of one the values in Table 2-6 shall be omitted from the <limits.h>
on specific implementations where the corresponding value is equal to or
greater than the stated minimum, but is indeterminate.*

Table 2-6 Run-time Invariant Values

Name	Description	Minimum Value
ARG_MAX	Maximum length of the arguments for the exec functions in bytes, including environment data	_POSIX_ARG_MAX
CHILD_MAX	Maximum number of simultaneous processes per real user ID	_POSIX_CHILD_MAX
OPEN_MAX	Maximum number of files that one process can have open at any given time	_POSIX_OPEN_MAX

*This might depend on the amount of available memory space on a specific
instance of a specific implementation. The actual value supported by a specific
instance shall be provided by the sysconf() function.*

2.8.5   Pathname Variable Values

The values in Table 2-7 may be constants within an implementation or may vary from one pathname to another. For example, file systems or directories may have different characteristics.

Table 2-7 Pathname Variable Values

LINK_MAX	Maximum value of a file's link count	_POSIX_LINK_MAX
MAX_CANON	Maximum number of bytes in a terminal canonical input line	_POSIX_MAX_CANON
MAX_INPUT	Minimum number of bytes for which space will be available in a terminal input queue; therefore maximum number of bytes that a portable application may require to be typed as input before reading them	_POSIX_MAX_INPUT
NAME_MAX	Maximum number of bytes in a filename (not a string length; count excludes a terminating null)	_POSIX_NAME_MAX
PATH_MAX	Maximum number of bytes in a pathname (not a string length; count excludes a terminating null)	_POSIX_PATH_MAX
PIPE_BUF	Maximum number of bytes that can be written atomically when writing to a pipe	_POSIX_PIPE_BUF

A definition of one of the values from Table 2-7 shall be omitted from the <limits.h> on specific implementations where the corresponding value is equal to or greater than the stated minimum, but where the value can vary depending on the file to which it is applied. The actual value supported for a specific pathname shall be provided by the pathconf() function.

2.9   Symbolic Constants

A conforming implementation shall have the header <unistd.h>. This header defines the symbolic constants and structure referenced. The constants defined by the header are described next. The actual values of the constants are implementation defined.

2.9.1   Symbolic Constants for the access() Function

The constants used by the access() function are shown in Table 2-8.

Table 2-8 Symbolic Constants for the access() Function

Constants	Description
R_OK	Test for read permission
W_OK	Test for write permission
X_OK	Test for execute or search permission
F_OK	Test for existence of file

The constants F_OK, R_OK, W_OK, and X_OK and the expressions R_OK | W_OK, R_OK | X_OK, and R_OK | W_OK | X_OK shall all have distinct values.

2.9.2   Symbolic Constants for the lseek() Function

The constants used by the lseek() function are shown in Table 2-9.

Table 2-9 Symbolic Constants for the lseek() Function

Constant	Description
SEEK_SET	Set file offset to offset
SEEK_CUR	Set file offset to the current plus offset
SEEK_END	Set file offset to EOF plus offset

2.9.3   Compile-time Symbolic Constants for Portability Specifications

The constants in Table 2-10 can be used by the application at compile time to determine which optional facilities are present and what actions shall be taken by the implementation.

Table 2-10 Compile-time Symbolic Constants

Name	Description
_POSIX_JOB_CONTROL	If this symbol is defined, it indicates that the implementation supports job control.
_POSIX_SAVED_IDS	If defined, each process has a saved set-user ID and a saved set-group ID.
_POSIX_VERSION	The integer value is 198808L. This value will change with each published version or revision of this standard to indicate the (4-digit) year and (2-digit) month for the standard as approved by the IEEE Standard Board.

Although a Strictly Conforming POSIX Application can rely on the values compiled from the <unistd.h> header to afford it portability on all instances of an implementation, it may choose to interrogate a value at runtime to take advantage of the current configuration. See sysconf() function for further information.

2.9.4 Execution-time Symbolic Constants for Portability Specifications

The constants in Table 2-11 can be used by the application, at execution time, to determine which optional facilities are present and what actions shall be taken by the implementation. If any of the contents in Table 2-11 are not defined in the header <unistd.h>, the value varies depending on the file to which it is applied. See pathconf().

If any of the constants in Table 2-11 are defined to have value -1 in the header <unistd.h>, the implementation shall not provide the option on any file; if any are defined to have a value other than -1 in the header <unistd.h>, the implementation shall provide the option on all applicable files.

Table 2-11 Execution-time Symbolic Constants

Name	Description
_POSIX_CHOWN_RESTRICTED	The use of the chown() function is restricted to a process with appropriate privileges and to changing the group ID of a file only to the effective group ID of the process or to one of its supplementary group IDs.
_POSIX_NO_TRUNC	Pathname components longer than NAME_MAX generate an error.
_POSIX_VDISABLE	Terminal special characters defined in <termios.h> can be disabled using this character value, if it is defined. See tcgetattr() and tcsetattr().

All the constants in Table 2-11 whether defined in <unistd.h> or not, may be queried with respect to a specific file using the pathconf() or fpathconf() functions.

2.10 Signals

2.10.1 Signal Names

The <signal.h> header declares the sigset_t type and the sigaction structure. It also defines the symbolic constants given in Table 2-12, each of which expands to a distinct constant expression of the type void(*)(), whose value matches no declarable function.

Table 2-12 Default and Ignore Signal Description

Symbolic Constant	Description
SIG_DFL	request for default signal handling
SIG_IGN	request that signal be ignored

The type sigset_t is used to represent sets of signals. It is always an integral or

*structure type. Several functions used to manipulate objects of type sigset_t are
defined in sigsetops.*

*The <signal.h> header also declares the constants that are used to refer to the
signals that occur in the system. Each of the signals defined by this standard
and supported by the implementation shall have distinct, positive integral values. The value zero is reserved for use as the null signal; see kill(). An implementation may define additional signals that may occur in the system.*

*The constants shown in Table 2-13 shall be supported by all implementation-
s.The constants shown in Table 2-14 shall be defined by all implementations.
However, implementations that do not support job control are not required to
support these signals. If these signals are supported by the implementations,
they shall behave in accordance with the IEEE POSIX standard. Otherwise,
the implementation shall not generate these signals, and attempts to send these
signals or to examine or specify their actions shall return an error condition.*

Table 2-13 POSIX Required Signals

Symbolic Constant	Default Action	Description
SIGABRT	1	Abnormal termination signal, such as is initiated by the abort() function
SIGALRM	1	Time-out signal, such as initiated by the alarm() function
SIGFPE	1	Erroneous arithmetic operation, such as division by zero or an operation resulting in overflow
SIGHUP	1	Hang-up detected on controlling terminal or death of controlling process
SIGILL	1	Detection of an invalid hardware instruction
SIGINT	1	Interactive attention signal
SIGKILL	1	Termination signal (cannot be caught or ignored)
SIGPIPE	1	Write on a pipe with no readers
SIGQUIT	1	Interactive termination signal
SIGSEGV	1	Detection of invalid memory reference
SIGTERM	1	Termination signal
SIGUSR1	1	Reserved as application defined signal 1
SIGUSR2	1	Reserved as application defined signal 2

Table 2-14 Job Control Signals

Symbolic Constant	Default Action	Description
SIGCHLD	2	Child process terminated or stopped.
SIGCONT	4	Continue if stopped.
SIGSTOP	3	Stop signal (cannot be caught or ignored).
SIGTSTP	3	Interactive stop signal
SIGTTIN	3	Read from control terminal attempted by a member of a background process group.
SIGTTOU	3	Write to control terminal attempted by a member of a background process group.

Default actions for Tables 2-13 and 2-14 are as shown in Table 2-15.

Table 2-15 Default Action Description for Signals

Default Actions	Description
1	Abnormal termination of the process
2	Ignore the signal
3	Stop the process
4	Continue the process if it is currently stopped; otherwise ignore the signal.

2.10.2 Signal Generation and Delivery

A signal is said to be generated for (or sent to) a process when the event that causes the signal first occurs. Examples of such events include detection of hardware faults, timer expiration, and terminal activity, as well as the invocation of the kill() function. In some circumstances, the same event generates signals for multiple processes.

Each process has an action to be taken in response to each signal defined by the system. A signal is said to be delivered to a process when the appropriate action for the process and signal is taken.

During the time between the generation of a signal and its delivery, the signal is said to be pending. Ordinarily, this interval cannot be detected by an application. However, a signal can be blocked from delivery to a process. If the action associated with a blocked signal is anything other than to ignore the signal, and if that signal is generated for the process, the signal shall remain pending until either it is unblocked or the action associated with it is set to ignore the signal and if that signal is generated for the process, it is unspecified whether the signal is discarded immediately upon generation or remains pending.

Each process has a signal mask that defines the set of signals currently blocked from delivery to it. The signal mask for a process is initialized from that of its parent. The sigaction(), sigprocmaks(), and sigsuspend() functions control the manipulation of the signal mask.

The determination of which action is taken in response to a signal is made at the time the signal is delivered, allowing for any changes since the time of generation. This determination is independent of the means by which the signal was originally generated. If a subsequent occurrence of a pending signal is generated, it is implementation defined as to whether the signal is delivered more than once. The order in which multiple, simultaneously pending signals are delivered to a process is unspecified.

When any stop signal (SIGSTOP, SIGTSTP, SIGTTIN, SIGTTOU) is generated for a process, any pending SIGCONT signals for that process shall be discarded. Conversely, when SIGCONT is generated for a process, all pending stop signals for that process shall be discarded. When SIGCONT is generated for a process that is stopped, the process shall be continued, even if the SIGCONT signal is blocked or ignored. If SIGCONT is blocked and not ignored, it shall remain pending until it is either unblocked or a stop signal is generated for the process.

Example

```
/* filename cuex1.c */

#include <stdio.h>
#include <unistd.h>
#include <signal.h>
```

```
void handler(signal)
int signal;
{
  if(signal == SIGALRM)
     printf("pass: received signal SIGALRM\n");
  else
     printf("error: expected=%d, received=%d\n", SIGALRM,
            signal);
}

main()
{
  pid_t   pid;

  pid = getpid();
  /* set alarm using signal */
  signal(SIGALRM, handler);
  kill(pid, SIGALRM);
}
```

Output

```
pass: received signal SIGALRM
```

```
/* filename cuex2.c */

#include <stdio.h>
#include <unistd.h>
#include <signal.h>

void handler(signal)

int signal;
{
  if(signal == SIGALRM)
     printf("pass: received signal SIGALRM\n");
  else
     printf("error: expected=%d, received=%d\n", SIGALRM,
            signal);
}
```

```
main()
{
  pid_t   pid;

  pid = getpid();
  /* set alarm using sigset */
  sigset(SIGALRM, handler);
  kill(pid, SIGALRM);
}
```

Output

```
pass: received signal SIGALRM
```

2.10.3 Signal Actions

There are three types of actions that can be associated with a signal: SIG_DFL, SIG_IGN, or a pointer to a function. Initially, all signals shall be set to SIG_DFL or SIG_IGN prior to entry of the main() routine. The actions pre-scribed by these values are as follows:

1. *SIG_DFL :- Signal specific default action*

(a) The default actions for the signals defined in this standard are specified in the preceding tables.

(b) If the default action is to stop the process, the execution of that process is temporarily suspended. When a process stops, a SIGCHLD signal shall be gen-erated for its parent process, unless the parent process has set the SA_NOCLD-STOP flag; see seduction(). While a process is stopped, any additional signals that are sent to the process shall not be delivered until the process is continued, except SIGKILL, which always terminates the receiving process. A process that is a member of an orphaned process shall not be allowed to stop in response to the SIGTSTP, SIGTTIN, or SIGTTOU signals. In cases where delivery of one of these signals would stop such a process, the signal shall be discarded.

Setting a signal action to SIG_DFL for a signal that is pending, and whose default action is to ignore the signal (for example, SIGCHLD) shall cause the pending signal to be discarded, whether or not it is blocked.

2.   *SIG_IGN :- ignore signal*

(a) *Delivery of the signal shall have no effect on the process. The behavior of a process is undefined after it ignores a SIGFPE, SIGILL<, or SIGSEGV signal that was not generated by the kill() function or the raise() function defined by the C Standard.*

(b) *The system shall not allow the action for the signals SIGKILL or SIGSTOP to be set to SIG_IGN.*

(c) *Setting a signal action to SIG_IGN for a signal that is pending shall cause the pending signal to be discarded, whether or not it is blocked.*

(d) *If a process sets the action for the SIGCHLD signal to SIG_IGN, the behavior is unspecified.*

3.   *Pointer to a function :- Catch a signal*

(a) *On delivery of the signal, the receiving process is to execute the signal-catching function, the receiving process shall resume execution at the point at which it was interrupted.*

(b) *The signal catching function shall be entered as a C language function call as*

> ***void func(signo)***
> ***int signo ;***

where func is the specified signal-catching function and signo is the signal number of the signal to be delivered.

(c) *The behavior of a process is undefined after it returns normally from a signal-catching function for a SIGFPE, SIGILL, or SIGSEGV signal that was not generated by the kill() function or the raise() function defined by the C Standard.*

(d) *The system shall not allow a process to catch the signals SIGKILL and SIGSTOP.*

(e) *If a process establishes a signal-catching function for the SIGCHLD signal while it has a terminated child process for which it has not waited, it is unspec-*

ified whether a SIGCHLD signal is generated to indicate that child process.

(f) When signal catching functions are invoked asynchronously with process execution, the behavior of some of the functions is unspecified if they are called from a signal-catching function.

Example

```
/* filename cuex3.c */

#include <stdio.h>
#include <unistd.h>
#include <signal.h>

void handler(signal)

int signal;
{
  if(signal == SIGALRM)
     printf("pass: received signal SIGALRM\n");
  else
     printf("error: expected=%d, received=%d\n", SIGALRM,
            signal);
}
main()
{
  int      sighold_value;
  pid_t    pid;

  pid = getpid();
  signal(SIGALRM, handler);
  sighold_value = sighold(SIGALRM);

  if (sighold_value == 0)
     printf("pass: sighold() call successful\n");
  else
     printf("error: sighold() call failed\n");
  printf("sighold holds the signal SIGALRM in queue\n");

  kill(pid, SIGALRM );
  printf("sigrelse releases the signal SIGALRM in queue\n");
```

```
    sigrelse(SIGALRM );
}
```

Output

```
pass: sighold() call successful
sighold holds the signal SIGALRM in queue
sigrelse releases the signal SIGALRM in queue
pass: received signal SIGALRM
```

```
/* filename cuex4.c */

#include <stdio.h>
#include <signal.h>

void handler(signal)
int signal;
{
  if(signal == SIGALRM)
     printf("pass: received signal SIGALRM\n");
  else
     printf("error: expected=%d, received=%d\n", SIGALRM,
             signal);
}

main()
{
  int       sigpending_value;
  int       member;
  sigset_t set;
  pid_t    pid;

  pid = getpid();
  signal(SIGALRM, handler);
  /* sighold shall hold SIGALRM in queue */
  sighold (SIGALRM);
  kill(pid, SIGALRM);
  sigpending_value = sigpending(&set);

  if (sigpending_value == 0) {
     printf("pass: sigpending() call successful\n");
     member = sigismember(&set, SIGALRM);
```

```
      if (member == 1)
         printf("signal SIGALRM is pending\n");
      else
         printf("error: SIGALRM is not pending\n");
   }
   else
      printf("error: sigpending() call failed\n");

   printf("release the signal SIGALRM in queue\n");
   sigrelse(SIGALRM );
}
```

Output

```
pass: sigpending() call successful
signal SIGALRM is pending
release the signal SIGALRM in queue
pass: received signal SIGALRM
```

```
/* filename cuex5.c */

#include <stdio.h>
#include <unistd.h>
#include <signal.h>
#include <sys/wait.h>

main()
{
   int      stat_loc;
   pid_t    child;

   child = fork();
   if (child == 0) {
      sigset(SIGPIPE, SIG_DFL);
      printf("sigpause suspends child process\n");
      sigpause (SIGPIPE);
      printf("error: sigpause did not suspend child\n");
   }
   /* parent sleeps for 2 seconds, child in suspension */
   sleep(2);
   /* wake up child */
```

```
    kill(child, SIGALRM);
    waitpid(child, &stat_loc, WUNTRACED);
}
```

Output

```
sigpause suspends child process
```

/* filename cuex6.c */

```
#include <stdio.h>
#include <signal.h>

void handler(signal)
int signal;
{
  if(signal == SIGALRM)
     printf("pass: received signal SIGALRM\n");
  else
     printf("error: expected=%d, received=%d\n", SIGALRM,
            signal);
}
main()
{
  int     sigaction_value;
  struct  sigaction  act, oact;

  /* example 1 */
  /* set the signal */
  sigemptyset(&act.sa_mask);
  sigemptyset(&oact.sa_mask);
  sigaddset(&act.sa_mask, SIGALRM);
  act.sa_handler = handler;
  act.sa_flags =  SA_ONSTACK;
  sigaction_value = sigaction(SIGALRM, &act, &oact);

  if (sigaction_value == 0) {
     printf("pass: sigaction() call successful\n");
     kill(getpid(), SIGALRM);
  }
  else
```

```
    printf("error: sigaction() call failed\n");

/* Now examine the signal */
sigemptyset (&act.sa_mask);
sigemptyset (&oact.sa_mask);
sigaddset (&act.sa_mask, SIGALRM);
act.sa_handler = handler;
act.sa_flags =  SA_ONSTACK;
sigaction_value = sigaction (SIGALRM, &act, &oact);

if ( sigaction_value == 0 ) {
    printf("pass: sigaction() call successful\n");
    sigaction(SIGALRM, &act, &oact);
    if ( sigismember(&oact.sa_mask, SIGALRM) == 1 )
        printf ("previous signal set was SIGALRM\n");
    else
        printf ("error: did not retrieve previous signal
                SIGALRM\n");
    if ( oact.sa_handler == handler )
        printf ("previous signal function set was
                handler\n");
    else
        printf ("error: did not retrieve previous signal
                handler\n");
  }
  else
    printf ("error: sigaction() call failed\n");
}
```

Output

```
pass: sigaction() call successful
pass: received signal SIGALRM
pass: sigaction() call successful
previous signal set was SIGALRM
previous signal function set was handler
```

2.10.4 Signal Effects on Other Functions

Signals affect the behavior of certain functions if delivered to a process while it is executing such a function. If the action of the signal is to terminate the pro-

cess, the process shall be terminated and the function shall not return. If the action of the signal is to stop the process, the process shall stop until continued or terminated. Generation of a SIGCONT signal for the process causes the process to be continued, and the original function shall continue at the point where the process was stopped. If the action of the signal is to invoke a signal-catching function, the signal-catching function shall be invoked; in this case the original function is said to be interrupted by the signal. If the signal-catching function executes a return, the behavior of the interrupted function shall be as described individually for that function. Signals that are ignored shall not affect the behavior of any function; signals that are blocked shall not affect the behavior of any function until they are delivered.

2.11   Error Numbers

Most functions provide an error number in the external variable errno, which is defined as

extern int errno ;

The value of this variable shall be defined only after a call to a function for which it is explicitly stated to be set, and until it is changed by the next function call. The variable errno should only be examined when it is indicated to be valid by a function's return value. No function sets errno to zero to indicate an error.

If more that one error occurs in processing a function call, this standard does not define in what order the errors are detected; therefore, any one of the possible errors may be returned.

Implementation may support additional errors not included in this list, may generate errors included in this list under circumstances other than those described here, or may contain extensions or limitations that prevent some errors from occurring. The Errors subsection in each function description specifies which error conditions shall be required and which may be implementation defined.

Example

```
/* filename cuex7.c  */

#include <stdio.h>
```

```
#include <sys/stat.h>
#include <errno.h>

/* errno is defined in errno.h header file */

main()
{
  int      ret_val;
  ret_val = chdir("testdir");

  if(ret_val == 0)
     printf("pass: chdir() call successful\n");
  else {
     printf("error: chdir() call failed\n");
     printf("error number: %d\n", errno);
     printf("error: %s\n", strerror(errno));
  }
}
```

Output

```
error: chdir() call failed
error number: 2
error: No such file or directory
```

/* filename cuex8.c */

```
#include <stdio.h>
#include <errno.h>
#include <string.h>
```

/* errno is defined in errno.h */
```
extern int  sys_nerr;
extern char *sys_errlist[];

main()
{
  char      *strerror_value;
  int       i;

  /* example 1 */
  /* delete a nonexisting file should generate error */
```

```
remove ("testfile");
strerror_value = strerror (errno);
if ( strerror_value != (char *)0 ) {
   printf ("pass: strerror() call successful\n");
   /* print  the error */
   printf ("error: %s\n" , strerror_value);
}
else
   printf ("error: strerror() call failed\n");

/* example 2 */
/* print all the errors from the database */
for (i = 1; i <= sys_nerr; i++ ) {
   strerror_value = strerror (i);
   printf ("error: %s\n" , strerror_value);
}

/* example 3 */
/* print all the errors from the array sys_errlist[] */
for (i = 1; i < sys_nerr; i++ ) {
   printf ("error: %s\n" , sys_errlist[i]);
}
}
```

Output

```
pass: strerror() call successful
error: No such file or directory
...
```

2.11.1 Generic Errors

The following symbolic names identify the possible error numbers, in the context of functions. The general descriptions are more precisely defined in ERRORS sections of functions that return them. Only these symbolic names should be used in programs. All values listed in this section shall be unique. The implementation defined values for these names shall be found in the header <errno.h>

[E2BIG] *Arg list tool long*
The sum of the number of bytes used by the new process image's argument list

and environment list was greater than the system imposed limit of {ARG_-MAX} bytes.

[EACCESS] *Permission denied*
An attempt was made to access a file in a way forbidden by its file access permissions.

[EAGAIN] *Resources temporarily unavailable*
This is a temporary condition and later calls to the same routine may complete normally.

[EBADF] *Bad file descriptor*
A file descriptor argument was out of range, referred to no open file, or a read (write) request was made to a file that was only open for writing (reading).

[EBUSY] *Resource busy*
An attempt was made to use a system resource that was not available at the time because it was being used by a process in a manner that would have conflicted with the request being made by this process.

[ECHILD] *No child processes*
A wait() or waitpid() function was executed by a process that had no existing or unwaited for child process.

[EDEADLK] *Resource deadlock avoided*
An attempt was made to lock a system resource that would have resulted in a deadlock situation.

[EDOM] *Domain error*
Defined in the C Standard; an input argument was outside the defined domain of the mathematical function.

[EEXIST] *File exists*
An existing file was specified in an inappropriate context, for instance, as the new link name in a link() function.

[EFAULT] *Bad address*
The system detected an invalid address in attempting to use an argument of a call. The reliable detection of this error is implementation defined; however, implementations that do detect this condition shall use this value.

[EFBIG] *File too large*
The size of a file would exceed an implementation-defined maximum file size.

[EIDRM] Identifier removed
Returned during interprocess communication if an identifier has been removed from the system.

[EINTR] *Interrupted function call*
An asynchronous signal (such as SIGINT or SIQUIT; see the description of header <signal.h>) was caught by the process during the execution of an interruptible function. If the signal handler performs a normal return, the interrupted function shall return this error condition.

[EINVAL] *Invalid argument*
Some invalid argument was supplied. For example, specifying an undefined signal to a signal() or kill() function.

[EIO] *Input / output error*
Some physical input or output error occurred. This error may be reported on a subsequent operation on the same file descriptor. Any other error-causing operation on the same file descriptor may cause the [EIO] error indication to be lost.

[EISDIR] *Is a directory*
An attempt was made to open a directory with write mode specified.

[EMFILE] *Too many open files*
An attempt was made to open more than the maximum number of {OPEN_-MAX} file descriptors allowed in this process.

[EMLINK] *Too many links*
An attempt was made to have the link count of a single file exceed {LINK_-MAX}.

[ENAMETOOLONG] *Filename tool long*
The size of a pathname string exceeded {PATH_MAX}, or a pathname component was longer than {NAME_MAX} and {_POSIX_NO_TRUC} was in effect for that file.

[ENFILE] *Too many open files in system*
Too many files are currently open in the system. The system reached its predefined limit for simultaneously open files and temporarily could not accept requests to open another one.

[ENODEV] *No such device*
An attempt was made to apply an inappropriate function to a device; for example, trying to read a write-only device such as a printer.

[ENOENT] *No such file or directory*
A component of a specified pathname did not exist, or the pathname was an empty string.

[ENOEXEC] *Exec format error*
A request was made to execute a file that, although it had the appropriate permissions, was not in the format required by the implementation for executable files.

[ENOLCK] *No locks available*
A system imposed limit on the number of simultaneous file and record locks was reached and no more are available at that time.

[ENOMEM] *Not enough space*
The new process image required more memory than was allowed by the hardware or by system imposed memory management constraints.

[ENOMSG] No message of desired type
The message queue does not contain a message of the required type during interprocess communications.

[ENOSPC] *No space left on device*
During a write() function on a regular file, or when extending a directory, there was no free space left on the device.

[ENOTDIR] *Not a directory*
A component of the specified pathname existed, but it was not a directory, when a directory was expected.

[ENOTEMPTY] *Directory not empty*
A directory with entries other than dot and dot-dot was supplied when an empty directory was expected.

[ENOTTY] *Inappropriate I/O control operation*
A control function was attempted for a file or special fie for which operation was inappropriate.

[ENXIO] *No such device or address*
Input or output on a special file referred to a device that did not exist, or made a request beyond the limits of the device. This error may also occur when, for example, a tape drive is not on-line or no disk pack is loaded on a drive.

[EPERM] *Operation not permitted*
An attempt was made to perform an operation limited to processes with appropriate privileges or to the owner of a file or other resource.

[EPIPE] *Broken pipe*
A write was attempted on a pipe or FIFO for which there was no process to read the data.

[ERANGE] *Result too large*
Defined in the C Standard; the result of the function was too large to fit in the available space.

[EROFS] *Read only file system*
An attempt was made to modify a file or directory on a file system that was read-only at that time.

[ESPIPE] *Invalid seek*
An lseek() function was issued on a pipe or FIFO.

[ESRCH] *No such process*
No process could be found corresponding to that specified by the given process ID.

[ETXTBSY] Text file busy
An attempt has been made to execute a pure-procedure program that is currently open for writing, or an attempt has been made to open for writing a pure-procedure program that is being executed.

[EXDEV] *Improper link*
A link to a file on another file system was attempted.

2.11.2 Stream Errors

[EADV] Advertise error
This error is remote file sharing (RFS) specific. It occurs when users try to advertise a resource that has been advertised already, or try to stop RFS while

there are resources still advertised, or try to force unmount of a resource when it is still advertised.

[EBADFD] File descriptor in bad state
Either a file descriptor refers to no open file or a read request was made to a file that is open only for writing.

[EBADMSG] Trying to read unreadable message
During a read, getmsg, or ioctl system call to a STREAMS device, something has come to the head of the queue that cannot be processed.

[ECOMM] Communication error on send
This error is RFS specific. It occurs when the current process is waiting for a message from a remote machine, and the virtual circuit fails.

[EMULTIHOP] Multihop attempted
This error is RFS specific. It occurs when users try to access remote resources that are not directly accessible.

[ENAMETOOLONG] Path name is too long
The length of the path argument exceeds PATH_MAX, or the length of a path component exceeds NAME_MAX while _POSIX_NO_TRUNC is in effect.

[ENODATA] No data available
There are no data available on stream.

[ENOLINK] The link has been severed
This error is RFS specific. It occurs when the link (virtual circuit) connecting to a remote machine is gone.

[ENONET] Machine is not on the network
This error is RFS specific. It occurs when users try to advertise, unadvertise, mount, or unmount remote resources while the machine has not done the proper start-up to connect to the network.

[ENOPKG] Package not installed
This error occurs when users attempt to use a system call from a package that has not been installed.

[ENOSR] Out of streams resources
During a STREAMS open, either no STREAMS queues or no STREAMS head data structures were available. This is a temporary condition; one may recover

from it if other processes release resources.

[ENOSTR] Device not a stream
A putmsg or getmsg system call was attempted on a file descriptor that is not
a STREAMS device.

[ENOTUNIQ] Name not unique on network
Given log name not unique.

[EOVERFLOW] Value too large to be stored in data type
Value too large for defined data type.

[EPROTO] Protocol error
Some protocol error occurred. This error is device specific, but is generally not
related to a hardware failure.

[EREMCHG] Remote address changed
Address of the remote machine changed.

[EREMOTE] The object is remote
This error is RFS specific. It occurs when users try to advertise a resource that
is not on the local machine, or try to mount/unmount a device (or pathname)
that is on a remote machine.

[ESRMNT] Srmount error
This error is RFS specific. It occurs when an attempt is made to stop RFS
while resources are still mounted by remote machines, or when a resource is
readvertised with a client list that does not include a remote machine that
currently has the resource mounted.

[ETIME] Timer expired
The timer set for a STREAMS ioctl call has expired.

2.11.3 Shared Library Errors

[EILSEQ] Illegal byte sequence.
Handle multiple characters as a single character.

[ELIBACC] Cannot access a needed shared library
Trying to exec an a.out that requires a static shared library and the static
shared library does not exist or the user does not have permission to use it.

[ELIBBAD] Accessing a corrupted shared library
Trying to exec an a.out that requires a static shared library (to be linked in) and exec could not load the static shared library. The library is probably corrupted.

[ELIBEXEC] Attempting to exec a shared library
Attempting to exec a shared library directly.

[ELIBMAX] Attempting to link in too many libraries.
Trying to exec an a.out that requires more static shared libraries than is allowed on the current configuration of the system.

[ELIBSCN] .lib section in a.out corrupted
Trying to exec an a.out that requires a static shared library (to be linked in) and there were erroneous data in the .lib section of the a.out. The .lib section tells exec what static shared libraries are needed. The a.out is probably corrupted.

[ELOOP] Symbolic link loop
Number of symbolic links encountered during path name traversal exceeds MAXSYMLINKS.

[ENOSYS] Unsupported file system operation
File system operation not supported.

[ENOTEMPTY] Directory not empty
Directory contains some files.

[ERESTART] Restartable system call
Interrupted system call should be restarted.

[ESTRPIPE] If pipe/FIFO, do not sleep in stream head
Streams pipe error (not externally visible).

[EUSERS] Too many users (for UFS)
Too many users.

2.11.4 BSD Networking Software Errors

[EADDRINUSE] Address already in use

The address is already in use by some other process.

[EADDRNOTAVAIL] Can not assign requested address
The specified address is not available on the local or remote machine.

[EAFNOSUPPORT] Address family not supported by protocol family
Addresses in the specified address family cannot be used with this socket.

[EALREADY] operation already in progress
The socket is nonblocking and a previous connection attempt has not yet been completed.

[ECONNABORTED] Software caused connection abort
A connection abort was caused internal to your host machine.

[ECONNREFUSED] Connection refused
The attempt to connect was forcefully rejected. The calling program should close() the socket descriptor, and issue another socket() call to obtain a new descriptor before attempting another connect() call.

[ECONNRESET] Connection reset by peer
Connection has been reset by the peer.

[EDESTADDRREQ] Destination address required.
A required address was omitted from an operation.

[EHOSTDOWN] Host is down
A transport provider operation failed because the destination host was down.

[EHOSTUNREACH] No route to host
A transport provider operation was attempted to an unreachable host.

[EINPROGRESS] Operation now in progress
The socket is nonblocking and the connection cannot be completed immediately. It is possible to select() for completion by selecting the socket for writing. However, this is only possible if the socket STREAMS module is the topmost module on the protocol stack with a write service procedure.

[EISCONN] Socket is already connected
A connect request was made on an already connected socket.

[EMSGSIZE] Message too long

The socket requires that the message be sent atomically, and the message was too long.

[ENETDOWN] Network is down
Operation encountered a dead network.

[ENETRESET] Network dropped connection because of reset
The host you were connected to crashed and rebooted.

[ENETUNREACH] Network is unreachable
The network is not reachable from this host.

[ENOBUFS] No buffer space available
The system ran out of memory for fragmentation buffers or other internal data structure.

[ENOPROTOOPT] Protocol not available
The option is unknown at the level indicated.

[ENOTCONN] Socket is not connected
The specified socket is not connected.

[ENOTSOCK] Socket operation on nonsocket
Attempt to do socket operation on nonsocket.

[EOPNOTSUPP] Operation not supported on socket
The referenced socket is not of type SOCK_STREAMS.

[EPFNOSUPPORT] Protocol family not supported
The protocol family has not been configured into the system or no implementation for it exists.

[EPROTONOSUPPORT] Protocol not supported
The protocol type or the specified protocol is not supported within this domain.

[EPROTOTYPE] Protocol wrong type for socket
The file referred to by name is a socket of a type other than type s (for example, s is a SOCK_DGRAM socket, while name refers to a SOCK_STREAM socket).

[ESHUTDOWN] Can not send after socket shut down
A request to send data was disallowed because the socket has already been

shut down.

[ESOCKTNOSUPPORT] Socket type not supported
The support for the socket type has not been configured into the system or no implementation for it exists.

[ETIMEDOUT] Connection timed out
Connection establishment timed out without establishing a connection.

[ETOOMANYREFS] Too many references: can't splice
There are too many references unable to break.

[EWOULDBLOCK] Block the socket operation
The socket is marked nonblocking and the requested operation would block.

2.11.5 TLI Network Services Library Errors

[TACCES] Incorrect permissions
The user does not have permission to use the specified address or options.

[TBADADDR] Incorrect address format
The specified protocol address was in an incorrect format or contained illegal information.

[TBADDATA] Illegal amount of data
The amount of user data specified was not within the bounds allowed by the transport provider.

[TBADF] Illegal transport file descriptor
The specified file descriptor does not refer to a transport end point.

[TBADFLAG] Bad flags
An invalid flag is specified.

[TBADOPT] Incorrect option format
The specified protocol options were in an incorrect format or contained illegal information.

[TBADSEQ] Bad call sequence number
An invalid sequence number was specified.

[TBUFOVFLW] Buffer not large enough
The number of bytes allocated for an incoming argument is not sufficient to store the value of that argument.

[TFLOW] Flow control
O_NDELAY or O_NONBLOCK was set, but the flow control mechanism prevented the transport provider from accepting the function at this time.

[TLOOK] Event requires attention
An asynchronous event has occurred on this transport end point and requires immediate attention.

[TNOADDR] Could not allocate address
The transport provider could not allocate an address.

[TNODATA] No data
O_NDELAY or O_NONBLOCK was set, so the function successfully initiated the connection establishment procedure, but did not wait for a response from the remote user.

[TNODIS] No disconnect indication
No disconnect indication currently exists on the specified transport end point.

[TNOREL] No orderly release indication
No orderly release indication currently exists on the specified transport end point.

[TNOTSUPPORT] Primitive not supported
This function is not supported by the underlying transport provider.

[TNOUDERR] Unit data error not found
No unit data error indication currently exists on the specified transport end point.

[TOUTSTATE] Out of state
The function was issued in the wrong sequence.

[TSTATECHNG] State is in the process of changing
The transport provider is undergoing a state change.

[TSYSERR] System error
A system error has occurred during the execution of this function, errno will

be set to the specific error.

2.11.6 Exercises

2.1   Draw the UNIX system architecture diagram.

2.2   What is a library and a header file in UNIX operating system context?

2.3   Write a program so that when an input with newline is typed on standard input the signal-handling function writes the input to standard output. *Hint*: Use SIGIO.

2.4   Write a program that saves the calling environment when an error and/or interrupts are encountered in a low-level subroutine and that later restores the saved environment and continues with program execution. Print to standard output the values before and after the error and/or interrupts. *Hint*: Use sigsetjmp(), siglongjmp().

2.5   Implement a program to change and/or examine calling the process's signal mask. Print to standard output the mask value. *Hint*: Use sigprocmask().

2.6   Implement a program to add signal SIGALRM to the set pointed by the *sigset*. Check whether the signal specified by the value of SIGALRM is a member of set or not. Hint: Use sigaddset() and sigismember().

2.7   Write a program to generate error EACESS (permission denied). The error message text should contain the error number and error description. Display the error message text on standard output.

2.8   Write a program to generate error EBADF (bad file descriptor). The error message text should contain the error number and error description. Display the error message text on standard output.

Software Design and Testing

3.1　Introduction

Today, programming is done by students of any discipline. Good software design and testing are crucial for any program. The focus of this chapter is on some of the basics of software designing, coding, documentation, and testing. An X application program, xdtool, based on the motif widget set, is presented as a case study to discuss the details of different techniques. This will help anyone who wishes to write a program without getting lost in the intricate theoretical details of software analysis, design, coding, and testing methods. This view of software analysis, software design, software coding, testing, and final product process is illustrated in Figure 3-1. The software analysis section covers program requirements, program specifications, and quality specifications. The software design section discusses the different design methodologies and algorithm selection for given functions. The software coding section covers language selection criteria, Application Programmer's Interface (API) coding based on given program requirements. The programming style and evaluation of code at the completion of the coding of the application are also discussed. The software testing section discusses various testing methodologies. The software documentation section discusses the user and release documentation process. Application portability levels and a guide to writing application software are covered at the end of the chapter.

Since each application has specific requirements applicable to that category of applications only (for instance, network applications need protocol specifications, database applications need database file format and access specifications, and object-oriented programs need object-oriented representations), it is impossible to cover all the program requirements in a single software production process example. The xdtool application that displays a description of an input word is used as an example to explain the key program parameters and illustrates the overall process of software production. This process can be effectively applied to most of the application production with some variations.

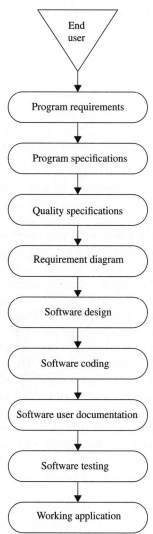

Figure 3-1
The software development process

3.2   Software Analysis

Given a task to be performed by an application, one needs to know exactly what the problem is and what to develop. The problem should be fully analyzed and investigated before it is coded. The analysis depends on the type of application being developed. The software application can be classified into the six broad categories shown in Table 3-1.

Table 3-1 Software Category

Software	Examples
Accounting software	Accounts payable, accounts receivable, financial Applications
Horizontal software	CAD, CAE, image processing, office productivity tools
Vertical software	Advertising, agriculture, engineering, scientific applications
System software	Access control, compilers, device drivers, debuggers
Communications software	LAN, WAN, Mac-to-UNIX, PC-to-UNIX, network servers
Application tools	Text editors, libraries, development languages (C, C++)

Depending on the type of software, the application should be further investigated in the following areas:

<u>Data-specific questions</u>
1. Data input
2. Data validation
3. Data manipulation
4. Data format
5. Data output

<u>System specific questions</u>
1. Compatibility
2. Interoperability
3. Internationalization
4. Localization
5. Portability
6. Program language
7. Scalability

8. Testability

Development time-specific questions

1. Labor estimates
2. Project milestones
3. System resources
4. Testing procedures

Market and cost-specific questions

1. Development cost
2. Selling cost
3. Software documentation guide
4. Target market areas

Once the software has been categorized and requirements fully studied by the user and developer, the program requirements should be documented.

In this section we will do a case study on a real-life X application program and use it as a benchmark program for software analysis and design.

3.2.1 Program Requirements

Program requirements are documentation of the user's requirements so that the application program's desired intent and properties are well understood by the user and developer.

The user who wants the program should be very specific about the program's use and the task it should perform. The program's use should be explained to the developer with examples. For commercial applications, the independent software vendor (ISV) should study the user and market requirements before developing the software. Any software application can be described in terms of the activities comprising the system and the flow of data among these activities referred to as requirement diagrams.

3.2.1.1 Input/Output Specifications

The software application in its basic form can be described in terms of input, black box (software application), and output, as shown in Figure 3-2, represents the basic primitive form of a program requirement diagram for most of the application. The input and output are usually associated with the user. In some automated software applications the input is supplied by the software driver and the output is manipulated in some form for later use.

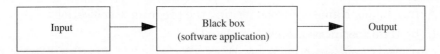

Figure 3-2
Basic program requirement diagram (black-box representation)

3.2.1.2 Models

The program requirements can also be expressed in the form of a model. Complex requirements can be expressed in an accurate and efficient way. Four different types of models are commonly used: mathematical, functional, timing, and object.

1. **Mathematical models:** A mathematical model uses relations to describe the software's behavior. Mathematical models are very useful for linear programming, navigation, econometric, signal processing and weather analysis types of applications.

2. **Functional models:** A functional model provides mapping from inputs to outputs. A functional model can be used to specify the response of a previously described mathematical model in the form of a finite state machine. Function models, finite state machines, or Petri nets can help identify and define various features of the software or can demonstrate the intended operation of the system.

3. **Timing models:** A timing model specifies the timing constraints. For real-time systems, the timing model can be used to specify the form and details of the software's behavior.

4. **Object models:** An object model specifies the problem domain in terms of objects and classes. Similar objects are defined in their common class. An object has state, behavior, and identity. The complete behavior of a system is expressed in terms of relationships between objects.

3.2.2 Program Specifications

Program specifications call for writing precise, detailed descriptions of the program requirements. The program requirements also describe the planned set of inputs, the desired processing, and the planned set of outputs of a program. Ideally the specification does not recommend the particular algorithms or techniques the program should use. The specifications should contain:

- Project name: Name of the software application
- Author name: Name of person writing the program specifications
- Date: Date specifications are completed
- Category: Category of the application
- Synopsis: Name and command line options of the application
- Description: Detailed description of the program and its behavior
- External interfaces: Detailed user interface and/or GUI button description, if any
- System resources: Memory (RAM), disk space, and other system requirements
- Security: Access to software application issues
- Diagnostics: Error messages provided to users
- Issues: Open items, system requirements, built tools

Some server or client server types of applications like X server and database types of applications may need detailed descriptions of the type of system resources needed for applications to function properly.

3.2.3   Program Quality Specifications

Program quality specifications are the precise statement of a set of program characteristics, each characteristic being called a quality attribute. The quality attribute can be measured in terms of a metric value. For each quality attribute, a minimum acceptable level, a maximum desired level, and an expected or planned level are specified. A priority ranking or level is given to each quality attribute.

The unit of the attribute should be well defined. For example, the performance of the application under a heavy load should be measured in the time unit of seconds. The minimum level specifies the lowest value achievable for a given quality attribute; for example, the automated testing of the software on a machine with good computing power could be done in 10 minutes. The maximum level specifies the highest limit allowable. For example, automated testing of a system with less computing power and memory could take about 30 minutes to test the whole software. The planned level is the targeted attribute level for a given attribute; in most cases its value is between the maximum and minimum limits. The priority level could be as in Table 3-2.

Table 3-2   Priority Levels

Priority	Level
High	1
Medium	2
Low	3

Following are some program attributes that should be considered:

- **Completeness:** This is the most important quality attribute. This attribute provides the overall picture of the project's development. The completeness quality attribute can be measured in terms of the ratio of completed software components or documents compared to the total number of software components or documents.

- **Consistency:** The software program should be consistent in the use of notations, terminologies, and symbols. Code should be indented in a consistent manner. This attribute can be measured in terms of the ratio of variation per number of lines of the source code. Variation is the deviation in usage of symbols, comments, and the like, and could result from the previously discussed design specifications. This attribute can also be measured in terms of the ratio of software components or documents that are free of variation to the total number of software components or documents.

- **Correctness:** The correctness of the software is very important. This quality attribute specifies how well the software requirements and design specifications have been implemented. It can be measured in the terms of the ratio of correctly implemented specifications in software components to total the number of software components.

- **Interoperability:** This quality is the ability of two or more components or systems to exchange information. This attribute can be measured in terms of the number of software components whose interfaces are compatible compared to the total number of software components.

- **Internationalization:** The software application should contain internationalization functions for future localization. The internationalization attribute is measured in terms of the number of languages the software can run on if the localized message catalog files are provided. The software application should also provide the correct directory tree structure for language-specific message catalog files to reside in after the translation of the message catalog file is completed.

- **Learning ease:** The user should be able to get familiar with the tool in a short amount of time. The learning curve of the tool should be minimum. The interface should be user friendly with spot help messages for all the buttons and fields. This guides the user through the tool in a concise and easy manner without having to resort to explanations in the user's guide. This attribute can be measured in terms of minutes.

- **Localization:** The program should a contain country-specific directory for deposition of localized message catalog files. The localization attribute is also measured in terms of the number of languages, but with a slight difference— it means the number of different language interfaces for which the localized message catalog files are currently provided.

- **Maintainability:** The software should be easy to maintain. Failed operations should be easy to restore to satisfactory conditions with easy bug identification. This attribute can be measured in terms of the ratio of total error correction labor time required to the total number of corrections.

- **Modifiability:** Change and enhancement to the program should be easy to implement. Modifiability depends on the type of upgrade to be made to the software. If it is a minor fix, it could done be in days, if a major change is to be incorporated, it could take months or years. Modifiability is usually associated with upward revision of the software to incorporate new features of the upgraded operating system and/or computing power.

- **Performance:** The program should be able to continue execution under certain imperfect conditions, such as input data out of order or part of input data missing. If the system is under a heavy load the application should distribute the task and if the immediate output is not required, it should return to the user. The performance attribute of response time can be measured in seconds.

- **Portability:** The program should be able to run on different computers by using standardized features of the programming language. The unit of measurement of the portability attribute is the number of operating systems the software application can be ported to.

- **Reliability:** The software application should be error and bug free. Ideally, under no condition should the software hang up or freeze. The unit of measurement can be the ratio of computer runs that produce correct outputs to the total number of invocations or runs.

- **Testability:** The application software should produce quality outputs for easy testability. Useful messages should be provided for testing and debugging purposes. The attribute unit of measurement can be identification of independent paths for testing. In a crude way, this attribute can also be measured in terms of the number of minutes it takes the software to be tested. Like some of the other attributes, the testing time depends on the computing power of the machine.

3.2.4 Software Specification Form (SSF)

The software specification form (SSF) consists of all the key items of the program requirements, specifications, and quality specifications. The SSF document can be submitted for review and/or presentation within an organization and may contain items as listed in Table 3-3. Alpha and beta are test releases. FCS stands for first customer support, a complete product that a vendor can buy.

Table 3-3 Software Specification Form (SSF)

Item	Program...	Item	Program...
1	Name	2	Author name
3	Date	4	Category
5	Synopsis	6	Requirements
7	Diagram	8	Description
9	External interfaces	10	System resources
11	Security	12	Diagnostics
13	Quality specifications	14	System requirements
15	Development tools	16	Executable file name
17	Labor estimates	18	Design time
19	Design review	20	Coding time
21	Integration time	22	Documentation
23	Alpha release	24	Alpha testing
25	Alpha bug fixes	26	Beta release
27	Beta release	28	Beta bug fixes
29	Packaging time	30	FCS
31	Cost estimates	32	Issues

Items 16 to 32 are rough estimates. They cannot be quantified until the software design issues are fully studied and documented. The alpha, beta, and FCS releases for a big project can have N number of minor releases like alpha 1.0, 1.1.., beta 1.0, 1.1.., and pre-FCS 1.0, 1.1...

3.2.5   Software Specification Document (SSD)

The software specification document (SSD) is detailed documentation of all the items in the software specification form (SSF). It is the first document in a software production cycle that details the end-user requirements. This document should be given to the end-user for review to get feedback on whether all requirements are covered or not.

Consider the following software project involving the development of the X window system-based tool to automate the search of a word from a dictionary database and the display of its meaning, analogous to manually searching for a word in a dictionary and finding its meaning. The tool can also be used to display the meaning of a UNIX glossary word or to check the spelling of a word.

The xdtool SSF can now be documented to create the SSD. Some of the quality specifications are for the sake of explanation only and are not implemented.

Example: xdtool Software Specification Document (SSD)

Project overview

Develop an X window-based tool with Graphical User Interface (GUI) to search for a word from a dictionary database file and display the meaning of the word.

After careful analysis of the given problem, the following are some of the important software specifications.

1. **Project name:** Dictionary Tool
2. **Author name:** <your name here>
3. **Date:** 10/01/1993
4. **Category:** Application Tools
5. **Synopsis:** xdtool [-d directory] [-h help] [X options]

6. **Requirements**

   - User to input a dictionary word.

   - The software application to search for the word in the dictionary database file.

   - Display exact match of a word with description or closest possible active dictionary word list.

   - Internationalization for input usage of character set, character collation and word separation for a given locale [e.g., strxfrm(), strcoll()].

7. **Requirement diagram:** Program Requirement Diagram can now be easily drawn as in Figure 3-3.

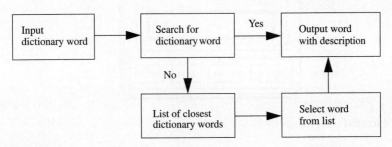

Figure 3-3
Program requirement diagram for xdtool application

8. **Description:** xdtool application finds detailed description and the equivalent of a given dictionary word. If the dictionary word is not found, it gives the closest available word list. By default, xdtool searches for the token from the database files in the current directory. The default directory path can be changed through the xdtool environment variable XDTOOLDIR or *XDtoolres* resource file.

9. **External interfaces**

The external interfaces are as shown in Figure 3-4.

Figure 3-4
xdtool external interfaces

- **Match:** Text Field; gives the exact match of the
  dictionary word or equivalent closest match to select
  from the list. The default text field is 20 characters
  with the scrollbar after that. By default, a list of the
  10 closest match words can be seen with the scrollbar
  beyond it.

- **Search:** Text Field; use the search text field to specify
  the name of the dictionary word to be searched for. The
  default text field is 20 characters with the scrollbar
  after that. After entering the word, carriage return
  causes a search for the description in a dictionary
  database. If found, the description is displayed in the
  form of a panel.

- **Apply:** Push Button; if the dictionary token has been
  entered in the search field, allows the dictionary token

to be searched on a single click of the left mouse button. If found, display the description in the form of a panel.

- **Reset:** Push Button; initializes and refreshes the xdtool application and destroys the previous contents in the Search and Match text fields.
- **Quit:** Push Button; on a single click of the left mouse button, allows quitting the xdtool application.
- **Help:** Push Button; on a single click of the left mouse button, invokes the help panel for the xdtool.

10. **System resources:** The xdtool application needs at least 1MB (megabyte) of RAM (random-access memory) and 2MB of disk space for executable binaries, libraries, and dictionary files.

11. **Security:** Can only be accessed by the user with valid identification key.

12. **Diagnostics:**
Match found: Description for the dictionary word exists in the database file.

No match: Invalid word, not in the dictionary database.

Signal Errors: Uncatchable signals via signal handler.

X errors: Unable to open display, font, color not found, bad atom as values and so on.

Xt errors: Xt instrinsic specific errors.

13. **Quality specifications:** Table 3-4 lists the program quality specifications of the xdtool example application with minimum, maximum and planned levels with priority rankings for each attribute. See the section on software documentation for the total number of documents required by a given completed software product.

14. **System requirements:** The xdtool application will need the UNIX operating system with static and shared systems, X11R5, and motif release 1.2 libraries.

Table 3-4 Quality Specifications for xdtool Application

Attribute	Unit	Minimum	Maximum	Planned	Priority
Completeness	Completed documents/total documents	5/6	6/6	6/6	1
Consistency	Consistent documents/total documents	4/6	6/6	5/6	2
Correctness	Correct components/total components	3/5	5/5	4/5	1
Interoperability	Interoperable components/total components	7/10	10/10	8/10	2
Internationalization	Number of languages	1	All languages	2	3
Learning Ease	Learning time in minutes, hours, days	5 minutes	1 day	15 minutes	1
Localization	Number of languages	1	All languages	2	3
Maintainability	Bug identification speed in minutes, hours, days	10 minutes	1 day	30 minutes	1
Modifiability	Number of days to upgrade	1 day	10 days	5 days	2
Performance	Response time in seconds	1 second	3 seconds	2 seconds	1
Portability	Number of operating system	3	All OS	5	1
Reliability	Failure/number of operations	1/500	1/infinity	1/5,000	1
Testability	Testing time in minutes	10 minutes	30 minutes	20 minutes	2

15. **Development tools:**
    - C compiler
    - GUI builder
    - Makefile generator
    - Source code control tools (sccs, rcs, etc.)
    - debuggers
16. **Executable file name:** xdtool
17. **Labor estimates:** 1 programmer
18. **Design time:** 10 days/2 working weeks
19. **Design review:** 5 days/1 working week
20. **Coding time:** 10 days/2 working weeks
21. **Integration time:** Integrating all source modules, source cleanup, 2 days
22. **Documentation:** 5 days/1 working week
23. **Alpha release:** 11/15/93
24. **Alpha testing:** 1 day
25. **Alpha bug fixes:** 1 day
26. **Beta release:** 11/17/93
27. **Beta testing:** 1 day
28. **Beta bug fixes:** 1 day
29. **Packaging time:** 5 days
30. **Cost estimates:** <location dependent>
31. **FCS:** 11/22/93
32. **Issues:** dictionary files availability and format; GUI development tools

3.3 Software Design

Software design is a process of implementing software specifications. First, the specification is analyzed to provide a precise breakdown of the functions desired. This procedure is intended to uncover any inconsistencies and shortcomings in the specification and, at the same time, to prepare for the development of test cases. The working drawings and outline allow improvement of the specification by providing the modification and growth of the required software application and for good communication facilities between the program and user. Software design also outlines how a desired program will perform its intended function. This way the major details of a proposed solution can be determined before coding begins so that the solution can be compared with alternative solutions, and the intended program can be improved before committing to specific programming details.

Software design is the blueprint of the intended software functions and algorithms before coding. Some of the programming paradigms used are:

- Procedure oriented
- Object oriented
- Logic oriented
- Rule oriented
- Client-server oriented

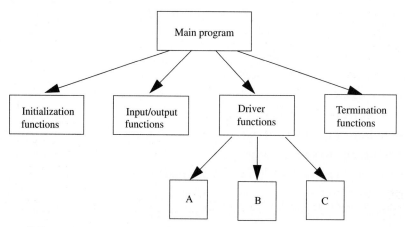

Figure 3-5
Standard form for program structure

A further study on the determination of major data entities, major functions, type of design, and algorithms is carefully organized. At the same time it is determined if the program is feasible. Quality specifications are analyzed again and whether the desired speed and capacity are achievable using present or planned system resources. This section will focus on some of the software design methods. All these designs are presented as tools for software design. A given application program may not fit into any of the design methods discussed; the designer may have to adopt a hybrid of design methods. But in real life almost all the applications fall into one of the categories. Most programs can be organized as shown in Figure 3-5. The structure of the standard program is usually the main program module, initialization, input/output, driver, and termination functions.

A standard form for most commercial applications can now be derived consisting of main() function, initialization or initialization function, a basic set of read(), write() functions, a driver function calling set of functions A(), B(), and others for data manipulation, and an exit() routine to terminate the program. Figure 3-6 depicts the standard form for most commercial applications.

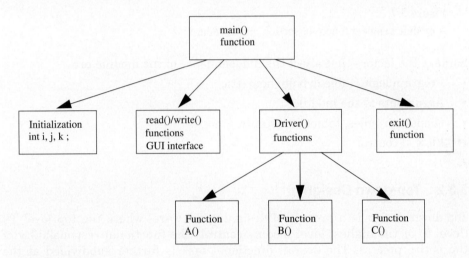

Figure 3-6
Standard form for commercial application

3.3.1 Modular Design

Modular design is a process in which any logical portion can be changed without affecting the rest of the program. In a modular program, each module (for example, each function, section, or procedure as shown in Figure 3-7) is independent of the others. This implies that it can be changed or modified without affecting other modules. In practice, this independence is difficult to achieve. A 100% independence may be utopian thinking, but even if a modularity of 90% is achieved, it could lead to less testing, debugging, and maintenance time.

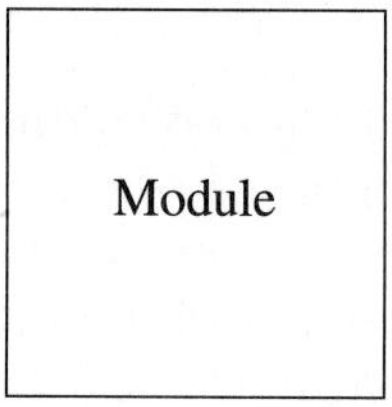

Figure 3-7
A module can be a function, section, or procedure

Some of the factors that affect the independence of the module are

- Program logic (table driven, heuristic)
- Arguments to the module
- Global variables, tables, constants
- Flow of control

3.3.2 Top-down Design

Top-down design is a process of designing software, where the top level T0 (level 0) or the highest-level module controls the functional responsibility of the entire process. The overall functional task is further subdivided at the next level, T1, T2, Tn (level 1), among a set of subsidiary modules, and so on. In its most elementary conceptual form it can be represented as in Figure 3-8(a).

Topddown design coding can be arranged in two ways, horizontally and vertically as shown in Figures 3-8 (b) and (c), respectively. The horizontal approach is good for an overview of the program. From a debugging or maintenance point of view, the vertical approach may be more convenient.

A top-down design is usually good for programs written from scratch. A top-down design involves breaking a large problem into smaller subproblems that can be dealt with individually. The key to successful top-down design seems to be a formal and rigorous effort on the part of the designer to specify the input, the function, and the output of each module in a program or system.

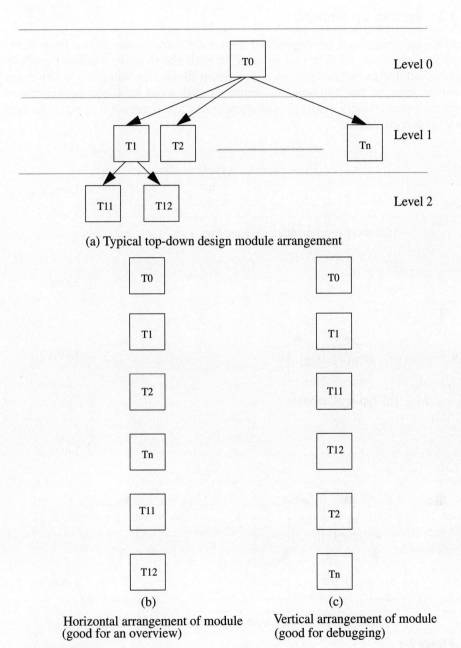

(a) Typical top-down design module arrangement

(b)

Horizontal arrangement of module
(good for an overview)

(c)

Vertical arrangement of module
(good for debugging)

Figure 3-8
Top-down design

3.3.3   Bottom-up Design

Bottom-up design is a process of designing software in which the lower-level modules are designed first and integrated with the main or top-level module. Bottom-up design is the inverse of top-down design. In some cases the main level or some of the top-level modules already exist or could be generated fromthe commercially available software packages. Figure 3-9 depicts the bottom-up design stages.

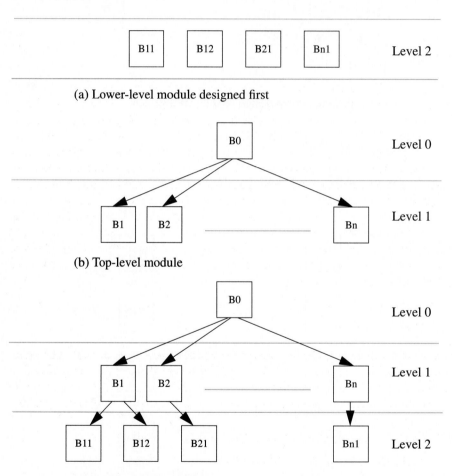

(a) Lower-level module designed first

(b) Top-level module

(c) Modules b and c integrated to generate bottom-up design

Figure 3-9
Bottom-up design

As shown in Figure 3-9(a), the lower modules B11, B12, B21, and Bn1 are designed first; a test driver is then coded to help test the modules and their interfaces. These modules are then integrated with a module subsystem at the next higher level, which coordinates the operations of these modules. Modules B11 and B12 are integrated with the higher-level module B1, module B21 is integrated with the higher-level module B2, and so forth. Figure 3-9(b) shows the higher-level modules. The union of all lower-level and corresponding upper-level module subsystems generates the complete bottom-up design shown in Figure 3-9(c).

3.3.4 Structured Design

Structured design is the process of designing a software program with well-structured branching and control statements. It includes the concept of top-down program design. In structured design the use of goto statements is taboo. In this scheme, an entire program is considered a subroutine from the operating systems point of view. The program interacts with the operating system with one entry and one exit point. Structured programming sometimes involves duplication of the code. The duplication of the code is required when, after making a decision, the task to be performed is common. The duplication can be avoided by writing a generalized subroutine and calling that routine after making the decision. The routine should return a range of valid and invalid values to the caller instead of making a decision and exiting. It is the prerogative of the caller to test the return value and then continue or return from the routine.

3.3.5 Object -oriented Design

In object-oriented design writing the programming revolves around the logical entity object. It is a new approach to write large complex programs by dividing the task into smaller modules. Object-oriented design is based on the principle of structured and modular design, unlike conventional procedural design. The design is centered on:

- Objects: A logical entity that contains both data and code
- Encapsulation: Linkage of code and data
- Polymorphism: One name that can be used for several different purposes
- Inheritance: A process by which one object can acquire the properties of another object

Object-oriented analysis (OOA) analyzes the problem domain in terms of objects and classes, while object-oriented design (OOD) reflects the system to be built in the same term. The usual progression is from OOA -> OOD -> OOP in an implementation. OOA and OOD differ from OOP in that the notations are graphical instead of the usual textual declarative form. This allows easier visualization and makes dependencies more explicit.

3.3.6   Simulation Models

A software simulation model is a process of designing a software program in which components of the application represent the components of the system of interest on a one-for-one basis and each software component mimics the behavior of the represented component.

The simulation model ensures that the entities of the software system explicitly correspond to the entities of the underlying real-world system. The programs are easy to understand and maintain if the entities of the software system mirror those of the real world.

A software flight simulator is a classical example based on the simulation model. The take-off, flight patterns, altitude, wind speed, and landing are based on real-life airplane data. Effects of changes to any parameter can be easily studied, which helps in designing better and advanced airplanes. It also helps in simulated flight instruction.

3.3.7   Design Tools

Currently, a number of commercial design tools are available that allow automation of parts of the design process. The efficient use of these tools can sharply cut down the development time and cost. A number of design tools available that help in designing the graphical user interface (GUI), makefiles, grammar generator, check for memory leaks in logic, source code maintenance tools, and more. One can also use the parts of previously written programs and/or design instead of writing from scratch. Some important factors that should be considered when selecting the GUI builders:

1. Multiple operating systems
2. Multiple libraries
3. Same look and feel

The tools should be able to generate code that can be compiled and run on different architectures and operating systems. The GUI tools should also be able to generate code having functions from different libraries, for instance Motif libraries, OPENLOOK, InterViews, and MS Windows libraries without any loss of external interface looks. This way the user interface has the identical look and feel across the platforms and different architectures.

3.3.8 Documenting Design

The purpose of the software design documentation is to put forward a concrete, feasible proposal. The solution is outlined to show the overall approach, and resolution of the critical issues is discussed. It sets assumptions and restrictions. The proposal should be clearly written so as to convince the reader that the design can be implemented.

The design proposal format of the project should contain the following four major sections:

- **Design solution:** This section contains the program specifications, data input, data manipulations, and data output. The boundaries to input and output data are applied. This helps in stating an intended scope and the program specification in order to have a precise statement about the proposed program.
- **Design approach:** The design approach discusses how it intends to solve the problem. The overall design and techniques of the proposed program are now presented. The design technique can be any of the techniques discussed in previous sections. First, a list of major data blocks is given with a brief description of each block. Second, a list of major processing functions or routines is given with a brief description of each function.
- **Documenting the application programmer interface (API):** All the application functions should be documented. This leads to stricter quality controls during coding and reusable code for some future projects. The functions name, syntax, description, return values, and error diagnostics should be listed.
- **Design evaluation:** The proposed design is studied again to resolve deficiencies in any of the functions or routines. The design is studied for a typical input and worst-case input.

3.3.9   Software Design Form (SDF)

The software design form (SDF) consists of a list of important design parameters. Once documented, the design parameters shown in Table 3-5, should be studied and evaluated for any deficiencies in the design specifications.

Table 3-5 Software Design Form (SDF)

Item	Program...
1	Design type
2	Design tools
3	Process flow
4	Software architecture overview
5	Protocol specifications
6	Database specifications
7	Data structures
8	Key algorithms
9	System libraries
10	Application library names
11	API, Application programmers Interface specification
12	Application library functions
13	Design validation
14	Design review

3.3.10 Software Design Document (SDD)

The software design document (SDD) provides detailed documentation for all the items of the software design form (SDF). This design document is the single most important document in the software production cycle. This document should be reviewed very carefully. A good design with reusable functionality can cut down the cost of future software projects. The following example documents the xdtool application design in detail.

Example: xdtool Software Design Document (SDD)

1. **Design type:** Top-down, modular, procedure oriented

2. **Design tools:**
   · Project management tools
   · GUI builder
   · Project workspace
   · Source code control tools (sccs, rcs etc.)

3. **Process flow:** The process flow diagrams are as shown in Figure 3-10.

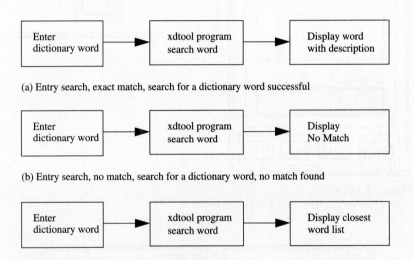

(a) Entry search, exact match, search for a dictionary word successful

(b) Entry search, no match, search for a dictionary word, no match found

(c) Entry search, close match. search for a dictionary word, displays closest words

Figure 3-10
Process flow diagram for xdtool

4. **Software architecture overview:** The software architecture overview diagrams can be drawn from the process flow as in Figure 3-11. The help message box is shown in Figure 3-12. There may also be spot help messages for every button and text field providing information to the user at every point. The online help should have hypertext links to navigate easily.

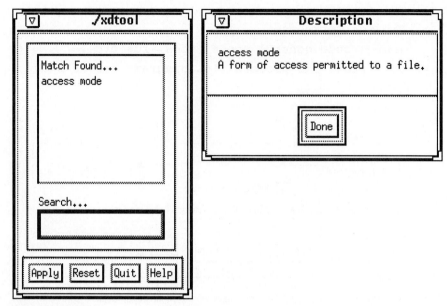

Figure 3-11 (a)
Search for dictionary word successful

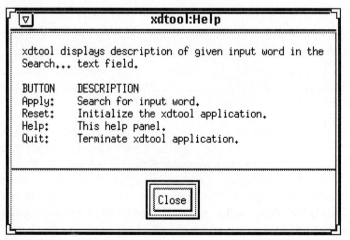

Figure 3-12
xdtool help message box

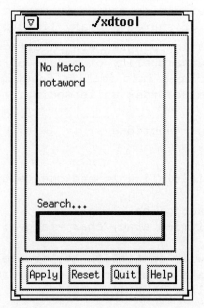

Figure 3-11 (b)
Search for dictionary word failed

5. **Protocol specifications:** None

6. **Database specifications:** Dictionary file formats
   - dict.list: List of all dictionary words separated by newline.
   - dict.desc: Dictionary words with descriptions. Each dictionary description end tagged with EOR (end of record) identifier on a separate line.

7. **Data structures:** No major user-defined data structures.

8. **Key Algorithms:** Linear search, fuzzy match. Algorithm should be able to perform comparisons of collated character set [use strcoll() and strxfrm() internationalization calls].

9. **System libraries:** libsys, libc, Motif release 1.2, and later libraries.

10. **Application library names:** The generic reusable application functions to reside in static library libxdtool.a and/or shared library libxdtool.so.1.

11. **API:** The application programmers interface list may contain major functionality of module or function. A module may be divided into smaller functions without loss of any predetermined task while coding.

· *Initialization Functions*

NAME
  AppInit - initialize Xt and create top-level shell
SYNOPSIS
  #include <xdtool.h>
  void AppInit(int argc, char **argv);
DESCRIPTION
  AppInit() will initialize Xt, create an application context, make a connection to the display and create a top-level application shell.
RETURN VALUE
  None

NAME
  AppGetOptions - extract command line options
SYNOPSIS
  #include <xdtool.h>
  void AppGetOptions(int argc, char **argv);
DESCRIPTION
  AppGetOptions() function will extract from the command all options used by the application and other valid X options.
RETURN VALUE
  None

NAME
  AppUsage - print to stdout the usage message
SYNOPSIS
  void AppUsage(char *app_name);
DESCRIPTION
  AppUsage will print to stdout the usage message of the application.

RETURN VALUE
None

· *Security Functions*

NAME
SecureApp - allows the use of application only by
licensed users
SYNOPSIS
void SecureApp()
DESCRIPTION
SecureApp() function will allow to access xdtool
by licensed users only. The users need to enter valid
key code to access the application for the first
time. This key will be matched with the applications
encrypted key.
RETURN VALUE
None
ERRORS
Not a valid key code.

· *Error-handling Functions*

NAME
SigHandler - print uncatchable signal error and
abort application
SYNOPSIS
#include <signal.h>
void sig_handler(int sig, int code);
DESCRIPTION
This routine will print uncatchable signal error
like SIGBUS, SIGSEGV, etc., and exit application.
The handler will be set by signal() function.
RETURN VALUE
None

NAME
XHandler - print X protocol error and abort
application
SYNOPSIS
int XHandler(Display *dpy, XErrorEvent *err_ev);

DESCRIPTION
This function will be invoked by application when a
X protocol error occurs. It will print the error
message and abort application. It will be set by
XSetErrorHandler() function.
RETURN VALUE
None

NAME
XioHandler - print X server disconnect error and
abort application
SYNOPSIS
int XioHandler(Display *dpy);
DESCRIPTION
This function will be invoked by application when a
X I/O error occurs, such as server disconnect.
It will print the error message and abort
application. It will be set by XSetIOErrorHandler()
function.
RETURN VALUE
None

NAME
XtHandler - print Xt intrinsic error and abort
application
SYNOPSIS
void XtHandler(String Name, String type,
String class, String defaultp, String *params,
Cardinal *num);
DESCRIPTION
This function will be invoked by application when
an Xt Intrinsic error occurs. It will be set by
XAppSetErrorMsgHandler() function.
RETURN VALUE
None

· *Search Functions*

NAME
GetWord - get input word and find a match in the list
SYNOPSIS

```
int GetWord(char *input);
```
DESCRIPTION
The GetWord() function gets the input word from the
search field and searches for an entry in the
dictionary database file.
RETURN VALUE
If the word is found, it returns zero; else it
returns the nonzero integer value.

- *Display Functions*

NAME
DisplayDesc() - display description for a given
input word in a message box
SYNOPSIS
```
Widget DisplayDesc(char *word, Widget parent);
```
DESCRIPTION
The DisplayDesc() function will print description of
given input dictionary word.
RETURN VALUE
Upon successful completion it returns
the message dialog widget.

- *Exit Functions*

NAME
QuitApp() - exit application
SYNOPSIS
```
void QuitApp()
```
DESCRIPTION
This QuitApp() will be registered as callback
function and will allow to exit xdtool application
by a single click on Quit push button.
RETURN VALUE
None

12. **Application library functions:**
AppGetOptions, AppInit, AppUsage, DisplayDesc, GetWord,
QuitApp, SecureApp, SigHandler, XHandler, XioHandler,
XtHandler

13. **Design validation:** Fuzzy match logic not implemented

14. **Design review:** To be presented to design group for critical comments, changes, etc.

3.4   Software Coding

The final stage in the software development cycle is writing code for the software design. This coding should be approached in a careful, cautious, and organized fashion. The coding should be implemented in top-down fashion as discussed earlier. Initially, avoid using the sophisticated algorithms that make a program complicated. The approach of entire software coding and designing on the fly is a recipe for disaster. The basic goal should be a working program. The algorithm of different modules can be changed at a later stage to make it more robust and error free. The code should be clean and readable with functionality at every stage documented; this makes it easy to modify and debug the code. This section discusses some of the finer points of coding software.

3.4.1   Programming Language

The choice of the programming language depends on the software design and problem. The appropriate language selection can greatly reduce coding time. Lately, the C and C++ languages have become very popular, and almost any application can be implemented using these languages. Part of their popularity stems from the fact that most operating systems are written in C language. Table 3-6 lists some of the languages with the applications they may be most suited for.

Table 3-6 Language-application Association

Language	Applications
ADA	Military data processing
BASIC	Interactive small applications
C	Any type of applications
C++	Object-oriented applications
COBOL	Business applications
FORTRAN	Numerical and scientific applications
LISP	Artificial intelligence applications
PASCAL	Structured and modular applications

3.4.2 Programming Style

Programming style refers to the way the programmer approaches writing the software code in a given language. A program has two functions; it directs a computer in the execution of an algorithm, and it also conveys design and techniques to other programmers who may need to change the program. The coding style refers to the manner in which these directions and ideas are expressed in the program text. The program text determines effectiveness in communicating with:

- **User:** Most programs interact with the user. This is a crucial aspect of any program with interactive processing, to let the user have information on the current activity in progress by displaying comment lines as:

  xdtool: Invoking xdtool application...
  xdtool: Searching dictionary database...

- **Tester:** Almost all the programs have to undergo some sort of testing. The output should be structured; this format helps the tester to automate the testing procedure.

- **Maintenance programmer:** The program should have comments, assertions, error detection, and debug statements. The debug statements can be of the form

  #ifdef DEBUG
  ...
  #endif

  This helps to diagnose the problem quickly in case of software failures.

- **Variable names:** Variable names are the symbolic basic data object names used by the program. The variable name should be meaningful, resembling its intended use in the program.

- **Function names:** Function names should ideally begin with the project acronym or an initially agreed upon convention. If the source code module or function is to be reused in some other application or projects, the names should be generic. The function name can be tagged with the type of operation it performs according to its intended use. For example, in the case of xdtool example, all the callback functions can be of the type XD_CB_func(), where XD is short for xdtool, and CB is short for CallBack and, similarly, the event handlers as XD_EH_func() (here EH identifies it as event handler function). If the name is to be generic, it can be ApplyCB, QuitCB, or the like.

- **Data structure names:** Structure names, like function names, may begin with the project acronym or initially agreed upon prefix. Also, a suffix of struct could be added. All the structures in the xdtool program can be of type XD_Struct_name() or XDS_name(). The C++ class name may look like XD_Class_name() or XDC_name().

3.4.3 Evaluation of Code

Many program qualities can be checked by examining the program code. Quality checklists can be used in code inspections and structured walk-throughs. Some of the criteria are:

1. Compatibility
2. Design validation
3. Efficiency
4. Error handling
5. Internationalization
6. Localization
7. Maintainability
8. Modifiability
9. Portability
10. Reliability
11. Testability

Some of other intuitive quality components connected with the general user interface of the program are:

1. Accuracy
2. Accessibility
3. Consistency
4. Communicativeness
5. Device efficiency
6. User-friendly interface

3.4.4 Software Coding Form (SCF)

The software coding form can be used to track the development of software, notation, documentation, and so on. Some important criteria to be considered are listed in Table 3-7.

Table 3-7 Software Coding Form (SCF)

Item	Program...
1	Language
2	Coding tools
3	Input
4	Output
5	External interfaces
6	Variable names
7	Data structure names
8	Function names
9	Application library functions
10	Source documentation
11	Source code
12	Design validation

3.4.5 Software Coding Document (SCD)

The software coding form (SCF) can be used to generate the software coding document (SCD). It contains detailed descriptions of all the items of the SCF. It should contain at least the programming language(s) used, coding tools, and complete source code listings, as well as reusable functions API. The following example contains the complete xdtool application software coding document.

Example: xdtool Software Coding Document (SCD)

1. **Language:** C-UNIX Programming Language
2. **Coding tools:**
    - C compiler
    - GUI builder
    - Makefile generator
    - Project workspace
    - Source code control tools (e.g., sccs, rcs, etc.)

- Debuggers

3. **Input:** Dictionary word

4. **Output:** Dictionary description

5. **External interfaces:** Will assume external GUI interface source code has been implemented using GUI builder. Although in reality the code has been implemented using previous program templates. The idea is to cover API listings for all major categories of functions because many applications may not be GUI based.

6. **Variable names:**
   - Counter variables: i, j, k, l, ...
   - Return values: ret_val, word, line, message
   - Filenames: prefix_file, dict.list, dict.desc

7. **Data structure names:** No major-user defined data structures

8. **Function names:**
   This function list may contain more functions than one specified in the API section of the software design document by subdividing the functionality at the time of coding.
   - Initialization functions
     AppGetOptions(), AppInit(), AppUsage()
   - Security functions
     SecureApp(), GetKeyStd(), GetKeyFile()
   - Error Handling functions
     SigHandler(), XHandler(), XioHandler(), XtHandler()
   - Search functions
     GetWord(), GetMessage()
   - Display functions
     GetDesc(), DisplayDesc()
   - Exit functions
     QuitApp()

9. **Application library functions:** Alphabetical listing of reusable library functions residing in library libxdtool.a/libxdool.so.1 with brief descriptions are listed in Table 3-8.

Table 3-8 Alphabetical Listing with Description of libxdtool Library Functions

Function	Brief Description
AppCsToRs()	Convert compound string to regular string.
AppGetOptions()	Extract the command line options used by the application.
AppInit()	Initialize Xt, creates a application context, connect to display and create top-level shell.
AppUsage()	Print to standard output usage message.
CreateHelp()	Create application help window.
DisplayDesc()	Display description for a given input word in a message box.
GetDesc()	Create popup shell to display description.
GetKeyFile()	Get application code key from file.
GetKeyStd()	Get application code key from standard input.
GetMessage()	Get description for given input word.
GetWord()	Get input word and find a match in the list.
QuitApp()	Exit application.
SecureApp()	Allows the use of application only by licensed users.
SigHandler()	Print uncatchable signal error and abort application.
XHandler()	Print X protocol error and abort application.
XioHandler()	Print X server disconnect error and abort application.
XtHandler()	Print Xt intrinsic error and abort application.

10. **Source documentation:** Complete
11. **Source code:** The source code for xdtool is listed in following section.

The Program

```
/*****************************************************************
* File:   xtool.c
*
* Project:  Display description of an input dictionary word
*
```

```
*************************************************************/
/* xdtool header file */
#include <xdtool.h>
/* Standard C headers */
#include <stdlib.h>
#include <stdio.h>
#include <sys/types.h>
#include <errno.h>
#include <string.h>
#include <limits.h>
#define MAX_ARGS   128
#define MAXHISTORY 128
#define MAX_ITEMS   50
#define MSG_LEN     80

extern int  errno;
extern char *sys_errlist[];
extern void SecureApp() ;
extern int XioHandler() ;
extern int XHandler() ;
extern void XtHandler() ;
char TopEnv[255];
Widget Command1;
Widget Frame0;
Widget Layout;
XmString itemTable[MAX_ITEMS];
void CommandChanged();
void FindDescription();
void CreateCmdBox(parent, firstTime, dependent)
Widget parent;
Boolean firstTime;
Widget dependent;
{
  Arg args[10];
  int n;
  if (!firstTime) {
    n = 0;
    XtSetArg (args[n], XmNtopAttachment, XmATTACH_FORM);  n++;
    XtSetArg (args[n], XmNleftAttachment, XmATTACH_FORM); n++;
    XtSetArg (args[n], XmNtopOffset, 5);                  n++;
    XtSetArg (args[n], XmNleftOffset, 5);                 n++;
    XtSetValues (dependent, args, n);
```

```
    XtDestroyWidget (Frame0);
    XtDestroyWidget (Command1);
  }
  n = 0;
  XtSetArg (args[n], XmNtopAttachment, XmATTACH_FORM);    n++;
  XtSetArg (args[n], XmNleftAttachment, XmATTACH_FORM);   n++;
  XtSetArg (args[n], XmNtopOffset, 10);                   n++;
  XtSetArg (args[n], XmNleftOffset, 10);                  n++;
  Frame0 = XmCreateFrame(parent, "Frame0", args, n);
  XtRealizeWidget(Frame0);
  XtManageChild(Frame0);
  n = 0;
  XtSetArg (args[n], XmNselectionLabelString,
        XmStringCreateSimple ("Search..."));              n++;
  Command1 = XmCreateCommand(Frame0, "Command1", args, n);
  XtRealizeWidget(Command1);
  XtManageChild(Command1);
  XtAddCallback (Command1, XmNcommandEnteredCallback, CommandChanged,
              (XtPointer) NULL);
  XtManageChild (Command1);
  if (!firstTime) {
    n = 0;
    XtSetArg (args[n], XmNtopAttachment, XmATTACH_WIDGET); n++;
    XtSetArg (args[n], XmNtopWidget, Frame0);             n++;
    XtSetValues (dependent, args, n);
  } /* end if */
}
void CommandChanged(w, client_data, call_data)
Widget w;
XtPointer client_data;
XtPointer call_data;
{
  char *word;
  XmCommandCallbackStruct *call_val = (XmCommandCallbackStruct *)call_data;
  word = AppCsToRs(call_val->value);
  FindDescription(word);
}
void ApplyCommand (w, client_data, call_data)
Widget w;
XtPointer client_data, call_data;
{
  Arg args[2];
```

```
  char *word;
  XmString textString;
  XtSetArg (args[0], XmNcommand, &textString);
  XtGetValues (Command1, args, 1);
  XmStringGetLtoR(textString, XmSTRING_DEFAULT_CHARSET, &word);
  FindDescription(word);
}
void FindDescription(word)
char *word;
{
  int n, ret_val, value;
  int description;
  Arg args[2];
  char *match = "Match Found...";
  char *no_match = "No Match";
  ret_val = GetWord(word);
  if (ret_val == 0) {
    itemTable[0] = XmStringCreateSimple (match);
    itemTable[1] = XmStringCreateSimple (word);
  } else {
    itemTable[0] = XmStringCreateSimple (no_match);
    itemTable[1] = XmStringCreateSimple (word);
  }
  value = 2;
  XtSetArg (args[0], XmNhistoryItems, itemTable);  n++;
  XtSetArg (args[1], XmNhistoryItemCount, value);  n++;
  XtSetValues (Command1, args, 2);
  if (ret_val == 0)
    GetDesc(word);
}
void ResetApp(w, client_data, call_data)
Widget w;
XtPointer client_data, call_data;
{
  CreateCmdBox (Layout, False, (Widget) client_data);
}
void HelpMenuList (w, client_data, call_data)
Widget w;
XtPointer client_data, call_data;
{
  int n, i;
  Arg args[1];
```

```
Widget CreateHelp();
Widget PopupShell;
static Widget message_box = NULL;
n = 0;
XtSetArg(args[n], XtNgeometry, "+500+0");          n++;
XtSetArg(args[n], XtNallowShellResize, True);      n++;
PopupShell = XtCreatePopupShell("Application Help",
            topLevelShellWidgetClass, Shell1, args, n);
if (!message_box) message_box = CreateHelp (PopupShell);
XtManageChild (message_box);
}
void QuitApp()
{
fprintf(stdout, "Exiting application...\n");
fflush(stdout);
exit(0);
}
void main(argc, argv)
int argc;
char **argv;
{
register int  n, i;
int      offset;
char     buf[32];
char     *str ;
Arg      args[MAX_ARGS];
Widget   Frame1, Frame2;
Widget   ApplyB, ResetB, QuitB, HelpB;
Widget   RowCol;
memset(TopEnv, '\0', 255);
str = getenv("XDTOOL");
if (str == (char *)0) {
   fprintf(stdout, "Please set XDTOOL environment variable\n");
   fprintf(stdout, "To set variable consult your installation notes.\n");
   exit(-1);
} else
   strcpy(TopEnv, str);
printf("%s\n", TopEnv);
/* Only valid users with code key can invoke application */
SecureApp();
/* X I/O handler */
XSetIOErrorHandler(XioHandler);
```

```
/* X Protocol errors */
XSetErrorHandler(XHandler);
AppInit(argc, argv);
XtRealizeWidget(Shell1);
/* setup xtToolkitError handler */
XtAppSetErrorMsgHandler(app_context, XtHandler);
/* Overall Plan:
 * Create Command box whose list resources can be set
 * and gotten by user-driven interface
 */
n = 0;
Layout = XmCreateForm (Shell1, "Layout", args, n);
XtRealizeWidget(Layout);
XtManageChild(Layout);
CreateCmdBox(Layout, True, NULL);
n = 0;
XtSetArg (args[n], XmNleftAttachment, XmATTACH_FORM);  n++;
XtSetArg (args[n], XmNrightAttachment, XmATTACH_FORM);  n++;
XtSetArg (args[n], XmNtopAttachment, XmATTACH_WIDGET); n++;
XtSetArg (args[n], XmNtopWidget, Frame0);          n++;
XtSetArg (args[n], XmNtopOffset, 5);          n++;
XtSetArg (args[n], XmNrightOffset, 5);          n++;
XtSetArg (args[n], XmNleftOffset, 5);          n++;
Frame1 = XmCreateFrame (Layout, "Frame1", args, n);
XtRealizeWidget(Frame1);
XtManageChild(Frame1);
n = 0;
XtSetArg (args[n], XmNleftAttachment, XmATTACH_FORM);  n++;
XtSetArg (args[n], XmNrightAttachment, XmATTACH_FORM);  n++;
XtSetArg (args[n], XmNbottomAttachment, XmATTACH_FORM); n++;
XtSetArg (args[n], XmNtopAttachment, XmATTACH_WIDGET); n++;
XtSetArg (args[n], XmNtopWidget, Frame1);          n++;
XtSetArg (args[n], XmNleftOffset, 5);          n++;
XtSetArg (args[n], XmNrightOffset, 5);          n++;
XtSetArg (args[n], XmNbottomOffset, 5);          n++;
Frame2 = XmCreateFrame (Layout, "Frame2", args, n);
XtRealizeWidget(Frame2);
XtManageChild(Frame2);
n = 0;
XtSetArg(args[n], XmNorientation, XmHORIZONTAL);     n++;
RowCol = XmCreateRowColumn(Frame2, "RowCol", args, n);
XtRealizeWidget(RowCol);
```

```
XtManageChild(RowCol);
n = 0;
XtSetArg (args[n], XmNlabelString,
        XmStringCreateSimple ("Apply"));        n++;
ApplyB = XmCreatePushButtonGadget(RowCol, "ApplyB", args, n);
XtRealizeWidget(ApplyB);
XtManageChild(ApplyB);
XtAddCallback (ApplyB, XmNactivateCallback, ApplyCommand,
                (XtPointer) NULL);
n = 0;
XtSetArg (args[n], XmNlabelString,
        XmStringCreateSimple("Reset"));        n++;
ResetB = XmCreatePushButtonGadget(RowCol, "ResetB", args, n);
XtRealizeWidget(ResetB);
XtManageChild(ResetB);
XtAddCallback (ResetB, XmNactivateCallback, ResetApp, Frame1);
n = 0;
XtSetArg (args[n], XmNlabelString,
        XmStringCreateSimple ("Quit"));        n++;
QuitB = XmCreatePushButtonGadget (RowCol, "QuitB", args, n);
XtRealizeWidget(QuitB);
XtManageChild(QuitB);
XtAddCallback (QuitB, XmNactivateCallback, QuitApp, NULL);
n = 0;
XtSetArg (args[n], XmNlabelString,
        XmStringCreateSimple ("Help"));        n++;
HelpB = XmCreatePushButtonGadget(RowCol, "HelpB", args, n);
XtRealizeWidget(HelpB);
XtManageChild(HelpB);
XtAddCallback (HelpB, XmNactivateCallback, HelpMenuList, NULL);
XtRealizeWidget(Shell1);
XtAppMainLoop(app_context);
}
/****************************************************************
*
* Name:        AppCsToRs()
*
* Function:    This function receives as input a Compound
*              string and returns to the user a Regular string
*              representation.
*
* Returns:     A Regular string corresponding to the inputs
```

```
*              Compound String. return NULL if string is NULL
*
*****************************************************************/
#include "xdtool.h"
#ifdef _NO_PROTO
char *AppCsToRs(cs)
XmString cs;
#else /* _NO_PROTO */
char *AppCsToRs(XmString cs)
#endif /* _NO_PROTO */
{
  XmStringContext context;
  XmStringCharSet charset;
  XmStringDirection direction;
  Boolean separator;
  char *primitive_string;
  /* No conversion if string is NULL */
  if (cs == NULL)
      return (NULL);
  XmStringInitContext(&context,cs);
  XmStringGetNextSegment(context,&primitive_string,
      &charset,&direction,&separator);
  XmStringFreeContext(context);
  return(primitive_string);
}
/*****************************************************************
*
* Name:      AppInit()
*
* Purpose:   This routine will Initialize Xt, create an app
*               context, create a connnection to the display,
*               and create a top-level application shell. Shell1
*               and display are global variables.
*
* Returns:   Nothing
*
*****************************************************************/
/* xdtool  header file */
#include "xdtool.h"
#define MAX_ARGS     128
XtAppContext app_context; /* Global Application Context */
Display *display;             /* Global Display variable */
```

```
Widget Shell1;              /* Global TopLevel Application Shell */
Window rootWindow;          /* Global TopLevel Root Window */
Screen *screen;             /* Global TopLevel screen */
char AppResource[100] = "XDtoolres";
/* signal handler declaration */
extern void SigHandler();
#ifdef _NO_PROTO
void AppInit(argc, argv)
int argc;
char **argv;
#else /* _NO_PROTO */
void AppInit(int argc, char **argv)
#endif /* _NO_PROTO */
{
  int n, i;
  Arg args[MAX_ARGS];
  signal(SIGHUP,  SigHandler);
  signal(SIGINT,  SigHandler);
  signal(SIGQUIT, SigHandler);
  signal(SIGKILL, SigHandler);
  signal(SIGBUS,  SigHandler);
  signal(SIGSEGV, SigHandler);
  XtToolkitInitialize();
  app_context = XtCreateApplicationContext();
  display = XtOpenDisplay(app_context, NULL, argv[0], AppResource,
                     NULL, 0, &argc, argv);
  if (display == NULL) {
    fprintf(stderr, "%s:  Cannot open display\n", argv[0]);
    exit(-1);
  }
  n = 0 ;
  AppGetOptions(&argc, argv);
  rootWindow = XDefaultRootWindow(display);
  XtSetArg(args[n], XmNallowShellResize, True);       n++;
  Shell1 = XtAppCreateShell(argv[0], AppResource,
              applicationShellWidgetClass, display, args, n);
  screen = XtScreen(Shell1);
}
/* xdtool header file */
#include "xdtool.h"
#include <string.h>
#include <fcntl.h>
```

```c
#include <limits.h>
#include <unistd.h>
#include <stdio.h>
#if defined(__STDC__)
#include <stdlib.h>
#endif
#define MAX_FILE        128
char default_dir[_POSIX_PATH_MAX];
char  *AppName;                        /* Name of application */
/****************************************************************
*
* Name:        AppUsage()
*
* Purpose:     This function will print to stdout the current
*               usage message.
*
* Flags:
*               -h : Prints the usage message
*               -p : directory path
*
* Returns:     Nothing
*
****************************************************************/
#ifdef _NO_PROTO
void AppUsage(app_name)
char *app_name;
#else /* _NO_PROTO */
void AppUsage(char *app_name)
#endif /* _NO_PROTO */
{
  fprintf(stdout, "Usage: %s \n", app_name);
  fprintf(stdout, "[-d <default_dir>] [-help] [X Options]\n");
}
/****************************************************************
*
* Name:           AppGetOptions()
*
* Purpose:        This function will extract from the command all
*                 options used by the application and arguments
*                 that are not valid for the application are
*                 passed on so that X can properly act on them.
*
```

```
 *  Flags:
 *                   -h : Prints the usage message
 *                   -p : directory path
 *
 *  Returns:         Nothing
 *
 **********************************************************************/
/* globals */
extern char *optarg;
extern int optind, opterr;

#ifdef _NO_PROTO
void  AppGetOptions (argc, argv)
int   *argc;
char  **argv;
#else /* _NO_PROTO */
void  AppGetOptions (int *argc, char **argv)
#endif /* _NO_PROTO */
{
  int c;
  Boolean default_dir_used = False;
  static char app_name[MAX_FILE];
  /* initializations */
  static int errflag = 0;
  /* disable warnings */
  opterr = 0;
  strcpy (app_name, argv[0]);
  AppName = app_name;
  if (*argc > 1) {
    while ((c = getopt(*argc, argv, "h:p:")) != EOF) {
     switch (c) {
       case 'p': if (strlen (optarg) >= (int)_POSIX_PATH_MAX) {
               printf ("Error: Directory name %s too long\n", optarg);
               errflag++;
               break;
               }
           default_dir_used = True;
           strcpy (default_dir, optarg);
           break;
       case 'h': AppUsage(app_name);
           exit(0);
           break;
```

```
    } /* end switch */
    if (optind >= *argc) break;
    } /* end while getopt */
   } /* if *argc >= 1 */
   if (errflag) {
    AppUsage(app_name);
    exit (1);
   }
}
/*****************************************************************
*
* Name:        CreateHelp()
*
* Purpose:     This Function will create help window.
*
* Returns:     message dialog widget
*
*****************************************************************/
#include <stdio.h>
#include <fcntl.h>
#include <errno.h>
#include <xdtool.h>
extern int errno;
extern char TopEnv[255];
#define HELP_MSG_LEN  1024
Widget CreateHelp (parent)
Widget parent;        /* parent widget */
{
 int   bytes, fildes ;
 Widget button;
 Widget message_box;   /* Message Dialog */
 Arg   args[20];      /* arg list */
 register int n;       /* arg count */
 char help_file[255];
 static char message[HELP_MSG_LEN]; /* help text */
 XmString      title_string = NULL;
 XmString      message_string = NULL;
 XmString      button_string = NULL;
 memset(help_file, '\0', 255);
 strcpy(help_file, TopEnv);
 strcat(help_file, "/help/xdtool.hel");
 /* Generate message to display. */
```

```
  memset(message, '\0', HELP_MSG_LEN);
  fildes = open (help_file, O_RDONLY) ;
  bytes = read (fildes, message, HELP_MSG_LEN) ;
  if (!bytes)
   fprintf(stdout, "Error: %s\n", strerror(errno));
   message_string = XmStringCreateLtoR (message,
                          XmSTRING_DEFAULT_CHARSET);
  button_string = XmStringCreateLtoR ("Close", XmSTRING_DEFAULT_CHARSET);
  title_string = XmStringCreateLtoR ("xdtool:Help",
                          XmSTRING_DEFAULT_CHARSET);
  /* Create MessageBox dialog. */
  n = 0;
  XtSetArg (args[n], XmNdialogTitle, title_string);  n++;
  XtSetArg (args[n], XmNokLabelString, button_string);  n++;
  XtSetArg (args[n], XmNmessageString, message_string);  n++;
  message_box = XmCreateMessageDialog (parent, "helpbox", args, n);
  button = XmMessageBoxGetChild (message_box, XmDIALOG_CANCEL_BUTTON);
  XtUnmanageChild (button);
  button = XmMessageBoxGetChild (message_box, XmDIALOG_HELP_BUTTON);
  XtUnmanageChild (button);
  /*  Free strings and return MessageBox. */
  if (title_string) XmStringFree (title_string);
  if (message_string) XmStringFree (message_string);
  if (button_string) XmStringFree (button_string);
    return (message_box);
}
/****************************************************************
*
* Name:      DisplayDesc()
*
* Purpose:    This Function will print description window
*
* Returns:    message dialog widget
*
*****************************************************************/
#include <stdio.h>
#include <fcntl.h>
#include <errno.h>
#include <limits.h>
#include <stdlib.h>
#include <xdtool.h>
extern int errno;
```

```
extern char *sys_errlist[];
#define LIST_FILE  "dict.lis"
#define DESC_FILE  "dict.des"
#define LINE_LEN   80
#define MSG_LEN    512
extern char default_dir[255];
extern char TopEnv[255];
int GetWord(input)
char input[];
{
 int    fildes, ret_val;
 char   *env_val, *str, buf[LINE_LEN];
 char   list_file[_POSIX_PATH_MAX];
 FILE   *stream;
 memset (list_file, '\0', _POSIX_PATH_MAX);
 env_val = getenv("XDTOOLDIR");
 if (env_val == (char*)0) {
   if (strlen(default_dir) > 0)
     sprintf(list_file, "%s/%s", default_dir, LIST_FILE);
   else
     sprintf(list_file, "%s/data/%s", TopEnv, LIST_FILE);
 }
 else
   sprintf(list_file, "%s/%s", env_val, LIST_FILE);
 stream = fopen (list_file, "r");
 if ( stream == (FILE *)0 ) {
   fprintf (stdout, "Error: %s\n" , sys_errlist[errno]);
   fprintf (stdout, "%s specify correct dictionary path\n", list_file);
 }
 while((str = fgets (buf, LINE_LEN, stream) ) != NULL ) {
   ret_val = strncmp(buf, input, (strlen(buf)-1));
   if (ret_val == 0)
     break;
 } /* end while */
 fclose(stream);
 return(ret_val);
}
char *GetMessage(input)
char input[];
{
 int    fildes, flag, ret_val;
 char   *env_val, *str, buf[LINE_LEN];
```

```
char    desc_file[_POSIX_PATH_MAX];
char    message[MSG_LEN];
FILE    *stream;
env_val = getenv("XDTOOLDIR");
memset (desc_file, '\0', _POSIX_PATH_MAX);
if (env_val == (char *)0) {
  if (strlen(default_dir) > 0)
    sprintf(desc_file, "%s/%s", default_dir, DESC_FILE);
  else
    sprintf(desc_file, "%s/data/%s", TopEnv, DESC_FILE);
}
else
  sprintf(desc_file, "%s/%s", env_val, DESC_FILE);

stream = fopen (desc_file, "r");
if (stream == (FILE *)0) {
  fprintf(stdout, "Error: %s\n" , sys_errlist[errno]);
  fprintf (stdout, "%s specify correct dictionary path\n", desc_file);
}
while((str = fgets (buf, LINE_LEN, stream) ) != NULL ) {
    if (flag == 1) {
      ret_val = strncmp("EOR", buf,3);
      if (ret_val ==0)
        break;
      else {
        strcat(message, buf);
        continue;
      } /* end if ret_val */
    } /* end if flag */
    ret_val = strncmp(input, buf, strlen(input));
    if (ret_val == 0) {
      strcpy(message, buf);
      flag = 1;
      continue;
    }
  } /* end while */
 fclose(stream);
 return (message);
}
void GetDesc (word)
char *word;
{
```

```
  int n, i;
  Arg args[1];
  Widget DisplayDesc();
  Widget PopupShell;
  Widget message_box = NULL;
  n = 0;
  XtSetArg(args[n], XtNgeometry, "+500+0");          n++;
  XtSetArg(args[n], XtNallowShellResize, True);      n++;
  PopupShell = XtCreatePopupShell("Application Help",
                    topLevelShellWidgetClass, Shell1, args, n);
  if (!message_box) message_box = DisplayDesc (word, PopupShell);
  XtManageChild (message_box);
}
Widget DisplayDesc (word, parent)
char *word;
Widget parent;        /* parent widget */
{
  int    bytes, fildes ;
  Widget button;
  Widget message_box;   /* Message Dialog */
  Arg    args[20];      /* arg list */
  register int n;       /* arg count */
  char *message;        /* description text */
  XmString     title_string = NULL;
  XmString     desc_string = NULL;
  XmString     button_string = NULL;
  /* Generate message to display. */
  message = (char *)malloc(MSG_LEN);
  memset(message, '\0', MSG_LEN);
  message = GetMessage(word);
#ifdef DEBUG
  fprintf(stdout, "message=%s\n", message);
#endif
  desc_string = XmStringCreateLtoR (message, XmSTRING_DEFAULT_CHARSET);
  button_string = XmStringCreateLtoR ("Done", XmSTRING_DEFAULT_CHARSET);
  title_string = XmStringCreateLtoR ("Description",
                        XmSTRING_DEFAULT_CHARSET);
  /* Create MessageBox dialog. */
  n = 0;
  XtSetArg (args[n], XmNdialogTitle, title_string); n++;
  XtSetArg (args[n], XmNokLabelString, button_string); n++;
  XtSetArg (args[n], XmNmessageString, desc_string); n++;
```

```
message_box = XmCreateMessageDialog (parent, "descbox", args, n);
button = XmMessageBoxGetChild (message_box, XmDIALOG_CANCEL_BUTTON);
XtUnmanageChild (button);
button = XmMessageBoxGetChild (message_box, XmDIALOG_HELP_BUTTON);
XtUnmanageChild (button);

/*  Free strings and return MessageBox. */
if (title_string) XmStringFree (title_string);
if (desc_string) XmStringFree (desc_string);
if (button_string) XmStringFree (button_string);
   return (message_box);
}
/******************************************************************
*
*  Name:       SecureApp()
*
*  Purpose:    This function allows to access xdtool by
*                 licensed users only. The users need to enter
*                 valid code key to access the application for
*                 for first time.
*
*  Returns:    Nothing
*
******************************************************************/
#include <stdio.h>
#include <stdlib.h>
#include <sys/stat.h>
#include <limits.h>
#include <unistd.h>
#define MSG_LEN    80
#define CODE_FILE   "license/code.key"
#define ACCESS_KEY  "1234"
extern char TopEnv[255];
void GetKeyStd();
void GetKeyFile();
int  MatchKey();
void GetKeyStd()
{
 int  i, c;
 int   fildes, ret_val;
 char  string[MSG_LEN];
 char  code_file[_POSIX_PATH_MAX];
```

```c
    FILE *stream;
    sprintf(code_file, "%s/%s", TopEnv, CODE_FILE);
    stream = fopen(code_file, "wb");
    fprintf(stdout, "Please type in Code Key:");
    i = 0;
    while((c = getchar() ) != '\n')
     string[i++] = c;
     string[i] = '\0';
     ret_val = MatchKey(string);
     if (ret_val)
        fwrite(string, sizeof(char), strlen(string), stream);
    fclose(stream);
}
void GetKeyFile()
{
  int   i, c;
  int   fildes, ret_val;
  char  *str, buf[MSG_LEN];
  char  string[MSG_LEN];
  char  code_file[_POSIX_PATH_MAX];
  FILE *stream;
  sprintf(code_file, "%s/%s", TopEnv, CODE_FILE);
  stream = fopen(code_file, "r");
  if (stream != (FILE *)0){
     str = fgets (buf, MSG_LEN, stream);
     fclose(stream);
     if (strlen(str))
        MatchKey(str);
     else
        GetKeyStd();
  }
}
int MatchKey(string)
char *string;
{
  if(!strcmp(ACCESS_KEY, string)){
    fprintf(stdout, "Invoking application...\n");
    return (1);
  }
  else {
    fprintf(stdout, "Type in right Code Key to access application...\n");
    GetKeyStd();
```

```
  }
}
/* get code key from stdin or file for the first time only */
void SecureApp()
{
  int   ret_val;
  struct stat sbuf;
  char  code_file[_POSIX_PATH_MAX];
  sprintf(code_file, "%s/%s", TopEnv, CODE_FILE);
  ret_val = stat(code_file, &sbuf);
  if (ret_val != 0)
    GetKeyStd();
  else
    GetKeyFile();
}
/****************************************************************
 *
 * Name:        SigHandler()
 *
 * Purpose:     This routine will print uncatchable signal error.
 *
 * Returns:     aborts the current application
 *
 ****************************************************************/
#include <stdio.h>
#include <signal.h>
void  SigHandler(sig, code)
int sig, code;
{
  char sigstring[256];
  switch (sig) {
    case SIGHUP:   strcpy(sigstring, "hangup");
            break;
    case SIGINT:   strcpy(sigstring, "interrupt");
            break;
    case SIGQUIT:  strcpy(sigstring, "quit");
            break;
    case SIGKILL:  strcpy(sigstring, "kill");
            break;
    case SIGSEGV:  strcpy(sigstring, "segmentation fault");
            break;
    case SIGBUS:   strcpy(sigstring, "bus error");
```

```
              break;
   default:       strcpy(sigstring, "undetermined");
              break;
 }
 fprintf(stdout, "%s signal received: exiting application...\n", sigstring);
 fflush(stdout);
 exit(-1);
}
/****************************************************************
*
* Name:        XHandler()
*
* Purpose:     Invoked by X when a protocol error occurs;
*              used as XError handler with argument to
*              XSetErrorHandler(XHandler).
*
* Returns:     aborts current application
*
****************************************************************/
#include <stdio.h>
#include <string.h>
#include <X11/Xlib.h>
int XHandler(disp, error_event)
Display *disp;
XErrorEvent *error_event;
{
 char     *newline, *stars, *unexp;
 char      *routine, *errorwas, *serial;
 char     *res_id, *fatal, *of_the;
 char     proto_string[30], *proto_ptr;
 char     error_buf[80], *error_ptr;
 error_ptr = error_buf;
 proto_ptr = proto_string;
 /* set up the error message */
 newline = "\n" ;
 stars  = "\t****************************************************\n";
 unexp  = "\tAn XError occurred while invoking protocol request ";
 routine = "\tThe error was ";
 serial  = "\tNumber of requests sent over the network ";
 res_id  = "\tThe resource id, value, or atom for the failed request was";
 fatal   = "\tThis is a fatal condition. Please investigate the proper\n";
 of_the  = "\tinvocation of the protocol request in the application.\n";
```

```c
/* get the proper protocol request info */
switch(error_event->request_code) {
    case 1:
        strcpy(proto_string, "X_CreateWindow");
        break;
    case 2:
        strcpy(proto_string, "X_ChangeWindowAttributes");
        break;
    case 3:
        strcpy(proto_string, "X_GetWindowAttributes");
        break;
    case 4:
        strcpy(proto_string, "X_DestroyWindow");
        break;
    case 5:
        strcpy(proto_string, "X_DestroySubwindows");
        break;
    case 6:
        strcpy(proto_string, "X_ChangeSaveSet");
        break;
    case 7:
        strcpy(proto_string, "X_ReparentWindow");
        break;
    case 8:
        strcpy(proto_string, "X_MapWindow");
        break;
    case 9:
        strcpy(proto_string, "X_MapSubwindows");
        break;
    case 10:
        strcpy(proto_string, "X_UnmapWindow");
        break;
    case 11:
        strcpy(proto_string, "X_UnmapSubwindows");
        break;
    case 12:
        strcpy(proto_string, "X_ConfigureWindow");
        break;
    case 13:
        strcpy(proto_string, "X_CirculateWindow");
        break;
    case 14:
```

```
        strcpy(proto_string, "X_GetGeometry");
        break;
    case 15:
        strcpy(proto_string, "X_QueryTree");
        break;
    case 16:
        strcpy(proto_string, "X_InternAtom");
        break;
    case 17:
        strcpy(proto_string, "X_GetAtomName");
        break;
    case 18:
        strcpy(proto_string, "X_ChangeProperty");
        break;
    case 19:
        strcpy(proto_string, "X_DeleteProperty");
        break;
    case 20:
        strcpy(proto_string, "X_GetProperty");
        break;
    case 21:
        strcpy(proto_string, "X_ListProperties");
        break;
    case 22:
        strcpy(proto_string, "X_SetSelectionOwner");
        break;
    case 23:
        strcpy(proto_string, "X_GetSelectionOwner");
        break;
    case 24:
        strcpy(proto_string, "X_ConvertSelection");
        break;
    case 25:
        strcpy(proto_string, "X_SendEvent");
        break;
    case 26:
        strcpy(proto_string, "X_GrabPointer");
        break;
    case 27:
        strcpy(proto_string, "X_UngrabPointer");
        break;
    case 28:
```

```
            strcpy(proto_string, "X_GrabButton");
            break;
        case 29:
            strcpy(proto_string, "X_UngrabButton");
            break;
        case 30:
            strcpy(proto_string, "X_ChangeActivePointerGrab");
            break;
        case 31:
            strcpy(proto_string, "X_GrabKeyboard");
            break;
        case 32:
            strcpy(proto_string, "X_UngrabKeyboard");
            break;
        case 33:
            strcpy(proto_string, "X_GrabKey");
            break;
        case 34:
            strcpy(proto_string, "X_UngrabKey");
            break;
        case 35:
            strcpy(proto_string, "X_AllowEvents");
            break;
        case 36:
            strcpy(proto_string, "X_GrabServer");
            break;
        case 37:
            strcpy(proto_string, "X_UngrabServer");
            break;
        case 38:
            strcpy(proto_string, "X_QueryPointer");
            break;
        case 39:
            strcpy(proto_string, "X_GetMotionEvents");
            break;
        case 40:
            strcpy(proto_string, "X_TranslateCoords");
            break;
        case 41:
            strcpy(proto_string, "X_WarpPointer");
            break;
        case 42:
```

```
            strcpy(proto_string, "X_SetInputFocus");
            break;
      case 43:
            strcpy(proto_string, "X_GetInputFocus");
            break;
      case 44:
            strcpy(proto_string, "X_QueryKeymap");
            break;
      case 45:
            strcpy(proto_string, "X_OpenFont");
            break;
      case 46:
            strcpy(proto_string, "X_CloseFont");
            break;
      case 47:
            strcpy(proto_string, "X_QueryFont");
            break;
      case 48:
            strcpy(proto_string, "X_QueryTextExtents");
            break;
      case 49:
            strcpy(proto_string, "X_ListFonts");
            break;
      case 50:
            strcpy(proto_string, "X_ListFontsWithInfo");
            break;
      case 51:
            strcpy(proto_string, "X_SetFontPath");
            break;
      case 52:
            strcpy(proto_string, "X_GetFontPath");
            break;
      case 53:
            strcpy(proto_string, "X_CreatePixmap");
            break;
      case 54:
            strcpy(proto_string, "X_FreePixmap");
            break;
      case 55:
            strcpy(proto_string, "X_CreateGC");
            break;
      case 56:
```

```
        strcpy(proto_string, "X_ChangeGC");
        break;
    case 57:
        strcpy(proto_string, "X_CopyGC");
        break;
    case 58:
        strcpy(proto_string, "X_SetDashes");
        break;
    case 59:
        strcpy(proto_string, "X_SetClipRectangles");
        break;
    case 60:
        strcpy(proto_string, "X_FreeGC");
        break;
    case 61:
        strcpy(proto_string, "X_ClearArea");
        break;
    case 62:
        strcpy(proto_string, "X_CopyArea");
        break;
    case 63:
        strcpy(proto_string, "X_CopyPlane");
        break;
    case 64:
        strcpy(proto_string, "X_PolyPoint");
        break;
    case 65:
        strcpy(proto_string, "X_PolyLine");
        break;
    case 66:
        strcpy(proto_string, "X_PolySegment");
        break;
    case 67:
        strcpy(proto_string, "X_PolyRectangle");
        break;
    case 68:
        strcpy(proto_string, "X_PolyArc");
        break;
    case 69:
        strcpy(proto_string, "X_FillPoly");
        break;
    case 70:
```

```c
        strcpy(proto_string, "X_PolyFillRectangle");
        break;
    case 71:
        strcpy(proto_string, "X_PolyFillArc");
        break;
    case 72:
        strcpy(proto_string, "X_PutImage");
        break;
    case 73:
        strcpy(proto_string, "X_GetImage");
        break;
    case 74:
        strcpy(proto_string, "X_PolyText8");
        break;
    case 75:
        strcpy(proto_string, "X_PolyText16");
        break;
    case 76:
        strcpy(proto_string, "X_ImageText8");
        break;
    case 77:
        strcpy(proto_string, "X_ImageText16");
        break;
    case 78:
        strcpy(proto_string, "X_CreateColormap");
        break;
    case 79:
        strcpy(proto_string, "X_FreeColormap");
        break;
    case 80:
        strcpy(proto_string, "X_CopyColormapAndFree");
        break;
    case 81:
        strcpy(proto_string, "X_InstallColormap");
        break;
    case 82:
        strcpy(proto_string, "X_UninstallColormap");
        break;
    case 83:
        strcpy(proto_string, "X_ListInstalledColormaps");
        break;
    case 84:
```

```
          strcpy(proto_string, "X_AllocColor");
          break;
case 85:
          strcpy(proto_string, "X_AllocNamedColor");
          break;
case 86:
          strcpy(proto_string, "X_AllocColorCells");
          break;
case 87:
          strcpy(proto_string, "X_AllocColorPlanes");
          break;
case 88:
          strcpy(proto_string, "X_FreeColors");
          break;
case 89:
          strcpy(proto_string, "X_StoreColors");
          break;
case 90:
          strcpy(proto_string, "X_StoreNamedColor");
          break;
case 91:
          strcpy(proto_string, "X_QueryColors");
          break;
case 92:
          strcpy(proto_string, "X_LookupColor");
          break;
case 93:
          strcpy(proto_string, "X_CreateCursor");
          break;
case 94:
          strcpy(proto_string, "X_CreateGlyphCursor");
          break;
case 95:
          strcpy(proto_string, "X_FreeCursor");
          break;
case 96:
          strcpy(proto_string, "X_RecolorCursor");
          break;
case 97:
          strcpy(proto_string, "X_QueryBestSize");
          break;
case 98:
```

```
        strcpy(proto_string, "X_QueryExtension");
        break;
    case 99:
        strcpy(proto_string, "X_ListExtensions");
        break;
    case 100:
        strcpy(proto_string, "X_ChangeKeyboardMapping");
        break;
    case 101:
        strcpy(proto_string, "X_GetKeyboardMapping");
        break;
    case 102:
        strcpy(proto_string, "X_ChangeKeyboardControl");
        break;
    case 103:
        strcpy(proto_string, "X_GetKeyboardControl");
        break;
    case 104:
        strcpy(proto_string, "X_Bell");
        break;
    case 105:
        strcpy(proto_string, "X_ChangePointerControl");
        break;
    case 106:
        strcpy(proto_string, "X_GetPointerControl");
        break;
    case 107:
        strcpy(proto_string, "X_SetScreenSaver");
        break;
    case 108:
        strcpy(proto_string, "X_GetScreenSaver");
        break;
    case 109:
        strcpy(proto_string, "X_ChangeHosts");
        break;
    case 110:
        strcpy(proto_string, "X_ListHosts");
        break;
    case 111:
        strcpy(proto_string, "X_SetAccessControl");
        break;
    case 112:
```

```
        strcpy(proto_string, "X_SetCloseDownMode");
        break;
    case 113:
        strcpy(proto_string, "X_KillClient");
        break;
    case 114:
        strcpy(proto_string, "X_RotateProperties");
        break;
    case 115:
        strcpy(proto_string, "X_ForceScreenSaver");
        break;
    case 116:
        strcpy(proto_string, "X_SetPointerMapping");
        break;
    case 117:
        strcpy(proto_string, "X_GetPointerMapping");
        break;
    case 118:
        strcpy(proto_string, "X_SetModifierMapping");
        break;
    case 119:
        strcpy(proto_string, "X_GetModifierMapping");
        break;
    case 127:
        strcpy(proto_string, "X_NoOperation");
        break;
    case 128:
        strcpy(proto_string, "X_ShapeRectangles");
        break;
    case 129:
        strcpy(proto_string, "X_ShapeMask");
        break;
    case 130:
        strcpy(proto_string, "X_ShapeCombine");
        break;
    case 131:
        strcpy(proto_string, "X_ShapeOffset");
        break;
    case 132:
        strcpy(proto_string, "X_ShapeQueryExtents");
        break;
    case 133:
```

```
            strcpy(proto_string, "X_ShapeSelectInput");
            break;
        case 134:
            strcpy(proto_string, "X_ShapeInputSelected");
            break;
        case 135:
            strcpy(proto_string, "X_ShapeGetRectangles");
            break;
        default:
            strcpy(proto_string, "Unknown");
            break;
    }
    /* get the text for the XError */
    XGetErrorText(disp, error_event->error_code, error_ptr, 80);
    /* print the error message */
    fprintf(stdout, "%s %s %s %s %s %s %s %s = %d %s %s = %d %s %s %s",
        stars,
        unexp, proto_ptr, newline,
        routine, error_ptr, newline,
        serial, error_event->serial, newline,
        res_id, error_event->resourceid, newline,
        fatal,
        of_the
        );
    /* exit - this is a fatal error */
    exit(-1);
}
/***************************************************************
*
* Name:       XioHandler()
*
* Purpose:    Invoked by X when an IO error occurs (i.e. an unexpected server
*             disconnect). Used as X error handler with argument to
*             XSetIOErrorHandler(XioHandler)
*
* Returns:    aborts current application
*
***************************************************************/
#include <stdio.h>
#include <X11/Xlib.h>
int XioHandler(disp)
Display *disp;
```

```
{
 char *stars, *errormsg, *server, *fatal;
 /* set up the error message */
 stars    =   "\t****************************************\n";
 errormsg = "\tAn unexpected XIOError occurred. Check for\n";
 server   = "\tserver disconnect.\n";
 fatal    =   "\tFatal error. A B O R T I N G . . . .\n";

 /* abort the application */
 fprintf(stdout, "%s %s %s %s", stars, errormsg, server, fatal);
 exit(-1);
}
/*****************************************************************
 *
 * Name:        XtHandler()
 *
 * Purpose:     Invoked by Xt when an intrinsic error occurs.
 *              Used as Xt error handler with argument to
 *              XtAppSetErrorMsgHander(app_context, XtHandler)
 *
 * Returns:     aborts current application
 *
 *****************************************************************/
#include <stdio.h>
#include <X11/Intrinsic.h>
void XtHandler(name, type, class, defaultp, params, num_params)
String name;
String type;
String class;
String defaultp ;
String *params ;
Cardinal *num_params ;
{
 char *stars ;
 char *msg ;
 char *err ;
 char *res_name ;
 char *res_type ;
 char *handle ;
 char *newline ;
 char *tab ;
 stars  = "\t**************************************************\n" ;
```

```
 msg    = "\tXtToolkitError: During a toolkit call, the error was\n" ;
 err    =  "\tError:" ;
 res_name = "\tresource name = " ;
 res_type =   "\tresource type = " ;
 handle   =   "\tPlease investigate proper invocation of toolkit call.\n" ;
 newline  =   "\n" ;
 fprintf(stdout, "%s %s %s %s %s %s %s %s %s %s %s %s",
     stars, msg,
     err, defaultp, newline,
     res_name, name, newline,
     res_type, type, newline,
     handle);
 exit(-1) ;
}
```

12. **Design Validation:** Pass except for fuzzy match logic
    implementation.

3.5   Software Testing

Software testing is defined as set of programs to demonstrate the correct operation of a program within a controlled environment.

The controlled testing environment usually consists of:

1. **Static testing**: Static testing includes manual code inspection and structured walkthroughs and the use of automated tools that analyze the software by looking for certain kinds of common errors, such as argument data type and count mismatch in a function call, or missing parentheses.
2. **Dynamic testing:** It involves
    *   Observing the run-time effect the inputs have on the program
    *   Examining the program outputs to determine their acceptability

Thus, the purpose of testing is to expose the existence of bugs or to demonstrate conclusively the absence of any such bugs. The next section below covers the top-down and bottom-up testing methods.

3.5.1   Top Down Testing

Top-down testing involves testing to begin with the main program and one or two lower-level modules; the rest of the modules are dummy modules.

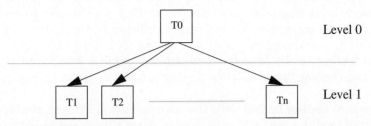

(a) All the modules called by T1, T2, and Tn are dummy modules and they
exit immediately.

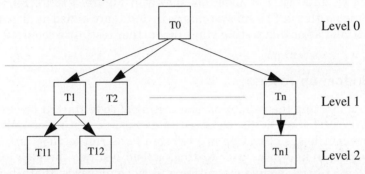

(b) Modules called by T11, T12, and Tn1 are dummies and they exit immediately

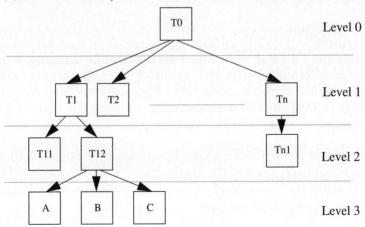

(c) Final stages: all subsystems are combined together and tested as whole unit.

Figure 3-13
Top-down testing

Once the testing on this is performed and all the interfaces are working properly, another level of module is added for testing, and so on. When the last module of the program is added and tested sufficiently, the testing is finished.

Top-down testing can be considered to go hand in hand with Top-down design and top-down coding. The top-down testing process is shown in Figure 3-13.

The process of testing begins with the main program T0 and possibly one or two levels of modules, as in Figure 3-13(a). After this skeleton is tested sufficiently, confirming that major interfaces are working, another level of logic modules (T11, T12, Tn1) is added as shown in Figure 3-13(b). Finally, last-level modules with the T12 subsystems A, B, and C are added as shown in Figure 3-13(c), and after this testing stage, no further testing is required.

3.5.2 Bottom-up Testing

In bottom-up testing the validation and testing of code start at the lowermost level. This lowest level is also referred to as module testing or unit testing. The subsequent levels of testing are referred to as run testing, and the final level of testing is known as user testing or field testing. The idea is to work from the lowest-level module or routine and move upwards, that is., from the leaf of the program tree to the main node of the program.

The bottom-up testing process is shown in Figure 3-14. The process of testing begins with module-or unit level testing of lowest-level modules A and B, and as shown in Figure 3-14(a). At the next level of testing, modules A, B, and C are incorporated into subsystem B12 as shown in Figure 3-14(b). Finally the highest-level module is added as shown in Figure 3-14(c); after this stage, the entire testing is finished. The testing is complete when the entire subsystems is integrated and tested as a unit.

It is easier to test software using bottom-up design, it offers comprehensive testing. Each and every level of the application is tested throughly. The drawback is bottom-up testing method needs to be changed every time the lower most module of the software changes.

To test software completely bottom-up testing may be employed.

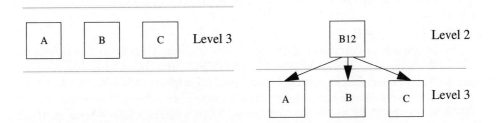

(a) Unit testing; individual function
modules are tested in a stand-alone
fashion.

(b) Module A, B, and C are incorporated
into subsystem T12.

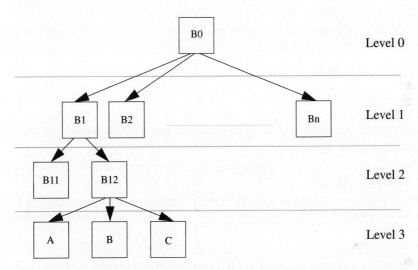

(c) In the final stages of integration, additional subsystems are combined
until the entire system is complete.

Figure 3-14
Bottom-up testing

3.5.3 Automated X Testing

Performing manual testing for X applications is a tedious, repetitive, and inef-
ficient task. Compounded with frequent releases and multiple platform ports,
manual testing cannot achieve its goals of assuring product quality prior to

release. Automation, in theory, should be the solution. Get the human operator out of test execution and into test design, while an automated tool executes a full suite of regression tests.

A new approach to computer-aided software testing (CAST) that emphasizes the specific needs of interactive applications has been developed. This approach has been implemented in commercial applications like the XRunner testing tool for X Window System applications. This section discusses the different methods used to create tests, and then presents how these methods combine into a single, integrated testing approach.

The conventional CAST tool uses a technique known as capture-replay-verify (CRV). However, those charged with testing GUI applications typically identify two problems with conventional CRV. First, automatic test execution has not been reliable enough to make test results of any use. Widgets move, windows change locations, and the tests crash. Second, the effort required to create and maintain the tests themselves makes automation more trouble than it is worth.

A useful automated testing tool for X applications should meet three simple criteria:

1. Automated tests must be easy to generate and easy to maintain throughout the application's life.
2. They must perform tests accurately, in spite of any variations in the tested applications.
3. Test automation must be useful throughout the entire software life cyle, from unit testing to heavy-duty regression across different platforms.

One of the biggest drawbacks of testing the graphics applications is that one has to perform manual testing, which requires the tester's physical presence to validate the user interface. The manual testing task itself is very tedious and time consuming. Further more most applications have periodic releases with upgrades on multiple platforms. Covering all the testing scenarios for a given graphical application requires lots of resources.

Obvious as it may be, CAST for X clients must bear in mind that the GUI was designed to put the user in control. Its neat, intuitive presentation of hundreds of options means that a large proportion of application operations involve selecting functions from what is displayed on screen.

For simplicity's sake, let's say there are two types of application operations that testing tools need to automate: (1) user actions, that drive the application, and (2) verification points, where the user confirms that the sequence of user actions led to the anticipated result. To imitate the human user, the automated test needs to work from a representation of the operations performed by the end user. This is known as a test script.

3.5.3.1 Analog Testing

A CAST tool records the sequence of user operations as a script and automates the test by repeating the sequence back to the application. The question is how does the automated tool should represent the sequence.

Unfortunately, there is no single standard in the X environment for monitoring user activities. There are a number of X-server extension variants that make it possible to record and replay user operations, such as XTrap, XTest, and others. These extensions allow test scripts to capture basic analog user actions, such as keystrokes and mouse movements, and bitmaps on screen. This analog approach can be represented as

```
set_mouse_absolute(500,300);
mouse_press();
move_mouse(0,50);
type(abcdefg);
type(<kReturn>);
mouse_release();
move_mouse(250,170);
```

This approach is useful in cases when input consists only of keystrokes or for drawing graphics using point-to-point mouse movements, since all the test has to do is repeat the same operations at the same spot in the display.

One disadvantage of analog recording is immediately obvious: It is difficult to discern much of anything about the test sequence from the script. The more significant flaw, however, is in its robustness. If the listbox and buttons are rearranged or the window pops up in a new location, the automated tool will point the mouse at objects that are no longer there and fail to execute the test sequence.

Verification points in analog testing are set into the script in a similar fashion. When the anticipated image appears on the screen, the tester incorporates it into the script by pressing a hot-key for point and shoot screen capture. When the test is repeated, the tool waits for the specified bitmap to appear.

An alternative approach is to represent user operations as GUI actions, instead of mouse movements (for example selecting a list item, pressing a button, or resizing a window). The automated testing tool can then overcome the variations typical of an X application.

The GUI applications consist essentially of drawing graphics involving keystrokes and mouse movements; the analog testing technique can be used to test the user interface to a certain extent. In analog automated testing a test script is generated consisting of basic analog user actions, such as keystrokes and mouse movements. This script can be played back again and again to simulate user actions and automate the tests. The analog testing is incomplete and cannot be applied to all the applications. The test script is difficult to read and cannot be modified easily. Further more, it does not capture, select items from a list, move scrollbars, resize widgets or windows, press buttons, enter items and so on. A different technique known as context-sensitive testing can be applied to test these features, as discussed in the next section.

The challenge is to establish a firm connection between the operation that the user performs and its context in the application. In other words, the testing tools need to know not only how to click the pointer, but how to find the right button to press. The test scripts would represent the GUI operations using a descriptive, logical command such as clickon-OK-button. Unfortunately, the X environment supplies no hooks from which to record such an operation.

Some testing tools have tackled the problem using object oriented programming to develop test scripts. To program such a script, one has to be intimately familiar with the application's internal GUI hierarchy and write all the class hierarchies and event handling mechanisms. It may look as below

```
PressButton("application_main.menu_bar1.File.sample_pull_down_1.Open");
PressButton("file_open_main.button_group_area_1.DummyWidget2.OK");
```

This is like programming the application GUI all over again, just for testing, but without any supporting toolkits. Programming the GUI in Xlib and automating the test itself is difficult.

3.5.3.2   Context-sensitive Testing

Instead of building an entire UI hierarchy just for testing, context-sensitive testing linking a firm connection between the user actions and the application behavior can be used. An object oriented approach (OOR) can be used to make test commands "context sensitive," that is, to make certain that test commands are applied correctly to objects in spite of changes in the UI. OOR employs a straightforward, descriptive syntax that combines user actions with application functions:

```
menu_select("File;Open");
button_press("OK");
```

The context sensitivity of these logical commands is achieved by directly mapping user actions (for example, selecting a menu item or pressing a button) to specific UI functions (opening a file or choosing OK).

Context-sensitive verification points also contribute robustness to the test scripts. Instead of comparing bitmaps, a logical test on the GUI to verify that application is ready. For instance, this approach makes certain that a check box is set to "on," which is more important to the test than the physical location of the check box.

This makes scripts easier to maintain through the development life cycle. As the application evolves through successive versions, buttons may move, list orders may change, and so forth. Like a discerning human user, context-sensitive tests overcome such variations without stumbling, executing test operations on UI elements wherever they may have moved.

To achieve this ambitious goal, the testing tool needs to query the underlying GUI layer for the content of graphical objects and widgets. This can be done by planting transparent hooks into the Xt layer as the tested application is run. The hooks give the CAST tool access to information about the application GUI based on low-level widget constructs. The logic is implemented in low-level messages. The logic works in two directions; It can map a high-level context sensitive command to a sequence of mouse movements and keystrokes while replaying a test. Alternatively, while it records a test, it can translate a sequence of low-level messages into high-level, context sensitive commands.

Recording test operations is the simplest, fastest way to create a script, because one can define it by performing it. This context-sensitive approach automatically creates the connection between user actions and application functions. The direct mapping into classes and widget hierarchies is created automatically when the test is replayed. For example, pull down a menu, pick a command and press the OK button, produces the following script:

```
menu_select("File:Print");
button_press("OK");
```

When the script is played back, it no longer matters where the OK button is found on the screen or where the Print command appears in the File menu. In addition, a self-explanatory test is created automatically—one that can be easily edited or modified later by anyone who reads it.

3.5.4   Software Testing Form (STF)

The software testing form (STF) is a set of well-defined testing items. The form can be used to evaluate the quality of the software before it is shipped to customers. Table 3-8 lists some important areas that may be covered during testing of an application.

Table 3-9 Software Testing Form (STF)

Item	Program...
1	Test tools
2	Test design specification
3	Test scripts/code
4	Static testing
5	Dynamic testing
6	Input testing
7	Output testing
8	Boundary testing
9	External interface testing
10	Positive testing
11	Negative testing
12	Error condition testing
13	Module testing
14	Quality specification testing
15	Test release notes
16	Test result documentation

3.5.5 Software Testing Document (STD)

The software testing document (STD) is a detailed description of all the test items listed in the software testing form (STF) and test results summary. The testing items should essentially validate the software design. The xdtool test document is given next as an example.

Example: xdtool Software Testing Document (STD)

1. **Test tools:** lint, automated GUI testers, memory leak testers, performance analyzers
2. **Test design specification:** None, manual testing and testing via available test tools
3. **Test scripts/code:** None
4. **Static testing:**
   - Code inspection: Complete pass
   - lint: Pass
   - Calling/called function argument count: Pass
   - Calling/called function argument data type: Pass
5. **Dynamic testing:** The xdtool invokes properly, and the dictionary directory specification via environment variable XDTOOLDIR functions properly. The directory specification in XDtoolres resource file fails.
6. **Input testing:** Passed dictionary word input testing
7. **Output testing:** Displayed description for all 20 dictionary word input entries
8. **Boundary testing:** Input of dictionary word "algori" did not display fuzzy list
9. **External interface testing:**
   - Match: The item box has 20 horizontal- and 10 vertical-character display field.
   - Search: The entry field is 20 characters long.
   - Apply, Reset, Quit, Help: All push buttons perform the assigned task properly.
10. **Positive testing:** Pass, known dictionary word displayed description, xdtool -h help displayed the application usage message. xdtool -d [default_dir] changed the

default dictionary directory. All the X options are passed to X functions and function as expected.

11. **Negative testing:** Pass, nondictionary word displayed diagnostics, No Match

12. **Error condition testing:** Pass, Invalid display, fonts, colors generated errors

13. **Module testing:** Ideally for each function or module a test design specification should be written. The test code/scripts generated from design should be used to test the modules. For discussions sake will assume all the modules work properly.

14. **Quality specification testing:** Table 3-4 quality specifications listed in xdtool software specification document should be tested and documented.

15. **Test release notes:** The test release notes should cover every aspect of test harness and test strategy. The test release notes contents are same as that of software release notes with additional items for tester to understand the results and file bug reports either in the test code or software code.

16. **Test result documentation:** Summary of preceding results

3.6   Software Documentation

The software documentation should be organized as shown in Figure 3-15. The software specification document (SSD), software design document (SDD), software coding document (SCD), and software testing document (STD) have been discussed in previous sections.

Once the software design document is complete, required user documents, the software product, its applications, and the audiences that will use the product must be identified. The software user's documentation is in parallel with the software design and software coding process.

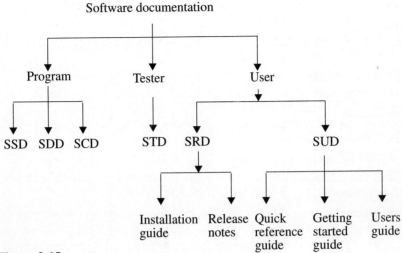

Figure 3-15
Software documentation tree

3.6.1   Release Documents

Every application should have an installation and release notes guide. These manuals guide the user in how to install and invoke the application. The release notes document changes and known bugs. The two can also be merged into a single document. The software release document may have:

1. Installation guide
2. Release notes

3.6.2   Software Release Form (SRF)

The software release form (SRF) specifies the contents of installation guides and release notes. Tables 3-10 and 3-11 list some important contents that may be considered while writing installation guides and release notes, respectively.

Table 3-10 Software Release Form (SRF), Installation Guide Contents

Item	Program...
1	Introduction
2	Supported platform
3	Distribution media
4	Installation
5	Contents
6	System setup
7	Environment setup
8	License setup
9	Invocation
10	Known problems
11	In case of difficulty

Table 3-11 Software Release Form (SRF), Release Notes Contents

Item	Program...
1	Introduction
2	Release number
3	New features
4	Changes
5	Status of reported problems
6	Known problems

All commercial software should have some sort of license key to access the software. This protects the unauthorized use or copying of the software application. Access can be through a code key that either creates a file with the encrypted key or tries to match the encrypted key in a file. Alternatively, a license daemon can be installed that communicates with the client application and allows only a fixed number of users to access the application. The license code should be implemented in such a way that it needs to be configured only once.

3.6.3 Software Release Document (SRD)

The software release document (SRD) contains a detailed description of software installation procedures, release changes, known problems, new features, changes from previous release, and the like. The xdtool installation and release notes document are given next as an example.

Example: xdtool Software Release Document (SRD)

A) xdtool Installation Manual

1. **Introduction:** This manual describes how to install the xdtool software package on UNIX-based workstations. It also contains setup information. The installation procedures should be performed by the system administrator.

2. **Supported platforms:** Table 3-12 shows the Operating systems used to build the application. The installation disk space shown is the maximum disk space in megabytes required to safely install the xdtool files.

Table 3-12 Platforms supported by xdtool

Platform	OS Built With	Disk Space/MB
HP PRO RISC	HP-UX	1.2
IBM/RS6000	SVR4.2	1.3
Silicon Graphics	IRIS	1.2
Sun SPARC	Solaris 2.3	1.1
Sun 486	Solaris 2.1	1.3
Univel/486	SVR4.2	1.3

3. **Distribution media:** The xdtool is distributed in both compressed tar format and SVR4 installation package format. It is available on 1.4MB 3 1/2 inch floppy diskette, Quick 150 cartridge tape, and CD-ROM. Check the media label installation instructions.

4. **Installation:** The xdtool is not directory sensitive. In other words, it does not matter where it is installed. The directory in which you choose to install xdtool is called XDTOOL directory. This can be any directory with read, write, and execute permissions. The installation procedure does not require root permissions. To install the package execute the following commands:

```
Loading tar file Format
csh% cd <XDTOOL>
csh% tar xvf <device_name>

Loading SVR4 package Format
csh% cd <XDTOOL>
csh% pkgadd -d <device> -a none all

You will be prompted
Enter path to package base directory [? q]

Enter the fullyqualified pathname of the directory
<XDTOOL> you just created.
For specific command line help, please consult the manual
entries for pkgadd and pgktrans
```

5. **Contents:** The software package after installation contains the software tree directory as shown in Table 3-13. The src directory tree will generally not be their for any commercial product. It is included here for the sake of completeness of the document.

Table 3-13 xdtool Directory Tree after Installation

Directory	Files
bin	xdtool executable
data	dictionary files
doc	xdtool documentation
help	help message file
include	xdtool include files
lib	library libxdtool.a and libxdtool.so.1

Table 3-13 xdtool Directory Tree after Installation (continued)

Directory	Files
license	xdtool users license file
src	xdtool.c main source code
src/lib	library source code

6. **System setup:** The xdtool can be run on both MONOCHROME and COLOR displays. To invoke the xdtool application, X server should be running.

7. **Environment setup:**
Set up top-level directory tree environment variable as under

```
%csh XDTOOL <xdtool directory>
```

Where <xdtool directory> is the complete absolute path name of the xdtool installation directory.

The path variable should contain the $XDTOOL/bin in the path to invoke xdtool application as follows

```
csh% setenv PATH "$PATH":$XDTOOL/bin
```

If you wish to install the dictionary database in different directory, you need to set variable XDTOOLDIR as follows

```
csh% setenv XDTOOLDIR <directory_path>
```

To access xdtool resource file set XENVIRONMENT variable as follows

```
csh% setenv XENVIRONMENT $XDTOOL/XDtoolres
```

To invoke shared version of xdtool set LD_LIBRARY_PATH variable as follows

```
csh% setenv LD_LIBRARY_PATH "LD_LIBRARY_PATH":$XDTOOL/lib
```

8. **License setup:**
   At the time of invocation of xdtool application, you will
   be prompted

   Please enter code key:
   Enter the code key 1234
9. **Invocation:** After system and environment setup execute
   following command to invoke the application:

   csh% xdtool

   You should see the xdtool GUI interface as shown in Figure
   3-16.

Figure 3-16
xdtool GUI interface after invocation

10. **Known problems:**
    Closest match: If the entered item is not found, the
    xdtool application does not display the fuzzy match list.
11. **In case of difficulty:** Your feedback is very important in
    shaping future releases. XYZ Inc. has created a mailing

list to keep people appraised of changes to xdtool. Clean problem reports (with vendor company names removed) will be distributed to the mailing list at the end of every quarter along with current status, answers to frequently asked questions, and so on. To subscribe to the mailing list, send mail to xdtool@xyz.net. To get the updated list of known problems, send an email with the Subject "#known problems". For technical support, call 1-800-<tel_number> between hours of 9 to 5 US PDT.

B) xdtool Release Manual

1. **Introduction:** This is the first release (1.0) of the xdtool application. This manual contains the release information. It describes new features and changes from previous release, if any. This manual is common to all xdtool-supported hardware and software platforms.

2. **Release number:** 1.0

3. **New features:** This is first release.

4. **Changes:** This is first release.

5. **Status of reported problems:** This is first release.

6. **Known problems:**
   Closest match: If the entered item is not found, the xdtool application does not display the fuzzy match list. This problem will be fixed in the next release.

3.6.4   User Document Requirement

There should be at least three sets of user's guides.

1. **Quick reference guide**
2. **Getting started guide**
3. **User's guide**

The contents of these guides should be organized in a clear and precise manner. This section discusses some of the guidelines that should be followed while writing the user's guides.

The user document requirements listing is analogous to that of the program requirements. Most of the software user interface, category of application, and the intended audience as specified in the program requirements and software design stage should be organized and listed in proper order to create the user documents. The documents should be augmented with examples to reduce the learning curve. In reference mode, on-line help for the user document should be provided to navigate through problems. Some of the important points that should be considered are:

- Document audience
- Instruction mode
- Number of document sets
- Reference mode
- User interface identification

3.6.5 User Document Contents

Once the user document requirements are available, user document components and the specific information about the components should be clearly documented.

3.6.6 Software User Form (SUF)

The software user form (SUF) specifies the set of listed user's items. This form should contain the items listed in Table 3-14.

Table 3-14 Software User Form (SUF), User's Guide

Item	Contents
1	Title page
2	Copyrights/Credits
3	Restrictions
4	Table of contents
5	Introduction
6	Body of document
7	Error messages
8	Appendixes
9	Glossary
10	Index

The document created should not be very big; the explanations should be succinct and augmented with example(s). Consistent symbols, figures, and stylistic conventions should be followed. Selected material of special material should be highlighted.

3.6.7 Software User Documents (SUD)

The software user documents (SUD) consist of detailed descriptions of the items listed in the software user form (SUF). This document's contents are very important from the user's viewpoint. The document should be able to convey all the information the user may need with examples. For commercial applications, the use of engineering terms should be avoided. It should discuss the on-line help and spot help messages that guide the user in case of difficulties, instead of resorting to the user documents. This section discusses only important parts of the user's guide. In reality, one should study many commercially available guides and use the style conventions best suited.

Example: xdtool Software User Documents (SUD), Users Guide

1. **Title page:** xdtool Users Guide
2. **Copyrights:** Copyright 1993, 1994 by XYZ Corporation,
   <Place>, <State>,<Country>
   All Rights Reserved
3. **Restrictions:** None
4. **Table of contents:**
   1.0 Introduction to the xdtool
   2.0 Setup the user environment
   3.0 Installing xdtool license
   4.0 xdtool External interfaces
   5.0 Diagnostic messages
5. **Introduction:** Brief description of Users Guide
6. **Body of document:** Describe table of contents
7. **Error messages:**
   Match Found: Description for dictionary word exists in
   database file.
   No Match: Invalid word, not in the dictionary database.
   Signal Errors: Uncatchable signals via signal handler.
   X Errors: Unable to open display, font, color not found,

```
bad atom, or value, etc.
Xt Errors: Xt Instrinsic specific errors.
```

8. **Appendixes:** None

9. **Glossary:** Alphabetical listing with description of all
    xdtool terms

10. **Index:** Alphabetical listing with page number(s) of all
    key words

3.7   Application Compatibility

An application is said to be compatible to the one system supporting the same interfaces over time, also referred to as backward compatibility. This implies that, although the system software and essential services are being upgraded, the application written on previous version will still run without any changes in binary form. The services include the machine-code instruction set, operating system services, and other system services such as networking, and X windows services.

3.8   System Compatibility

The compatibility can also be described as the copying, probably by reverse engineering, of one manufacturer's system by another and branding it as a compatible system thereby making the application running on the original system run on the cloned system in binary form. The advantage of compatibility is that the old software very rarely needs to change. The disadvantage of compatibility is that it does not allow the invention of innovative technologies. The makers of the compatible systems are often at the mercy of the market leader, who can manipulate the market to its own advantage. Also, there are no clear specifications, and if there are any, they are proprietary.

3.9   Application Portability

Portability is the ability to run UNIX applications on hardware platforms from multiple vendors. This offers users the capability of using the supplier of their choice based on such criteria as availability of local support. The main benefits of the open systems based on the UNIX operating systems stem from applications portability. The application portability at any level allows the software to be migrated across the systems with different architectures. It greatly reduces the cost to port to different systems, and the time involved in porting and allows a larger market segment to be tapped for the product. There are three levels of application portability: source-level portability, object-level portability, and binary-level portability. Figure 3-17 illustrates the relationship between portability levels.

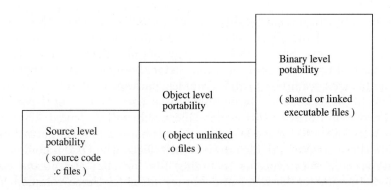

Figure 3-17
Portability hierarchy

3.9.1 Source-level Portability (SLP)

Source code is the way computer programs are written so that programmers can understand and manipulate work. They are essentially high-level languages like C, C++, FORTRAN, LISP, and COBOL that have their own specific definitions and grammatical rules. The application source is insulated from the underlying hardware architecture by defining the standards for the high-level language and the target environment. This makes it possible to develop applications that can run on widely different computer architectures.

Source code portability is the most widely applicable type of portability. It is source-level portability that first made the UNIX operating system so attractive to software developers and purchasers. The disadvantage of source-code portability is the independent software vendor (ISV), who still has to compile the application, thereby increasing overhead and cost. The other option is to sacrifice the source code to save time and money, but that is like digging your own grave. Still, source level portability is an excellent feature and reduces the headaches of keeping different versions of the application software for different architectures. Source-level portability is based on POSIX, ANSI C, SVID, X Window System, and networking standards. For UNIX System V

Release 4, the generic Application Binary Interchange (ABI) standards define the source-level portability.

3.9.2 Object-level Portability (OLP)

Object-level application portability is precompiled source, that is, the unlinked versions of the object code. Many application programs include not only binary programs, but also object programs or object libraries that are linked by the end user with their own code before being executed. Applications such as databases, compilers, and graphics packages all rely on shipping objects and libraries that are later linked by a user. Object-level portability defines the system libraries with which object code will be linked. The system interface is based on the same set of standards as source-level portability. In addition to these source-standard derived interfaces, the OLP includes object portability-specific specifications including file formats, subroutine calling conventions, assembler formats, and library formats. Since common object and library file formats, calling conventions, and system interfaces are supported on each OLP-compliant system, an OLP-compliant library or object can be linked to a system with the same architecture.

3.9.3 Binary-level Portability (BLP)

Binary-level portability (BLP) refers to the compiled and linked source code being able to be transported and executed on different hardware platforms using the same chip technology. Binary level portability defines specifications necessary to allow the portability of binary programs. It follows the same source standard and number of additional specifications specific to a binary portability standard, including executable file formats, memory maps, signal and exception handling.

Binary portability is the highest level of portability, combining the open systems benefits of source portability with the ease and convenience of binary portability. The processor-specific Application Binary Interchange (ABI) defines the binary level portability for UNIX System V Release 4. The BLP and OLP are the foundation of the shrinkwrapped software.

3.10 Conformance Levels

There are two types of conformance levels in an open systems environment: system conformance and application conformance.

3.10.1 System Conformance

System conformance is defined as the operating system, libraries, and utilities conforming to a well-defined set of standards. The conformance procedure usually involves unit testing of the functionality of the operating system, libraries, and utilities. A number of test suites are available in the industry to test the operating system, libraries and utilities such as the System V Verification Test Suite (SVVS), Interoperability Test Suite (ITS), and ABI Application Verification Suite (AVS).

3.10.2 Application Conformance

Application conformance is defined as the application program conforming to a well-defined set of standards (for example, ISO, ABI, POSIX, SVID, and ISO 9000) and language dependent services for the C and C++ programming language.

3.11 Guide to Writing Application Software

The forms listed next specifiy guidelines that can be followed to write application software. The guidelines cover some of the generic features that may be considered while writing application software. Some of the program features may not be relevant for a given application and some other program features may need to be added.

1. Document software specification form (SSF)
2. Document and implement software design form (SDF)
3. Document and implement software coding form (SCF)
4. Document and implement software testing form (STF)
5. Document software release form (SRF)
6. Document software user form (SUF)

3.12 Exercises

3.1 Rewrite the GetWord() function of the xdtool application of this chapter to internationalize input usage of character set, character collation, and word separation for a given locale. *Hint*: See section 4.6.2.

3.2 Localize the GUI buttons of xdtool application into a test language. Execute the xdtool program and display it in the pseudo test language. Hint: If the English text is "Apply", the pseudo test language text may look like "AApppllyy" (each English character is repeated twice).

3.3 Design a fuzzy match algorithm for the FuzzyMatch() function to display the closest word list for a given input word with the variable fuzzy distance, maximum distance limit to be 4. Assume input word and closest word list.

3.4 Write an application programmer's interface (API) for the algorithm of the FuzzyMatch() function in Exercise 3.2.

3.5 Implement software code for the API of the FuzzyMatch() function in Exercise 3.3.

3.6 Complete the program xdtool's software user documents (SUD) in Section 3.6.7.

3.7 Define application compatibility?

3.8 What is SLP, OLP, and BLP?

4

Internationalization

4.1   Introduction

This chapter describes the programming interface to the UNIX System V internationalization features. The intended audience is software engineers and translators. Knowledge of UNIX libraries, X window systems, and the C programming language are required. The chapter consists of a discussion on a character representation in multibyte and wide characters, a key in supporting the huge number of ideograms needed for input and output in an Asian language environment. A detailed look at the different locales encompassing the issues of character collation, date and time formatting, numeric formatting, message formatting, and monetary representation is also provided.

In addition the discussion concentrates on locale environment variables and on the System V implementation of ANSI standard C functions. To provide a practical approach, working examples are presented. The example programs have been tested on Sun Microsystems Solaris 1.1 and Solaris 2.3 and on the Univel SVR4.2 operating system.

4.2   Internationalization

Internationalization is the process of designing and building products that may be adapted to different languages and regions, conforming to local requirements and customs without engineering changes.

Internationalization is also the process of making software portable between languages or regions. International software in different languages can be developed using interfaces that modify program behavior at run time in accordance with specific cultural requirements.

Internationalization is often abbreviated as i18n because there are 18 characters between i and n. Software written using the System V release 4 internationalization interface is easy to migrate by merely translating messages and perhaps extending format databases.

4.3 Localization

Localization is the process of adapting software to a specific language or region. Localization involves establishing on-line information to support a specific language and/or region, called a locale.

Localization involves providing the necessary translations, format definitions, tables and other data to adapt an internationalized software product to local requirements.

Localization is referred to as l10n because there are 10 characters between letter l and n. If the software needs to be heavily modified for different languages and customs, localization is difficult and time consuming. For a given application, the larger the user messages are, the longer the time required to localize and test the application. The key to the localization process is a person being fluent in both English and the native language into which the application is to be localized.

4.4 Byte, Octet, and Character

Originally, interfaces were designed based on the assumption that a character consists of one byte of exactly 8 bits. To support the large number of ideograms, a byte can no longer mean 8 bits. The international standards bodies have redefined the terms byte, octet, and character.

- **Byte:** A unit of 8 bits or larger. Usually, sizes greater than 8 are relatively uncommon, but 9, 10, or even more bytes are possible.
- **Octet:** A byte of exactly 8 bits.
- **Character:** The sequence of one or more bytes representing a single graphic symbol or control code.

4.5   Character Representation

To support the large number of ideograms needed for input and output in an Asian language environment, SVR4 has adopted the Extended Unix Code (EUC) from AT&T's Multi-National Language Supplement (MNLS). Four single-byte and multibyte codesets can be represented in EUC at both the process level (internal to application) and file level (external to application).

EUC is used as file code for storing data internally in the CPU and main memory. It is essentially composed of one or more bytes and may be accompanied by single-shift characters.

EUC is composed of one primary codeset and three supplementary codesets as listed in Table 4-1. The primary codeset (codeset CS0) is used for ASCII and is always 7-bit U.S. ASCII. The three supplementary codesets CS1, CS2, and CS3, can be assigned to different character sets in LC_CTYPE directory.

Table 4-1 EUC Codeset Representation

Codeset	EUC Representation
CS0	0xxxxxxx
CS1	1xxxxxxx or 1xxxxxxx 1xxxxxxx or 1xxxxxxx 1xxxxxxx 1xxxxxxx
CS2	SS2 1xxxxxxx or SS2 1xxxxxxx 1xxxxxxx or SS2 1xxxxxxx 1xxxxxxx 1xxxxxxx
CS3	SS3 1xxxxxxx or SS3 1xxxxxxx 1xxxxxxx or SS3 1xxxxxxx 1xxxxxxx 1xxxxxxx

The primary codeset is defined as a single byte with the most significant bit (MSB) set to zero. The supplementary codesets can be multiple bytes, and the MSB of each byte is set to one. Codesets CS2 and CS3 are distinguished from codeset CS1 and each other by their use of a special shift byte (SS2 and SS3) before each character. The differentiation between codesets is done as follows: If the MSB is 0, the code is 1-byte ASCII. If it is 1, the byte is checked for shift characters SS2 or SS3 to determine the codeset. The multibyte EUC codeset has been further extended to implementation-defined integral-type wide characters that manipulate variable-width characters as uniformly sized data objects.

EUC has divided codeset space into graphic and special characters:

1.   Graphics Characters are those that can be displayed.
2.   Special Characters are space, delete, unassigned and the control character. control characters are nongraphic characters that initiate, modify, or stop a control operation. Table 4-2 indicates single-byte special characters.

Table 4-2 Single-byte Special Characters

Special Character	EUC Representation
Space	00100000
Delete	01111111
Primary Control codes	000xxxxx
Supplementary Control codes	100xxxxx

The programmers developing applications for less complex linguistic environments like European languages need not concern themselves with the details of multibyte and wide-character processing.

If an SVR3 application is being ported, it needs fixes. The application code should be 8-bit clean. Avoid using sign extension and character as indexes of array pitfalls. The sections below describe in detail how to avoid *dirty* code and write clean SVR4 code.

4.5.1   8-Bit Clean Codeset

For European languages, for instance, a single 8-bit codeset can hold all the characters of the major Western European languages. In these environments, at least one 8-bit character set will be represented in the EUC codesets, usually codesets CS0 and CS1. Other character sets may be represented simultaneously in various combinations. Applications based on European languages will work correctly with any standard 7- or 8-bit character set, provided they are 8-bit clean —they make no assumptions about the contents of high-order bits when processing characters.

Software applications written for 7-bit U.S. ASCII environments have assumed that the high-order bit is available for purposes other than character processing. In the computer industry, especially in data communications, it was often used as a parity bit. On receipt and after a parity check, the high-order bit was stripped either by the line discipline or the program to obtain the original 7-bit character.

Code that assumes that characters are only 7 bits long is dirty. The stripping of MSB is bad practice:

```
/* bad code */
#define CLEARMSB 0177
char c;


c &= CLEARMSB;
```

Code that explicitly uses the top bit for its own purposes is also dirty:

```
/* bad code */
#define SETMSB 0200
char c;


c |= SETMSB;
```

Neither of these two practices will work with 8-bit or larger code sets; instead, one should extend the data type to be unsigned short or unsigned int, and later set the top bit of the new data type. To clean the code one should search for constants like 0200, 0177, 127, 128, 0x80, and 0x7f.

4.5.2 Character Conversion

Code that assumes a particular range needs fixing, for example:

```
/* bad code */
if (c <= 037 || c == 0177)
```

Codeset-independent program should use isprint():

```
/* good code */
if (!isprint(c))
```

```
/* bad code */
if (c >= 'a' && c <= 'z')
```

Should be recoded with islower() function:

```
/* good code */
if (islower(c))
```

4.5.3 Sign Extension

In some C language software, character variables are not explicitly declared signed or unsigned and are treated as nonnegative quantities with a range of 0 to 255. In some other implementations, they are treated as signed quantities with a range typically from -128 to 127. When a signed object of type char is converted to a wider integer, the machine is obliged to propagate the sign, which is encoded in the high-order bit of the new integer object. If the character variable holds an 8-bit character with the high order bit set, the sign will be propagated to the full width of an object of type int or long, producing a negative value:

```
/ * bad code */
int i;
char c = 0200;

/* i is now negative */
i = c;
```

This problem can be avoided by declaring as unsigned any object of type char that is likely to be converted to a wider integer. This guarantees that on any implementation the values pointed at are nonnegative. The correct code should look like:

```
/* good code */
int i;
unsigned char c = 0200;

/* i is still positive */
i = c;
```

4.5.4   Characters Used as Indexes

Code that assumes characters fall in the range 0 to 127 needs fixing. If an array or table has been defined to contain only 128 possible characters, the amount of allocated memory will be exceeded if an 8-bit character whose value is greater than 127 is used as an index:

```
/* bad code */
char c;
int array[128];

/* ê is e with circumflex */
/* ê is 234 decimal in ISO-8859-1 */
c = ê;
array[ê] = 12;
```

The range of such tables should be extended to UCHAR_MAX, which is defined in <limits.h> on all ANSI C. Thus at least when dealing with 8-bit code sets, it is obvious to increase the size of the table from the 7-bit maximum of 128 to the 8-bit maximum of 256. Also, the object that will hold the character should be declared as unsigned char. For instance, Sun Openwindows 3.0 and above has standardized fonts ISO-8859-1, also known as ISO-Latin-1 for Western Europe. The fonts use the full 8-bit address space of a byte. The lower half of the ISO-8859-1 font contains all characters from the ASCII codeset, the upper half contains accented and special characters. The correct code is

```
/* good code */
#include <limits.h>
unsigned char c;
int array[UCHAR_MAX]; or
int array[256];

c = ê;
array[ê] = 12;
```

4.5.5   Multibyte Characters

The biggest difficulty in an Asian language environment is that of the huge number of ideograms needed for input and output. To work within the constraints of the usual computer architectures, these ideograms are encoded as a sequence of bytes. The associated application programs, operating systems, and terminals understand these sequences as individual ideograms. Because a single-byte character can be intermixed with multibyte characters, the sequence of bytes needed to encode an ideogram must be self-identifying. Regardless of the supplementary codeset used, each byte of a multibyte character will have the high-order bit set; if codesets CS2 or CS3 are used, each multibyte character will also be preceded by a shift byte. The difficulty associated with recognizing distinct ideograms depends on the encoding scheme used.

The term <u>multibyte character</u> is defined by ANSI C as a byte sequence that encodes a character, no matter what encoding scheme is employed. A single byte character is a special case of a multibyte character. All multibyte characters are members of the extended character set. A string is a contiguous sequence of bytes terminated by and including the NULL byte. It is an array of type char in C. The NULL byte has all its bits set to 0.

An empty multibyte character is one whose first element is NULL byte.

4.5.6   Wide Characters

In the case of multibyte characters, the difficulty associated with recongnising distinct ideograms depends on the encoding scheme used. The inconvenience of handling multibyte characters would be eliminated if all characters were of a uniform number of bytes. There can be thousands of ideograms in a character set, so a 16- or 32-bit sized integral value should be used to hold all its members. The Japanese Industry Standard requires about 6,400 ideograms, Korean about 5,000 ideograms, and the Chinese alphabet actually includes 6,800 ideograms. The unicode consortium defines the Far East Asian character sets as in Table 4-3.

Table 4-3 Far East Asian Character Standards

Country	Standard	Year	Characters
China	GB 2312	1980	6,763
Japan	JIS X0208	1983	6,349
Korea	KS C5601	1987	4,888
Taiwan	CNS 11643	1986	13,051

A <u>wide character</u> is an integral type large enough to hold any member of an extended character set. In program terms, ISO C provides the implementation-defined integral type wchar_t to manipulate variable characters as uniformly sized data objects called wide characters. A wide character string is a contiguous sequence of wide-characters terminated by and including the NULL wide character. It is an array of type wchar_t. The NULL wide character is a wchar_t value with all the bits set. Since there can be thousands of ideograms in an Asian- anguage set, programs should use a 32-bit-sized integral value to hold all members.

An empty wide-character string is one whose first element is the NULL wide character.

For each wide character there is a corresponding EUC representation, and vice versa. EUC codesets with 1, 2, or 3 bytes get mapped to wide characters, as shown in Table 4-4

Table 4-4 EUC and Wide-character Representation

Codeset	EUC Representation	Wide Character Representation
CS0	0xxxxxxx	00000000 00000000 00000000 0xxxxxxx
CS1	1xxxxxxx 1xxxxxxx	01100000 00000000 00xxxxxx 0xxxxxxx
CS2	SS2 1xxxxxxx 1xxxxxxx 1xxxxxxx	00100000 000xxxxx xxxxxxxx xxxxxxxx
CS3	SS3 1xxxxxxx 1xxxxxxx 1xxxxxxx	01000000 000xxxxx xxxxxxxx xxxxxxxx

Wide characters provide standard character size that is useful for indexing, memory management, interprocess communication, and other tasks that use character counts and known array sizes. The wide character method is stateless and unambiguous within a given locale.

4.5.7 Conversion Functions

For each multibyte character there is a corresponding wide-character code, and vice versa. The ISO C provides five library functions that manage multibyte and wide characters, as shown in Table 4-5.

Table 4-5 Multibyte and Wide-character Conversion Functions

Function	Description
mblen()	Length of next multibyte character
mbtowc()	Convert multibyte character to wide-character code
wctomb()	Convert wide-character code to multibyte character
mbstowcs()	Convert multibyte character string to wide-character string
wcstombs()	Convert wide-character string to multibyte character string

For a good number of application programs, there is no need to convert multi-byte characters to wide characters. Programs such as *diff*, for example, will read in and write out multibyte characters. needing only to check for an exact byte-for-byte match. More complicated programs such as *grep* that use regular expression pattern matching may need to understand multibyte characters, but only the common set of functions that manages the regular expression needs this knowledge. However, this knowledge can be localized to the functions that manage the regular functions. The program *grep* itself requires no other special multibyte-character handling.

4.5.8 C Language Features

To provide more flexibility to the application programmers in an Asian environment, ISO C provides 32-bit wide-character constants and wide string literals. These have the same form as their nonwide versions except they are immediately prefixed by the letter L. With the Sun Microsystems regular type-4 keyboard, the keyboard sequence Compose, A, ", produces Ä (known as A umlaut).

```
'a' regular character constant
'Ä' regular character constant
L'a' wide character constant
L'Ä' wide character constant
"abcÄxyz" regular string literal
L"abcÄxyz" wide string literal
```

Notice that multibyte characters are valid in both the regular and wide versions. The sequence of bytes necessary to produce the ideogram Ä is encoding specific, but if it consists of more than 1 byte, the value of the character constant Ä is implementation defined.

When the compilation system encounters a wide-character constant or wide string literal, each multibyte character is converted, as if by calling the mbtowc() function into a wide character. The following is an example:

```
L'Ä' /* is of type wchar_t */
L"abcÄxyz" /* is of array of type wchar_t[8] */
```

Just as with regular string literals, each wide string literal has an extra zero-valued element appended, but in this case it is wchar_t with value zero.

Like regular string literals, which can be used for character array initialization, wide string literals can be used to initialize wchar_t arrays.

```
wchar_t *wide_ptr = L"aÄz";
wchar_t i[] = L"aÄz";

wchar_t j[] = { L'a', L'Ä', L'z', 0 };
wchar_t k[] = { L'a', L'Ä', L'z', '\0' };
```

In this example, the three arrays i, j, and k and the array pointed to by wide_ptr have the same length and all are initialized with identical values.
The adjacent wide string literals are concatenated, just as with regular string literals. Adjacent regular and wide string literals cannot be concatenated and may produce undefined behavior.

4.6   Locales

A locale is the description of the subset of a user's environment as defined by X/Open that depends on language and cultural conventions. Alternatively, it can be described as the international environment of a computer program defining the localized behavior of that program at runtime. Locale name is specified by the LANG environment variable. Locale is made up of one or more categories. Each category is identified by its name and controls specific aspects of the behavior of components of the system. Category names correspond to the environment variable names with descriptions listed in Table 4-6.

Table 4-6 Locales partitioned into categories

Locale Category	Description
LC_CTYPE	Character representation information
LC_COLLATE	Collation order
LC_TIME	Date and time formats
LC_NUMERIC	Numeric formats
LC_MONETARY	Monetary formats
LC_MESSAGES	Message formats

Each programs begins in the C or English language locale known as POSIX Locale, by default, which causes the library functions to behave in a certain way. Any other locale will cause certain of these functions to behave in the appropriate language or culture-dependent ways. Locales can have names that are strings like "German", "French", or "Swedish" etc. (or "de", "fr", "sv", following ISO conventions). Locale can be changed by providing the second argument as the string to function setlocale().

A locale name is always composed of a language name, with a territory name appended if any. Language names, all lowercase, are defined in the ISO 639 standard specifications. Territory names, all uppercase, are in the ISO 3166 standard. Language is separated from the territory by an underscore, and territory is optional. Some standard accepted language and territory names are listed in Table 4-7 as defined for Solaris 2.1 and later operating environments and on Univel SVR4.2.

From the system implementation point of view, the locale categories are files in directories named for each locale they support; the directories themselves are usually kept in the */usr/lib/locale*

```
/* contains German character representation files */
/usr/lib/locale/de/LC_CTYPE

/* contains French collation order files */
/usr/lib/locale/fr/LC_COLLATE
```

Table 4-7 Standard Language and Territory Names

Locale	Language and Territory	Locale	Language and Territory
C	Default C locale	ga	Irish
ar	Arabic	gd	Scots Gaelic
bg	Bulgarian	hu	Hungarian
ca	Catalan	is	Icelandic
co	Corsican	it	Italian
cs	Czech	iw	Hebrew
cy	Welsh	ja	Japanese
da	Danish	ji	Yiddish
de	German	kl	Greenlandic
de_CH	Swiss German	ko	Korean
el	Greek	lv	Latvian
en	English	nl	Dutch
en_UK	English (UK)	no	Norwegian
en_US	English (US)	pl	Polish
eo	Esperanto	pt	Portuguese
es	Spanish	ro	Romanian
eu	Basque	ru	Russian
fa	Persian	sh	Serbo-Croatian
fi	Finnish	sk	Slovak
fr	French	sr	Serbian
fr_BE	Belgian French	sv	Swedish
fr_CA	Canadian French	tr	Turkish
fr_CH	French Swiss	zh	Chinese
fy	Frisian	zh_TW	Taiwanese Chinese

From the user's view, the categories are environment variables that can be set to a given locale:

```
/*set date and time formats to Italian */
LC_TIME=it
export LC_TIME
```

```
/*set message information to Swedish */
LC_MESSAGES=sv
export LC_MESSAGES
```

From the program's view, the categories are macros that can be passed as the first argument to function setlocale() to specify that it change the program's locale for that category. If the macro is LC_CTIME;

```
setlocale(LC_TIME, "fr");
```

tells the program to use date and time printing information in French, but leaves other categories unchanged. LC_ALL is the macro that specifies the entire locale. If the function is invoked with an empty string, such as

```
setlocale (LC_ALL, "");
```

the value of the corresponding environment variable is used. If the environment variable is unset or is set to the empty string, the environment set is implementation defined. Incidentally, the LANG environment variable is the user equivalent of the program's macro LC_ALL. The environment variable LANG is checked after environment variables for individual categories.

Locales other than those supplied by the implementation can be created by the application via the localedef utility.

Function setlocale(), then, is the interface to the program's locale. Any program that has a need to use language or cultural conventions should put a call such as

```
#include <locale.h>

/* call this at the beginning of program */
setlocale (LC_ALL, "");
```

early in its execution path. The second argument of empty string forces the value of the corresponding environment variable to be used. If there are parts of programs that need only the ASCII upper- and lowercase characters guaranteed by ANSI C in the <ctype.h> header, setlocale should be called with locale category LC_CTYPE and the C locale.

setlocale() returns the name of the current locale for a given category and serves in query only capacity when its second argument is a null pointer. The code may look like this:

Example

/* filename clex1.c */

```
#include <locale. h>

main()
{
  char *locale_category;
  setlocale(LC_CTYPE, "de");

  /* query current LC_CTYPE locale category */
  locale_category = setlocale(LC_CTYPE, NULL);
  printf ("category LC_CTYPE=%s\n", locale_category);
  setlocale(LC_MESSAGES, "fr");

  /* query current LC_MESSAGES locale category */
  locale_category = setlocale(LC_MESSAGES, NULL);
  printf ("category LC_MESSAGES=%s\n", locale_category);
  setlocale(LC_ALL, "it");

  /* query current locale */
  locale_category = setlocale(LC_ALL, NULL);
  printf ("category LC_ALL=%s\n", locale_category);
}
```

Output

```
category LC_CTYPE=de
category LC_MESSAGES=fr
category LC_ALL=it
```

Table 4-8 lists setlocale() calling sequences to query current environment and programs locale categories.

Table 4-8

Call	Description
setlocale(LC_Category, "")	Query environment locale category
setlocale(LC_Category, NULL)	Query program locale category

A complete discussion on the setlocale() function can be found in the manual pages.

4.6.1 LC_CTYPE: Character Classification and Case Conversion

The locale category LC_CTYPE defines rules for character classification, case conversion, and other character attributes. Character classification affects command line processing, recognition of white space, display of non printable characters by the editors, default field separator in sort and so on.

The LC_CTYPE information for libraries and utilities resides under directory */usr/lib/locale/<lang_territory>/LC_CTYPE*. The variable determines the locale category for character-handling functions, such as tolower(), toupper(), and isalpha(). It also determines the interpretation of sequences of bytes of text data as characters, the classification of characters (for example alpha, digit, and graph), and the behavior of character classes. The international software should be 8-bit clean and free of hard-coded case conversion; watch for sign extension problems and avoid using undeclared character type as indexes to the array. The software should use library routines under <ctype.h>, as listed in Tables 4-9 and 4-10.

Table 4-9 Query Character Type

Function	Character is....
isalnum()	Letter or digit
isalpha()	Letter
isascii()	7-Bit ASCII character
iscntrl()	Control code
isdigit()	Digit
isgraph()	Visible
islower()	Lowercase

Table 4-9 Query Character Type (continued)

Function	Character is....
isprint()	Printable
ispunct()	Punctuation mark
isspace()	White space
isupper()	Uppercase
isxdigit()	Hexadecimal digit

Table 4-10 Set Character

Function	Convert character to...
toascii()	Ascii
tolower()	Lowercase
toupper()	Uppercase

Example

```c
/* filename clex2.c */

#include <locale.h>
#include <ctype.h>

main()
{
  unsigned char c;

  /* set LC_CTYPE to German locale */
  setlocale (LC_CTYPE, "de");
  printf ("All graphic characters\n");
  for ( c = 0 ; c < 255; c++ ) {
    if ( isgraph(c) )
      printf ("%c", c);
  }
  printf ("\n");

  c = 'a';
```

```
    printf ("Convert lowercase to uppercase character\n");
    printf ("%c uppercase is %c\n", c, toupper(c));
}
```

Output

```
All graphic characters
!"#$%&'()*+,-.0123456789:;<=>?@ABCDEFGHIJKLMNOPQRSTUVWXYZ
[\]abcdefghijklmnopqrstuvwxyz...ÀÁÂÃÄ...(etc.)
Convert lowercase to uppercase character
a uppercase is A
```

4.6.2   LC_COLLATE: Collation

The locale category LC_COLLATE determines the locale category for character collation. It determines collation information for sorting and regular
expressions, including equivalence classes and multicharacter collating elements. The LC_COLLATE information for libraries and utilities resides under
directory */usr/lib/locale/<lang_territory>/LC_COLLATE*.

For string collation, sort orders may vary for different languages. ISO C provides two library functions strcoll() and strxfrm() routines to perform string
comparisons, which use locale-specific collation order according to the LC_CO-
LLATE category of the current locale. Conceptually, collation occurs in two
phases to obtain an appropriate ordering of accented characters, as in the case
of a two-character sequence that should be treated as one (the Spanish character *ch*, for example) and single characters that should be treated as two (the
sharp *s* in German). The function call strcoll() is more expensive than
strcmp(); therefore, strxfrm(), which transforms the string in such a way that
if the strcmp() function is applied to two transformed strings it will return the
same result as strcoll() applied to the same two original strings. should be
used if strings are compared number of times.

POSIX defines five rules governing complex collation order:
1. Byte or machine code ordering
2. Character ordering
3. String ordering
4. Text search ordering
5. Semantic-level ordering

Table 4-11 String Collation Functions

Function	Description
strcoll()	compare two strings
strxfrm()	transform string for comparison

Example

```
/* filename clex3.c */

#include <locale.h>
#include <ctype.h>

main()
{
  int ret_cmp;
  char *string1 = "êfg";
  char *string2 = "efg";

  /* set LC_COLLATE to French locale */
  setlocale (LC_COLLATE, "fr");
  ret_cmp = strcoll(string1, string2);
  printf ("string comparison return value=%d\n", ret_cmp);
}
```

Output

```
sring comparision return value=3
```

Example

```
/* filename clex4.c */

#include <locale.h>
#include <stdio.h>
#include <ctype.h>
main()
{
  int ret_cmp;
```

```
    size_t len1, len2;
    char *trans1;
    char *trans2;
    char *string1 = "êfg";
    char *string2 = "efg";

    /* set LC_COLLATE to French locale */
    setlocale (LC_COLLATE, "fr");
    len1 = strxfrm(NULL, string1, 0) + 1;
    len2 = strxfrm(NULL, string2, 0) + 1;

    trans1 = (char *)malloc(len1);
    trans2 = (char *)malloc(len2);

    strxfrm(trans1, string1, len1);
    strxfrm(trans2, string2, len2);

    ret_cmp = strcmp(trans1, string2);
    free (trans1) ; free (trans2);

    printf ("string comparison return value=%d\n", ret_cmp);

}
```

Output

```
string comparision return value=-83
```

4.6.3   LC_TIME: Date and Time Formatting

The locale category variable LC_TIME determines date and time formatting information. If affects the behavior of the time functions strftime() and nl_langinfo(). It defines the interpretation of the field descriptors supported by the date utility. The LC_TIME information for libraries and utilities resides under directory */usr/lib/locale/<lang_territory>/LC_TIME*. Some international date formats are given in Table 4-12. Table 4-13 lists the date and time library routines.

Table 4-12 International Date Conventions

Language	Convention	Example
French	dd/mm/yy	21/10/93
German	dd.mm.yy	21.10.93
Italian	dd.mm.yy	21.10.93
Spanish	dd-mm-yy	21-10-93
Swedish	yy-mm-dd	93-10-21
UK-English	dd/mm/yy	21/10/93
US-English	mm-dd-yy	10-21-93

Table 4-13 Date and Time function

Function	Description
strftime()	Convert date and time to string

The directive %x provides an implementation-defined date representation appropriate to the locale. The directive %X, on the other hand, obtains the locale's appropriate time representation. The format %Z yields the timezone.

The date and time format can also be controlled with the message retrieval functions gettxt() or catgets(), but these require more work. The %n$ form of conversion specification allows conversion of the nth argument in a printf list; For example:

```
printf(gettxt("progtime:5", %d/%d/%d\n"),
            tm_pointer->tm.mon,
            tm_pointer->tm.mday,
            tm_pointer->tm.year);
```

will produce the locale-dependent date displays as long as the string whose index is 5 in the message file progtime reads in different locale as follows:

```
Swedish locale "%3$d-%1$d-%2$d\n"
US-locale "%1$d/%2$d/%3$d\n"
```

The function scanf() can be used in a similar way to interpret formatted dates
in the input. The next example explains strftime() to print the current date in
a locale-dependent way.

Example

```
/* filename clex5.c */

#include <stdio.h>
#include <locale.h>
#include <time.h>

main()
{
  time_t time_struct;
  struct tm *tm_pointer;
  char buf [BUFSIZ];

  /* set LC_TIME to Swedish locale */
  setlocale (LC_TIME, "sv");
  time_struct = time(NULL);
  tm_pointer = localtime(&time_struct);

  /* %x : date representation */
  /* %X : time representation */
  strftime(buf, BUFSIZ, "%x %X", tm_pointer );
  printf ("date and time: %s\n", buf);

  /* %c : both date and time representation */
  strftime(buf, BUFSIZ, "%c", tm_pointer);
  printf ("date and time: %s\n", buf);
}
```

Output

```
date and time: 93-11-06 13:21:17
date and time: lör  6 nov 93 kl 13:21:17 PST
```

4.6.4   LC_NUMERIC: Numeric Formatting

The locale category LC_NUMERIC defines the rules and symbols that are used to format nonmonetary information. The LC_NUMERIC information for libraries and utilities resides under */usr/lib/locale/<lang_territory>/ LC_NUMERIC*. The information can be obtained through the localeconv() function. The function returns the pointer to a structure containing information useful for formatting numeric and monetary information appropriate to the current locale. The macro nl_langinfo() with the appropriate constant as argument returns the thousand and decimal separator.

Some conventions used by different countries are listed below in Table 4-14. Table 4-15 lists the numeric formatting functions.

Table 4-14 International Numeric Conventions

Language	Convention
French	1.234.567,00
German	1 234 567,00
Italian	1.234.567,00
Spanish	1.234.567,00
Swedish	1 234.567,00
US-English	1,234,567.00

Table 4-15 Numeric Formatting Function

Function	Description
localeconv()	Returns structure containing numeric and monetary format

Consider an example to print the numeric format in French.

Example

```
/* filename clex6.c */

#include <locale.h>
#include <langinfo.h>

main()
{
```

```
    int thousands = 1;
    int hundreds = 234;
    int fraction = 56;
    char *tsep, *dsep;
    char thousand_sep[2];
    char decimal_sep[2];
    struct lconv *numeric_ptr;

    /* set LC_NUMERIC to Italian locale */
    setlocale(LC_NUMERIC, "it");
    tsep = nl_langinfo(THOUSEP);
    strcpy(thousand_sep, tsep);
    dsep = nl_langinfo(RADIXCHAR);
    strcpy(decimal_sep, dsep);

    printf ("%d%s%d%s%d\n", thousands, thousand_sep, hundreds,
                            decimal_sep, fraction);

}
```

Output

```
1.234,56
```

4.6.5 LC_MONETARY: Monetary Formatting

The locale category LC_MONETARY defines the rules and symbols that are used
to format monetary numeric information. The LC_MONETARY information for
libraries and utilities resides under the directory */usr/lib/locale/<lang_terri-
tory>/LC_MONETARY*. Currency units and presentation order vary greatly
around the world. This information is available through the localeconv() function and is used by the strfmon() function. Table 4-16 shows monetary formats
in some countries.

Table 4-16 International Currency Conventions

Language	Currency	Example
French	Franc	F1.234,56
German	Deutsche Mark	1 234,56DM
Italian	Lira	L1234,56

Table 4-16 International Currency Conventions (continued)

Language	Currency	Example
Japanese	Yen	Y1,234
Spanish	Peseta	1.234,56Pts
Swedish	Krona	1234.56KR
US-English	Dollar	$1,234.56

Like the numeric format, the localeconv() function (Table 4-17) can be used to obtain currency formats. The localeconv() function returns a pointer to the filled in object, with monetary and numeric information. localeconv() uses the decimal point character rather than the period when the LC_NUMERIC category of the current locale is other than "C".

Table 4-17 Monetary Formatting Function

Function	Description
localeconv()	Returns structure containing monetary and numeric format

Example

```
/* filename clex7.c */

#include <locale.h>

main()
{
   int thousands = 1;
   int hundreds = 234;
   int fraction = 56;
   struct lconv *numeric_ptr;

   /* set LC_MONETARY to German locale */
   setlocale(LC_MONETARY, "de");
   numeric_ptr = localeconv();

   printf ("%s%d%c%d%c%d\n", numeric_ptr->currency_symbol,
     thousands, numeric_ptr->mon_thousands_sep[0], hundreds,
     numeric_ptr->mon_decimal_point[0], fraction);
```

}

Output

DM1 234,56

4.6.6   LC_MESSAGES: Message Formatting

The locale category LC_MESSAGES defines the application's usage summaries, error diagnostics, help text, menu choices, button labels, and affirmative and negative responses in given language and cultural conventions. There should be no explicit strings in an international application except those passed to gettext(). The message files should be translated stand-alone.

The message files reside under directory the */usr/lib/locale/<lang_territory>/LC_MESSAGES/application*. For message handling within the application source code, the standard X/Open function is catgets(), but gettext() is a better programming interface.Table 4-18 and 4-19 list message formatting library functions.

Table 4-18 Message Formatting Library Functions

Function	Description
catopen()	Open message catalog
catgets()	Get message from catalog
catgetmsg()	Get buffered message from catalog
catclose()	Close message catalog
gettext()	Get message from catalog
dgettext()	Get message from catalog domain

Table 4-19 Solaris 2.1 and up Version Specific Functions

Function	Description
bindtextdomain()	Associate pathname with message domain
textdomain()	Open message catalog domain

4.7 Other Locale Variables

- **LANG**: The environment variable LANG determines the locale category for the native language, local customs, coded character set, numeric format, time and date formats, monetary formats, message formats in the absence of LC_ALL, or any of the other locale categories; LC_COLLATE, LC_CTYPE, LC_NUMERIC, LC_TIME, LC_MONETARY, and LC_MESSAGES environment variables.

- **LC_ALL**: The variable LC_ALL is the programmer's equivalent of the environment variable LANG; it determines the values for all the locale categories in the program. The value of LC_ALL has precedence over any of the other environment variables: LANG, LC_COLLATE, LC_CTYPE. LC_NUMERIC, LC_TIME, LC_MONETARY, and LC_MESSAGES.

- **NLSPATH**: The environment variable NLSPATH contains a sequence of templates that the catopen() function uses when attempting to locate message catalogs. Each template consists of an optional prefix, one or more substitution fields, a filename, and an optional suffix. If set, NLSPATH specifies the search path to be used for locating the message catalog. The syntax for setting this environment variable is shown next:

```
NLSPATH=[:][/directory][substitution field][/
fliename][:alternative pathname]
```

A leading colon indicates the current directory, whereas subsequent colons act solely as field separators. Substitution fields consist of a % symbol followed by a single-letter keyword. The following keywords are currently defined:

```
%N Value of the name parameter passed to catopen()
%L Value of the LC_MESSAGES category
%l Language element from the LC_MESSAGES category
%t Territory element from the LC_MESSAGES category
%c Codeset element from the LC_MESSAGES category
%% A single character
```

A usual NLSPATH will look something like this

```
NLSPATH=:%N.cat:/usr/lib/locale/%L/%N.cat
```

4.8   Input Method

Input method is the way in which users enter the text of a language.

Many phonetic-based languages like English and European languages are easy to type on a keyboard. In the case of European languages, special keyboards are available with accented characters required by the language. For instance, on the German keyboard the characters Ä and Ö are present. If the characters are not available, one can generate them using the compose key. This type of input method can be implemented with the keyboard hardware or through the operating system software.

Asian languages such as Chinese, Japanese, and Korean, etc. are ideographic languages that consist of multiple alphabets and require several keystrokes to create one character. The ideograms are stored in a tabular form. To access the ideograms, the input server should be running. The input method for each language may be different, depending on the linguistic structure and conventions of that language. Usually, the user types the word, which appears on the screen in reverse video in an area called the pre-edit region. The user then commits the word or can invoke the Select Start key. This causes the alternative ideogram selections to be displayed in an area called the lookup choice region. The user can select the most appropriate word. The selected word replaces the word in the pre-edit region. The commit keystroke sends the text to the client.

4.9   Application Software Localization

The application software that needs to be localized for any language should be written with internationalization functions. The functions allow the program strings, user messages, error messages, text for buttons, and menu to be displayed in the language of the user's choice for which message translation is available. The date and time formats should also be in the locale-specific language. The software design and code should be based on table-driven algorithms and modular replacement techniques. The user-interface text, together with its position and size control, should be separate from the code that presents it. In this way, the text can be easily accessed for translation. The software should use the locale category specific functions discussed in previous sections.

The following are the important points to be considered when writing international software:

User interfaces
Text expansion
Text positioning
Writing direction
Thousands separators
Decimal separators
Paragraph numbering
Positive values
Negative values
Currency
Dates
Times

Currently, Sun Microsystems Solaris 2.1 operating environment and later versions supports French, German, Italian, Spanish, Swedish, Chinese, Taiwanese, Japanese, and Korean. The libraries, frequently used commands, and toolkit user interfaces have been localized.The application software can be localized using two methods:

1. Message catalog scheme using catgets()

2. Message catalog scheme using gettext()

The gettext source code is in the public domain and freely available. The source code can be downloaded from Sun Microsystems public domain ftp sites.

4.9.1   Message Catalog Scheme Using catgets()

The message catalog scheme using catgets() as suggested by the X/Open XPG3, is based on the catalog functions catopen(), catgets(), catgetmsg(), and catclose(). From the programmer's point of view, these functions allow one to open and read a message catalog file that consists of translated messages. Figure 4-1 illustrates the application localization using the catgets() message catalog scheme. The process involves adding message catalog functions with a set directive and message number. The strings are then extracted from the source code and localized.

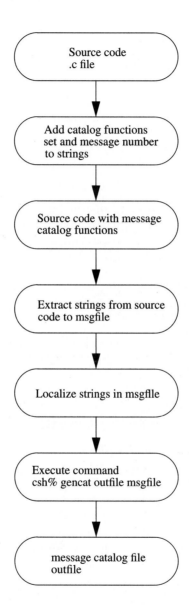

Figure 4-1
Application localization using catgets() message catalog scheme

The functions can be best explained with an example.

Example

```
/* filename clex8.c */

#include <stdio.h>
#include <nl_types.h>
#include <string.h>
#include <locale.h>

#define LENGTH 20
char yesstr[LENGTH];

main()
{
  int yes();
  nl_catd catd;
  setlocale (LC_ALL, "");

  /* open message catalog file */
  catd = catopen("progmsgs", 0);

  /* read translated message if NLSPATH is set properly */
  /* else print in English */
  print (catgets(catd, 1, 1, "Hello World\n"));
  strcpy (yesstr, catgets(catd, 1, 2, "yes"));

  while (1) {
    printf(catgets(catd, 1, 3, "Quit (y/n)"));
    if (yes()) {
      printf(yesstr);
      printf("\n");
      break;
    }
    else
    printf (catgets(catd, 2, 1, "no"));

  printf("\n");

  } /* end while */
```

```
   printf(catgets(catd, 2, 2, "Good Bye!\n"));

   /* close the catalog file */
   caclose(catd);

}

static int yes()
{

   int i, b;
   i = b = getchar();

   while (b != '\n' && b != '\0' && b != EOF)
       b = getchar();

   return (i == (int) yesstr[0]);

}
```

Consider messages.de file with German translations

```
$set 1
1 Hallo Welt\n
2 ja
3 Ende (j/n)
$set 2
1 nein
2 Auf Wiedersehen!\n
```

The $set 1 directive specifies that the first three messages are members of set 1. A subsequent $set 2 specifies that messages are from set 2 and so on.

The gencat command can be used to store the strings for a given locale in a catalog file to be used by the catopen() and catgets() calls. In this example

```
$ gencat progmsgs messages.de
```

will generate the catalog file progmsgs.

From the user's point of view, the user should specify the message catalog search paths with the NLSPATH environment variable.

The value of NLSPATH is used by function catopen() to locate the message catalog named in its first argument. If env variable NLSPATH is set to

```
$ NLSPATH=":%N.cat:/tmp/%L/%N.cat" ; export NLSPATH
```

and if LC_MESSAGES is set to the de (German) locale and the message catalog file name is progmsgs, the catopen() call will look for the requested message catalog in the current directory as progmsgs or progmsgs.cat; it would then search directory

/tmp/de/progmsgs.cat.

The output of this program is

Output

```
Hallo Welt
Ende (j/n)j
ja
Auf Wiedersehen!
```

The message catalog scheme has a shortcoming: for the catgets() one must pass two extra numeric parameters, one for the catalog descriptor, and another for the message set number. It also requires a numeric ID for each message. This makes code confusing and difficult to maintain.

4.9.2 Message Catalog Scheme using gettext()

The gettext() scheme is used by Sun Microsystems. This scheme uses international library (libintl.a) functions bindtextdomain(), textdomain(), gettext(), and dgettext(). The code is easy to maintain and write using this technique. Figure 4-2 depicts application localization using the gettext() message scheme. The gettext() scheme calls are added to the source code. The command xgettext then generates the messages.po file for localization. Finally, the command msgfmt is used to create the binary messages.mo file.

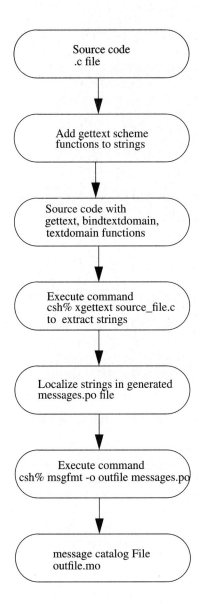

Figure 4-2
Application localization using the gettext() message catalog scheme

From the programmer's point of view, all the string literals should be enclosed inside the gettext() calls as follows:

Example

```
/* filename clex9.c */

#include <stdio.h>
#include <string.h>
#include <locale.h>

#define LENGTH 20
char yesstr[LENGTH];

main()
{
  int yes();
  setlocale (LC_ALL, "");

  /* arguments to bindtextdomain are filename, directory */
  bindtextdomain("progmsgs", "/tmp");

  /* domainname in progmsg file */
  textdomain("progmsgs");
  printf (gettext("Hello World\n"));
  strcpy (yesstr, gettext("yes"));

  while (1) {
    printf(gettext("Quit (y/n)"));
    if (yes()) {
      printf(yesstr);
      printf("\n");
      break;
    }
    else
    printf (gettext("no"));
  printf("\n");
  }
  printf(gettext("Good Bye!\n"));
}

static int yes()
```

```
{
  int i, b;
  i = b = getchar();
  while (b != '\n' && b != '\n' && b != EOF ) b = getchar();
  return (i == (int) yesstr[0]);
}
```

The function bindtextdomain() associates the pathname in the second argument with the message domain. Passing a null pointer as the second argument causes bindtextdomain() to return the pathname associated with the first argument's message domain. The function textdomain() sets or queries the name of the current domain of the active LC_MESSAGES locale category.

The strings file can be generated by the xgettext() command on the C source files to create a message file. This produces a readable .po file (the portable object) for translation by translators. In the preceding example,

```
$ xgettext getcalls.c
```

produces the following `messages.po` file

```
domain "messages"
# File:clex9.c, line:19, textdomain("progmsgs");
msgid "Hello World\n"
msgstr
msgid "yes"
msgstr
msgid "Quit (y/n)"
msgstr
msgid "no"
msgstr
msgid "Good Bye!\n"
msgstr
```

domain **domainname**
Specifies that all the target strings are contained in domainname until another domain directive.

msgid **message identifier**
Specifies the value of the message identifier associated with the following msgstr directive, the string associated with the gettext.

`msgstr` **message string**
Specifies the target translated string associated with the msgid. All statements containing a msgstr directive must be immediately preceded by a msgid statement.

The portable object file messages.po is then given to a translator to append the translated version of msgid to the msgstr line.

In the preceding example, the file `messages.po` (after translation to German) looks like

```
domain "messages"
# File:clex9.c, line:19, textdomain("progmsgs");
msgid "Hello World\n"
msgstr "Hallo Welt\n"
msgid "yes"
msgstr "ja"
msgid "Quit (y/n)"
msgstr "Ende (j/n)"
msgid "no"
msgstr "nein"
msgid "Good Bye!\n"
msgstr "Auf Wiedersehen!\n"
```

Once the file has been translated, the command msgfmt is executed against the portable object file. The output from msgfmt is a message object (suffix .mo) file:

```
$ msgfmt -o progmsgs.mo messages.po
```

This produces the binary `progmsgs.mo` file.

From the user's point of view, if the environment variable LANG or LC_MESSAGES is set to de (German), and if the progmsgs.mo file is placed in the directory

```
/tmp/de/LC_MESSAGES
```

the program when executed will look for the translated messages in file progmsgs.mo file and the output will be

Output

```
Hallo Welt
Ende (j/n)j
ja
Auf Wiedersehen!
```

4.10 Localization Examples

4.10.1 French, German, Italian, Spanish, Swedish

The following sections consist of translated strings of example getcalls.c for
French, German, Italian, Spanish, Swedish.

- **French**

```
domain "messages"
# File:clex9.c, line:19, textdomain("progmsgs");
msgid "Hello World\n"
msgstr "Bonjour tout le Monde\n"
msgid "yes"
msgstr "oui"
msgid "Quit (y/n)"
msgstr "Quitter (o/n)"
msgid "no"
msgstr "non"
msgid "Good Bye!\n"
msgstr "Aurevoir!\n"
```

- **German**

```
domain "messages"
# File:clex9.c, line:19, textdomain("progmsgs");
msgid "Hello World\n"
msgstr "Hallo Welt\n"
msgid "yes"
msgstr "ja"
msgid "Quit (y/n)"
msgstr "Ende (j/n)"
msgid "no"
msgstr "nein"
msgid "Good Bye!\n"
msgstr "Auf Wiedersehen!\n"
```

- **Italian**
```
domain "messages"
# File:clex9.c, line:19, textdomain("progmsgs");
msgid "Hello World\n"
msgstr "Hallo Mondo\n"
msgid "yes"
msgstr "Si"
msgid "Quit (y/n)"
msgstr "Fini (s/n)"
msgid "no"
msgstr "no"
msgid "Good Bye!\n"
msgstr "Arrivederla!\n"
```
- **Spanish**
```
domain "messages"
# File:clex9.c, line:19, textdomain("progmsgs");
msgid "Hello World\n"
msgstr "Hola Mundo\n"
msgid "yes"
msgstr "sí"
msgid "Quit (y/n)"
msgstr "Terminado? (s/n)"
msgid "no"
msgstr "no"
msgid "Good Bye!\n"
msgstr "Adios!\n"
```
- **Swedish**
```
domain "messages"
# File:clex9.c, line:19, textdomain("progmsgs");
msgid "Hello World\n"
msgstr "Hej världen\n"
msgid "yes"
msgstr "ja"
msgid "Quit (y/n)"
msgstr "Avsluta (j/n)"
msgid "no"
msgstr "nej"
msgid "Good Bye!\n"
msgstr "Hej då!\n"
```

4.10.2 Chinese, Taiwanese, Japanese, Korean

The following sections consist of translated strings of example getcalls.c for Chinese, Taiwanese, Japanese and Korean languages.

- **Chinese**

```
# File:getcalls.c, line:17, textdomain("progmsgs");
msgid  "Hello World\n"
msgstr "你好\n"
msgid  "yes"
msgstr "是"
msgid  "Quit (y/n)"
msgstr "退出 (y/n)"
msgid  "no"
msgstr "不"
msgid  "Good Bye!\n"
msgstr "再见!\n
```

- **Taiwanese**

```
domain "messages"
# File:getcalls.c, line:17, textdomain("progmsgs");
msgid  "Hello World\n"
msgstr "哈囉世界\n"
msgid  "yes"
msgstr "是"
msgid  "Quit (y/n)"
msgstr "結束 (y/n)"
msgid  "no"
msgstr "否"
msgid  "Good Bye!\n"
msgstr "再見!\n"
```

- **Japanese**

```
domain "messages"
# File:getcalls.c, line:17, textdomain("progmsgs");
msgid  "Hello World¥n"
msgstr "ハロー・ワールド¥n"
msgid  "yes"
msgstr "はい"
msgid  "Quit (y/n)"
msgstr "終了(y/n)"
msgid  "no"
msgstr "いいえ"
msgid  "Good Bye!¥n"
msgstr "さようなら¥n"
```

- **Korean**

```
domain "messages"
# File:getcalls.c, line:17, textdomain("progmsgs");
msgid  "Hello World\n"
msgstr "안녕하세요\n"
msgid  "yes"
msgstr "예"
msgid  "Quit (y/n)"
msgstr "끝 (y/n)"
msgid  "no"
msgstr "아니오"
msgid  "Good Bye!\n"
msgstr "안녕히 가세요\n"
```

4.11 Guide to Writing Internationalized Application

<u>The Localization or L rule</u>: Since there are 12 important rules to be followed for writing international software, it will be referred to here as the L rule, for L is also the twelfth character of the alphabet.

1. Set the desired locale by calling the setlocale() function to initialize language and cultural conventions.

2. Make international software 8-bit clean without using the most significant bit (MSB) of the byte.

3. Do character conversion with ctype library functions to identify character ranges.

4. Make sure all the characters are unsigned, thereby eliminating the sign extension problem.

5. Avoid using the signed characters as indexes to reference an array.

6. Use standard codesets such as Extended UNIX Code or ISO Latin-1.

7. Use the strcoll() function for string comparisons or transform strings for comparison using the strxfrm() function and then use the strcmp() function.

8. For printing date and time in local formats, use the strftime() function.

9. Use the nl_langinfo() and localeconv() functions for numeric and currency formats. Many countries will need a comma (,) instead of period (.) for numeric and currency formats.

10. Use the printf and scanf commands for formatted output and input.

11. Use wide-character and multibyte characters for the Asian languages.

12. The international application program should contain the gettext() or catgets() function for any message strings. There should not be any hard-coded locale-specific characters or strings in the application.

4.12 Exercises

4.1 Define software Internationalization?

4.2 Define software Localization?

4.3 Write a program that assumes characters are only 7 bits long; then make this code 8-bit clean.

4.4 Implement a codeset-independent program to print all the ASCII characters.

4.5 Define multibyte and wide character.

4.6 Write a program that prints the current locale of the environment and that of the program.

4.7 Implement a program to print the environments of six locale category values. Change these category values within the program and print the new values.

4.8 Investigate the tools needed to create LC_CTYPE, LC_COLLATE, LC_MESSAGES, and LC_MONETARY locale category files. Study the format of the ASCII files LC_NUMERIC and LC_TIME.

4.9 Compare the catgets and gettext message catalog schemes.

4.10 Write a program containing an English interface. Generate a message catalog file. Now translate the text in the message catalog file to a pseudo test language. Execute the program and display it in the pseudo test language. *Hint*: If the English text is "String", the pseudo test language text may look like "SSttrriinngg" (each English character is repeated twice).

4.11 Investigate the procedure needed to create a new locale.

5

The C Language

5.1   Introduction

The C programming language is one of the most popular of high-level languages. C allows the programmer to program closer to lower-level hardware functionality compared to other high-level languages like FORTRAN, Pascal, and Lisp. The C programming language was developed at Bell Laboratories in the early 1970s. It was designed for and implemented on the UNIX operating system.

C is a general-purpose structured programming language. The source code written for one hardware is not tied to it and can be directly compiled and linked onto another system (sometimes the code may need to be ported).

The purpose of this chapter is to learn C language basics by examples. Each section is example driven. Static and dynamic library development process is discussed in detail. P rule to assign a pointer to a memory address is also presented. The advanced functionality of C is covered at the end of the chapter. Familiarity with the data structures and pointer is not necessary but advisable.

5.2   C Reserved Keywords

The tokens or identifiers shown in Table 5-1 lowercase are reserved for use as keywords, and should not be used as variable names.

Table 5-1 C Reserved Keywords

asm	auto	break	case	char	const
continue	default	do	double	else	entry
enum	extern	float	for	goto	if
int	long	register	return	short	signed
sizeof	static	struct	switch	typedef	union
unsigned	void	volatile	while		

5.3   C Program Structure

The C program structure is well defined. It essentially consists of include files at the beginning, followed by the global declarations, user-defined functions, and main() function, as shown in Figure 5-1.

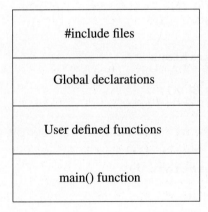

Figure 5-1
C program structure diagram

The following example gives the general structure of the C program.

```
/* include files */
#include <some.h>
#include <headers.h>
```

```
...

/* global declarations */
int integer;
char character;
...

/* user-defined function */
data_type function1(f1parm1, f1parm2, ...)
data_type f1parm1;
data_type f1parm2;
{
    /* local declarations */
    statements
    return(data_type x);
}

/* user-defined function */
data_type function2(f2parm1, f2parm2, ...)
data_type f2parm1;
data_type f2parm2;
{
    /* local declarations */
    statements
    return(data_type x);
}

main()
{
    /* local declarations */
    int value1;
    int value2;

    value1 = function1(f1arg1, f1arg2, ...);
    value2 = function2(f2arg1, f2arg2, ...);
    ...

    /* process the return values */
    ...

    statements
}
```

The source program coded in C exists in three forms; C source file, object file, and executable file. The compiler is responsible for translating the source file to the object file, and the linker is responsible for converting the object file to an executable file, as shown in Figure 5-2.

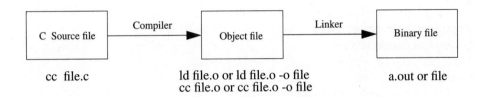

Figure 5-2
C source file to binary file translation process

The C compiler used to translate the source file to object file is usually known as cc and the linker or loader to convert the object file into executable file as ld. The following sections describe the three types of files in details. The C source files end with the suffix .c. The object files have .o as the suffix. The binary of the executable file generated by default is a.out. The compiler and/or linker -o filename option allows specification of a user-defined binary filename.

5.3.1   Source File

The C source file name in the UNIX environment should contain the last two characters '.c'. The prefix can be any name. Some valid filenames are prog.c, hello.c, 1.c, and 2.c. The C source file can be best described by an example in the form of C program structure. Consider the following C program. The characters /* introduce a comment, except within a character constant, a string literal, or a comment. The characters */ terminate it.

Example

```
/* filename cex1.c */

#include <stdio.h>
```

```
main()
{
   printf("Programming in C UNIX\n");
   printf("C Source Code File\n");
}
```

Output

```
Programming in C UNIX
C Source Code File
```

Example

```
/* filename cex2.c */

/* include files */
#include <stdio.h>

/* global declarations */
int i = 100;

/* User-defined functions */
int function(parm1, parm2)
int parm1;
int parm2;
{
  /* local declarations */
  int value = 0;

  /* statements */
  printf("Inside function\n");
  printf("Global value of i in function=%d\n", i);
  value = parm2 - parm1;
  return(value);
}

main()
{
  /* local declarations */
  int ret_func;
  int arg1 = 1;
```

```
    int arg2 = 2;

    /* statements */
    printf("Global value of i in main=%d\n", i);
    printf("Calling function\n");
    ret_func = function(arg1,arg2);
    printf("return value of function=%d\n", ret_func);
}
```

Output

```
Global value of i in main=100
Calling function
Inside function
Global value of i in function=100
return value of function=1
```

5.3.2   Object File

The source code, when compiled through the compiler, usually of the form

```
cc -c file.c
```

creates an object file with the suffix .o, in this case file.o.

During the first stage of the compilation process, each program statement is examined by the compiler to ensure that it conforms to the syntax and semantics of the language. If the complier encounters a syntax error, it is reported to the user and the compilation process terminates without creating an object file. Once all the syntactic and semantic errors are removed from the source program, the compiler translates each statement into a lower form. The intermediate lower form is the assembly program. The assembler converts each assembly language program into a binary format known as object code. The library functions remain unresolved at this stage.

5.3.3   Binary File

Once the source code has been converted into object code, it is ready to be linked. The linker combines relocatable object files, performs relocation, and resolves external symbols. The general form of the compilation command is

```
cc  file.c func1.c funcN.c -o file -lA -lB -lN
ld  file.o func1.o funcN.o -o file -lA -lB -lN
```

The compiler automatically calls the loader or linker ld, that there is no need to invoke ld command separately. The linker ld command is often used when only some of the source files have changed. The changed source files can be selectively compiled to create corresponding .o object files. This avoids recompilation of all modules.

Linker operates in two modes: static and dynamic. In static mode the relocatable object files given as arguments to the linker are combined to produce an executable object file. In dynamic mode the relocatable object files given as arguments to the linker are combined to produce an executable object file that will be linked at execution with any shared object files given as arguments.

If any of the arguments is a library, it is searched exactly once at the point it is encountered in the argument list. The library may be either a relocatable archive or a shared object. For an archive library, only those routines defining an unresolved external reference are loaded. For a shared library, the functions are loaded only at the execution time. The final executable object code format is stored by default in a.out file. The -o option allows specification of the user-defined filename.

5.3.4 Static Library

Static libraries consists of a collection of related functions in object file format. These object files are then combined in archive or library form. The static library name has lib as its prefix and .a as suffix. For example, the C library is called libc.a, and the X Window library is called libX.a. The compilation line is generally of the form

```
cc  -dn file.c func1.c funcN.c -o file -lA -lB -lN
```

The option -dn turns off the dynamic linking default. If the option is not specified the linker will search for unresolved references in shared libraries. The option -l instructs the compiler to search for objects in a given library (libL.a); the prefix lib and suffix .a are omitted. For example

```
cc -dn file.c func1.c func2.c func3.c -o file -lm -lX
```

The compiler and/or link editor searches for the unresolved references in the static archives or libraries. The link editor loads only the object files in these archives that contain a function that the program has called. In the preceding example the linker will load the objects from the System, C, Math, and X library for functions referenced in the func1.c, func2.c, func3.c, and the file.c (most of the linkers include System and C library by default).

The option -lc to load objects from the C library is not needed because compilers are usually designed to search for the C library in standard places.

An application can have its own set of libraries. The static library can be created by executing the command

```
ar -r libapp.a func1.o func2.o func3.o
```

This will create an archive library (libapp.a) that consists of the named object files. To use these objects, the -Ldir option instructs the compiler or linker that the user-created static library is in directory dir. If the static library libapp.a resides under directory /usr/home, the compilation command to create the executable is

```
cc  -dn file.c -o file -L/usr/home -lapp
```

The list of directories to be searched for static or dynamic library by the link editor can be specified by setting

```
LD_LIBRARY_PATH=dir1:dir2:dir2; export LD_LIBRARY_PATH
```

where `dir1, dir2, dir3, ...,` etc., are the directory paths in which libraries reside.

5.3.5 Dynamic Library

The dynamic library is a single object file that contains the code for every function in the library. When the function of the library is called in the program, the entire contents of that library are mapped into the virtual address space of the application process at run time. External references in the program are connected with their definitions when the program is executed. The shared library has a .so suffix and the optional version number suffix (for example the C shared library is called libc.so and the C shared library version 1 is libc.so.1). The compilation line is generally of the form

```
cc  file.c func1.c funcN.c -o file -lA -lB -lN
```

Notice there is no -dn option. Again the option -l instructs the compiler to search for objects in a given library (libN.so); the prefix lib and suffix .so are omitted. For example,

```
cc  file.c func1.c func2.c func3.c -o file -lm -lX
```

The compiler and/or link editor searches for the unresolved references in the shared libraries. The link editor maps the contents of the shared object into a virtual address space of application processes. It does not load the objects itself but just keeps track of the unresolved references. In the preceding example the linker will map external references for the objects from the System, C, Math, and X library functions referenced in the func1.c, func2.c, func3.c, and the file.c (most of the linkers include System and C library by default).

The -lc option to resolve functions from the C shared library is not needed because compilers are usually designed to search for the C library in standard places.

An application can have its own set of shared libraries. The shared library can be created by executing the command

```
cc -G -o libapp.so func1.o func2.o func3.o
```

This will create a shared object (so) library (libapp.so) that consists of the named object files. To use these objects, the -Ldir option instructs the compiler or linker that the user created shared library is in directory dir. If the dynamic library libapp.so resides under directory /usr/home, the compilation command to create the executable is

```
cc  file.c -o file -L/usr/home -lapp
```

The list of directories to be searched for static or dynamic library by the link editor can be specified by setting

```
LD_LIBRARY_PATH=dir1:dir2:dir3; export LD_LIBRARY_PATH
```

where `dir1, dir2, dir3, ...,` etc., are the directory paths in which libraries reside.

5.4   Types, Modifiers, and Operators

5.4.1   Variable Names

Variable names are the symbolic basic data object names used by the program. The variable name should begin with a letter or underscore (_). A variable name beginning with a digit or other special character is not allowed. C keywords listed in Table 5-1 are also not allowed. If the program is eventually to be compiled on a C++ compiler, the additional C++ keywords are also not allowed. Some systems do not allow more than eight characters for variable names, but these are rare. The variable names ab and Ab are different; the C language allows distinguishes between upper- and lowercase. For a two-letter name ab, taking into consideration upper- and lowercase, there are eight distinct variable names: ab, aB, Ab, AB, ba, bA, Ba, and BA. The general form of variable declaration is

```
data_type variable_list;
```

The variable name should be readable and close to the intended use of the name. For example, consider the function named func1(): It returns a value, so the variable name should look something like ret_func1, specifying the return value of the function. The declaration (int, char, etc.) specifies the variable type, and the operator (+, -, etc.) allows the variables to be manipulated. Variables can be declared local or global depending on their declarations. Some valid and invalid variable names are given next:

```
/* valid variable names */
int integer;
char character;
struct *tree;

/* invalid variable names are */
int $value;
char ?string;
struct #rocket;
```

5.4.2   Data Types and Sizes

The C programming language contains five important data types: int, char, float, double, and void. The bit size of the data types varies from machine to machine. The short and long data types are used as qualifiers. The void declaration has two purposes. It either declares a function as returning no value or creates generic pointers.

```
int integer;
char character;
float decimal;
double large;
short int min;
long int max;
unsigned char value;
signed short int sig_short;
```

The following C program can be used to find data-type sizes.

Example

```
/* filename cex3.c */

#include <stdio.h>

main()
{
  int integer, character;
  int min, max;
  int decimal, large;

  /* size of data type */
  integer = sizeof(int); character = sizeof(char);
  min = sizeof(short); max = sizeof(long);
  decimal = sizeof(float); large = sizeof(double);
  printf("size of data types in bytes\n");
  printf("int\t char\t short\t long\t float\t double\n");
  printf("%d\t %d\t %d\t %d\t %d\t %d\n",
        integer, character, min, max, decimal, large);

  /* if 1 byte = 8 bits */
  printf("size of data types in bits\n");
  printf("%d\t %d\t %d\t %d\t %d\t %d\n",
  8*integer, 8*character, 8*min, 8*max, 8*decimal, 8*large);
}
```

Output

```
size of data types in bytes
int  char  short long  float  double
4    1     2     4     4      8
size of data types in bits
32   8     16    32    32     64
```

Table 5-2 gives basic data-type bit sizes of some machines.

Table 5-2 Size of Data Types in Bits

Data Type	int	char	short	long	float	double
HP PRO RISC	32	8	16	32	32	64
Honeywell 6000	36	9	36	36	36	72
IBM/RS6000	32	8	16	32	32	64
Silicon Graphics/MIPS	32	8	16	32	32	64
Sun Solaris/486	32	8	16	32	32	64
Sun Sparc 2/10	32	8	16	32	32	64
Univel/486	32	8	16	32	32	64

The data type char size can be changed by applying the qualifier unsigned, and the data type int size can be changed by using qualifiers short, unsigned, or long. The variables must be declared before they can be used. Some systems with languages and floating-point coprocessors support 64-bit integers and 128-bit reals, respectively.

5.4.3 Access-type Modifiers

The const and volatile keywords are two access types of modifiers that control the way the variable can be accessed or modified. The order of keywords is not significant in C.

• **const**

If the variable is of type const, the program cannot change the value. The compiler tags the variable as read only. The const variables are very useful because they protect the arguments to a function from being modified.

Example

```
/* filename cex4.c */

#include <stdio.h>

main()
{
   /* access modifier const */
   /* value cannot be modified */
   const int integer = 1;
   printf("integer=%d\n", integer);

   /* illegal statement integer not a modifiable value */
   /* will generate syntax error comment statement below */
   /* out to compile */
   integer = 2;
   printf("integer=%d\n", integer);
}
```

Output

```
cex4.c: left operand must be modifiable lvalue
```

• **volatile**

The variable of type volatile is tagged by the compiler so that the value may be changed in ways not explicitly specified by the program. The volatile declaration is used to describe an object corresponding to a memory-mapped input/output port, an object accessed by an asynchronously interrupting function, and an object that is shared between multiple concurrent processes. Consider the declaration of the time clock variable.

```
extern const volatile int clock_time;
extern const unsigned char *io_port = 0xAB;
```

In this case both const and volatile are used, the const variable will prevent the possibility of changing the value of the clock_time by the program and volatile will allow the value to be changed by the operating system function interacting with the application.

Example

```c
/*  filename cex5.c  */

#include <stdio.h>
#include <unistd.h>
#include <signal.h>


/* access modifier volatile */
/* changed in ways not explicitly modified by the program */
volatile int flag = 1;
void handler(signal)
int signal;
{
  if (signal == SIGALRM)
    printf("received signal SIGALRM\n");
  else
    printf("error: did not receieve SIGALRM\n");
  flag = 0;
}

main()
{
  unsigned int alarm_value;

  signal(SIGALRM, handler);

  /* set alarm of 5 seconds */
  alarm_value = alarm (5);
  if ( alarm_value == 0 )
     printf("alarm set to 5 seconds\n");
  else
     printf("error: alarm() call failed\n");

  /* infinite loop till flag is False i.e. 0 */
  while(flag)
     ;
}
```

Output

```
alarm set to 5 seconds
received signal SIGALRM
```

5.4.4   Storage-type Modifiers

The C programming language supports five types of storage modifiers that tell the compiler how the variable will be used:

```
typedef
extern
static
auto
register
```

- **typedef**

The typedef modifier specifies the synonym for the type specified.

```
typedef int complex, imaginary;
complex i; imaginary j;
```

The variables i and j are both of type int, the typedef complex and imaginary are synonyms of type int. These types of declarations make programs more readable. The compiler replaces the typedef complex and imaginary by int.

Example

```
/* filename cex6.c */

#include <stdio.h>

main()
{
  /* storage modifier typedef */
  /* specifies the synonym for a given data type */
  typedef int voltage, current, resistance;

  voltage v = 4;
```

```
   current i = 2;
   resistance r;
   r = v/i;
   printf("resistance=voltage/current=%d\n",r);
}
```

Output

```
resistance=voltage/current=2
```

- **extern**

The extern modifier allows the multiple files to access the same variable. It is convenient for handling large projects in which the programs are divided into modules and the modules may need to access the same variable. If the variable is used within the same source file, the extern declaration can be omitted. If source file file1.c has a variable and is to be used by the source file file2.c, then an extern definition is needed in source file file2.c. For example,

```
extern int project_value;
extern char *string;
```

Example

```
/* filename cex7.c */

#include <stdio.h>

int i;
void func()
{
  /* storage modifier extern */
  /* any module, function can access the variable */
  extern int i;

  i = 100;
}

main()
{
  /* storage modifier extern */
```

```
    /* any module, function can access the variable */
    extern int i;

    i = 1;
    printf("current value of external variable i=%d\n", i);
    func();
    printf("new value of external variable as changed by
            func(), i=%d\n",i);
}
```

Output

```
current value of external variable i=1
new value of external variable as changed by func() i=100
```

* **static**

The static modifier allows the value of the variable to be retained between calls. If it is within a function, it is called a local static variable; if the variable is used by multiple functions, it is declared before the two functions and is known as a global static variable.

```
static char *string;
static func();
```

Example

```
/* filename cex8.c */

#include <stdio.h>

void func1()
{
    /* storage modifier static */
    /* local static variable */
    /* initialization happens only once */
    static float real = 10;
    printf("real=%f\n", real);
    real = 20;
}
```

```
main()
{
  printf("first invocation of func1(), static variable
          value is\n");
  func1();
  printf("second invocation of func1(), static variable
          value is\n");
  func1();
}
```

Output

```
first invocation of func1(), static variable value is
real=10.000000
second invocation of func1(), static variable value is
real=20.000000
```

Example

/* filename cex9.c */

```
#include <stdio.h>

main()
{
  void func1(), func2();

  printf("func1 invocation, static variable value is\n");
  func1();
  printf("func2 invocation, static variable value is\n");
  func2();
}
```

/* global static variable */
/* value is valid from here to end of the program */
```
static int i = 4;

void func1()
{
  printf("i=%d\n", i);
  i = 8;
```

```
}

void func2()
{
  printf("i=%d\n", i);
}
```

Output

```
func1 invocation, static variable value is
i=4
func2 invocation, static variable value is
i=8
```

• **auto**

The auto modifier is used before a local variable within a function. Every time the functions are called they are automatically created. If auto is not used the compiler assumes by default that the variables are auto. The usual declaration within a function should be

```
char *func()
{
    auto int i, j, k;
    ...
    statements
    return i;
}
```

Example

```
/* filename cex10.c */

#include <stdio.h>

int func1()
{
  /* storage modifier auto */
  /* default declaration is also auto */
  /* variable is created every time func1 is invoked */
  auto int i = 5;
```

```
  printf("auto i=%d\n", i);
  i = 10;
  return(i);
}

main()
{
  int ret_value;

  printf("first invocation of func1, auto variable
         value is\n");
  ret_value = func1();
  printf("ret_value=%d\n", ret_value);
  printf("second invocation of func1, auto variable
         value is\n");
  ret_value = func1();
  printf("ret_value=%d\n", ret_value);
}
```

Output

```
first invocation of func1, auto variable value is
auto i=5
ret_value=10
second invocation of func1, auto variable value is
auto i=5
ret_value=10
```

- **register**

The storage modifier `register` specifies that a given variable will be frequently used. Usually the C compiler tags such variable values to be kept in the register of the CPU rather than in memory. The actual access method is implementation dependent. The modifier `register` allows access to the variable value to be as fast as possible.

Example

```
/* filename cex11.c */
```

```
#include <stdio.h>

void swap(a, b)
int *a, *b;
{
  /* storage modifier register */
  /* frequently used temporary variable */
  register int tmp;

  tmp = *a;
  *a = *b;
  *b = tmp;
}

main()
{
  int i = 1, j = 2;

  printf("Before swap [%d, %d]\n", i, j);
  swap(&i, &j);
  printf("After swap [%d, %d]\n", i, j);
}
```

Output

```
Before swap [1, 2]
After swap [2, 1]
```

5.4.5 Expression

An expression consists of one or more variables, identifiers, string literals, function calls, constants, and so on, with zero or more operators.

Example

```
c = 'a'; k = 0;
func = strcmp(string1, string2);
a = b + c * d;
a > b;
i & j;
```

5.4.6 Cast Operators

The value of an expression can be converted to a given type by placing a parenthesized type name before an expression. The general form is

```
(data_type) expression;
```

The operand and data_type must be a pointer or an arithmetic type.

Example

```
/* filename cex12.c */

#include <stdio.h>

void *func()
{
  char *str = "hello";
  return(str);
}

main()
{
  int i;
  char *string;

  /* cast to char */
  i = (char)'a';
  printf("i=%c\n", i);

  /* convert return value of func() to character pointer */
  string = (char *)func();
  printf("string=%s\n", string);
}
```

Output

```
i=a
string=hello
```

5.4.7   Conditional Operator

The conditional operator ?: can be used to evaluate an expression and execute the True or False part according to evaluation value. The general form is

```
variable = exp1 ? exp2 : exp3
```

This is equivalent to the following if, else statement pair

```
if (exp1)
  variable = exp2;
else
  variable = exp3;
```

If exp1 is nonzero, then exp2 is evaluated; otherwise, exp3 is evaluated.

Example

```
/* filename cex13.c */

#include <stdio.h>

main()
{
  int a, b;
  int result;

  /* conditional operator ?: is equivalent to */
  /* if else statement */
  a = 4; b = 5;
  result = (a > b) ? a - b : b - a;

  printf("result(a>b)=%d\n", result);
}
```

Output

```
result(a>b)=1
```

5.4.8 Arithmetic Operators

All high-level languages have arithmetic operators. The C language uses universal mathematical notations to denote the arithmetic operators. The operators are as listed in Table 5-3.

Table 5-3 Arithmetic Operators

Operator	Action	Precedence	Associativity
*	Multiply two variables	2	Left to right
/	Divide two variables	2	Left to right
%	Modulus operation	2	Left to right
+	Add two variables	1	Left to right
-	Subtract two variables	1	Left to right

The order of evaluation is analogous to mathematical evaluation, that is, left to right. The precedence is as follows, the higher the number, the higher the precedence order in evaluation; that is, operators *, /, % will be evaluated before + and - in an expression.

Example

```
/* filename cex14.c */

#include <stdio.h>

main()
{
   int a = 2, b = 4, c = 6;
   int result;

   /* arithmetic operators evaluation is */
   /* left to right */
   result = a + b + c;
   printf("%d + %d + %d=%d\n", a, b, c, result);

   result = a - b + c;
   printf("%d - %d + %d=%d\n", a, b, c, result);

   result = a / b + c;
```

```
    printf("%d / %d + %d=%d\n", a, b, c, result);

    result = a * b / c;
    printf("%d * %d / %d=%d\n", a, b, c, result);

    result = -a;
    printf("-a=%d\n", result);
}
```

Output

```
2 + 4 + 6=12
2 - 4 + 6=4
2 / 4 + 6=6
2 * 4 / 6=1
-a=-2
```

5.4.9   Increment and Decrement Operator

The C programming language has two special operators: increment (++) and decrement (--). The increment operator (++) adds 1 to its operand and the decrement operator (--) subtracts 1.The prefixes ++ and -- have higher precedence than their postfix versions (see Table 5-4).

Table 5-4 Increment and Decrement Operator

Operator	Action	Precedence	Associativity
++i	Prefix increment	2	Right to left
--i	Prefix decrement	2	Right to left
i++	Postfix increment	1	Right to left
i--	Postfix decrement	1	Right to left

*   **Prefix increment and decrement**

If the operator is before the variable, for example, ++i, --i, the value is incremented or decremented before obtaining the variable value.

Example

```
/* filename cex15.c */

#include <stdio.h>

main()
{
  int add = 100;
  int subtract = 100;
  int result;

  /* prefix increment and decrement operator
  /* evaluation is right to left */
  /* value is incremented/decremented before obtaining */
  /* variable value */
  result = ++add;
  printf("++add=%d\n", result);
  result = --subtract;
  printf("--subtract=%d\n", result);
}
```

Output

```
++add=101
--subtract=99
```

- **Postfix increment and decrement**

If the operator is after the variable, for example, i++, i--, C obtains the variable's value before incrementing or decrementing it.

Example

```
/* filename cex16.c */

#include <stdio.h>

main()
{
  int add = 100;
```

```
    int subtract = 100;
    int result;
    int post_increment;
    int post_decrement;

    /* prefix increment and decrement operator
    /* evaluation is right to left */
    /* value is incremented/decremented after obtaining */
    /* variable value */
    result = add++;
    /* value is still 100 */
    printf("add++=%d\n", result);
    post_increment = add;
    printf("post_increment=%d\n", post_increment);
    result = subtract--;
    /* value is still 100 */
    printf("subtract--=%d\n", result);
    post_decrement = subtract;
    printf("post_decrement=%d\n", post_decrement);
}
```

Output

```
add++=100
post_increment=101
subtract--=100
post_decrement=99
```

5.4.10 Relational and Logical Operators

The relational and logical operators allow the data objects or variables to be manipulated in a relational or logical way. They evaluate to be true or false and help in decision making or control flow. The precedence of relational and logical operators is lower than that of arithmetic operators.

• **Relational Operators**

The relational operators are listed in Table 5-5.

Table 5-5 Relational Operators

Operator	Action	Precedence	Associativity
<	Less than	2	Left to right
<=	Less than or equal	2	Left to right
>	Greater than	2	Left to right
>=	Greater than or equal	2	Left to right
==	Equal	1	Left to right
!=	Not equal	1	Left to right

Example

```
/* filename cex17.c */

#include <stdio.h>

main()
{
   int i = 1, j = 2, k = 3;
   int a = j;
   int true, false;

   /* relational expression evaluation is*/
   /* left to right */
   /* expression evaluates to either true=1 or false=0*/
   true = (i <= j);
   printf("True=%d\n", true);
   false = (i > j);
   printf("False=%d\n", false);
   if (i < j)
      printf("True (%d < %d)\n", i, j);
   if (j <= a)
      printf("True (%d <= %d)\n", j, a);
   if (k > j)
      printf("True (%d > %d)\n", k, j);
   if (j >= a)
      printf("True (%d >= %d)\n", j, a);
```

```
    if ( (i < j) <= ( k >= j ) )
        printf ("True (%d < %d) <= (%d >= %d)\n", i, j, k, j);
}
```

Output

```
True=1
False=0
True (1 < 2)
True (2 <= 2)
True (3 > 2)
True (2 >= 2)
True (1 < 2) <= (3 >= 2);
```

- **Logical Operators**

The logical operators are listed in Table 5-6:

.

Table 5-6 Logical Operators

Operator	Action	Precedence	Associativity
!	NOT	3	Right to left
&&	AND	2	Left to right
||	OR	1	Left to right

Example

```
/* filename cex18.c */

#include <stdio.h>

main()
{
    int i = 0, j = 1, k = 2;
    int true, false;
    /* logical expression evaluates to */
    /* true=1 or false=0 */
    true = (i || j);
    printf("True=%d\n", true);
    false = (i && j);
```

```
    printf("False=%d\n", false);
    if (j && k)
       printf("True (%d && %d)\n", j, k);
    if (i || j )
       printf("True [%d || %d]\n", i, j);
    if (!i)
       printf("True (!%d)\n", i);
    if ( (j && k) && (i || j) )
       printf("True (%d && %d) && (%d || %d)\n", j, k, i, j);
}
```

Output

```
True=1
False=0
True (1 && 2)
True [0 || 1]
True (!0)
True (1 && 2) && (0 || 1)
```

5.4.11 Bitwise Logical Operators

The C programming language supports a complete set of bitwise operators. C contains all the bit operations that can be performed in an assembly language. This makes it ideal to emulate the lower-level assembly language features of testing, setting, complementing, or shifting of the actual bits within are int or char type. Bitwise logical operations may not be performed on float, double, and void types. The bitwise operators with their actions are given in Table 5-7.

Table 5-7 The Bitwise Operators

Operator	Action	Precedence	Associativity
~	One's complement	5	Right to left
>>	Shift right	4	Left to right
<<	Shift left	4	Left to right
&	AND	3	Right to left
^	Exclusive OR	2	Left to right
|	OR	1	Left to right

The bitwise operations are used in modem programs, mouse programs, disk file functions, and device drivers.

Example

```
/* filename cex19.c */

#include <stdio.h>

main()
{
  /* assign octal value */
  int i = 01, j = 02, k = 03;
  int value;

  /* bitwise operators perform setting, shifting, etc. */
  /* operations to bit values */
  value = ( j & k );
  printf("(0%o & 0%o)=0%o\n", j, k, value);
  value = ( j | k );
  printf("(0%o | 0%o)=%o\n", j, k, value);
  value = ( i ^ j );
  printf("(0%o ^ 0%o)=0%o\n", i, j, value);
  value = ( ~i );
  printf("(~0%o)=0%d\n", i, value);
  value = ( j >> i );
  printf("(0%o >> 0%o)=0%o\n", j, i, value);
  value = ( j << i );
  printf("(0%o << 0%o)=0%o\n", j, i, value);
  if ( (i & j) || (j | k) )
      printf("True (0%o & 0%o)||(0%o | 0%o]\n", i, j, j, k);
}
```

Output

```
(02 & 03)=02
(02 | 03)=3
(01 ^ 02)=03
(~01)=0-2
(02 >> 01)=01
(02 << 01)=04
```

```
True (01 & 02) || (02 | 03)
```

5.4.12 Assignment Operators

The assignment operators, =, +=, -=, /=, *=, and others. allow the values to be assigned to any valid variable. The general form of assignment is

```
variable_name [optional operator]= expression
```

Example

```
a = b;
a += b;
a -= b;
a /= b;
a *= b;
```

The left part of the assignment should be a variable name or pointer, not a constant or function. Multiple assignments in a single statement are also allowed, as in this example:

```
a = b = c = d = 100;
a = b += c /= d = 10;
```

Example

```
/* filename cex20.c */

#include <stdio.h>

main()
{
  {
    int i = 2, j = 4, k = 8;
    int value;

    /* assignment operators allow value to be assigned */
    printf("i=%d j=%d k=%d\n", i, j, k, value);
    value = i;
    printf("i=%d\n", value);
    j += i;
```

```
   printf("(j += i)=%d\n", j); j = 4;
   j -= i;
   printf("(j -= i)=%d\n", j); j = 4;
   j *= i;
   printf("(j *= i)=%d\n", j); j = 4;
   j /=i;
   printf("(j /= i)=%d\n", j); j = 4;
   j %=i;
   printf("(j %= i)=%d\n", j);
 }
 {
 /* assign octal value */
 int i = 01, j = 02, k = 03;
 printf("i=0%o j=0%o k=0%o\n", i, j, k);
 j &= k;
 printf("(j &= k)=0%o\n", j); j = 02;
 j ^= k;
 printf("(j ^= k)=0%o\n", j); j = 02;
 j |= k;
 printf("(j |= k)=0%o\n", j); j = 02;
 j <<= i;
 printf("(j <<= k)=0%o\n", j); j = 02;
 j >>= i;
 printf("(j >>= k)=0%o\n", j);
 }
}
```

Output

```
i=2  j=4  k=8
i=2
(j += i)=6
(j -= i)=2
(j *= i)=8
(j /= i)=2
(j = i)=0
i=01 j=02 k=03
(j &= k)=02
(j ^= k)=01
(j |= k)=03
(j <<= k)=04
(j >>= k)=01
```

5.4.13 Precedence Table

Table 5-8 lists the associativity and precedence of all C operators. All the operators except the unary and ?: associate left to right. Unary +, -, and * have higher precedence than their binary versions. Prefixes ++ and -- have higher precedence than their postfix versions.

Table 5-8 Associativity and Precedence of Operators

Operator	Associativity	Precedence
() [] -> .	Left to right	Highest
! ~ ++ -- + - * & (type) sizeof	Right to left	
* / %	Left to right	
+ -	Left to right	
<< >>	Left to right	
< <= > >=	Left to right	
== !=	Left to right	
&	Left to right	
^	Left to right	
|	Left to right	
&&	Left to right	
||	Left to right	
?:	Right to left	
= += -= *= /= %= &= ^= |= <<= >>=	Right to left	
,	Left to right	Lowest

5.5   C Statements

The C statements specify an action to be performed; they control the computations and program flow.

ANSI C places C statements into categories as listed in Table 5-9. This section discusses the C statements in detail.

Table 5-9 C Statements

Statement Category	C Reserved Symbols
Expression	Valid C expression
Block	Set of statements
Selection	if, else, switch
Iteration	for, while, do
Jump	break, continue, return, goto
Label	case, default

Most C statements evaluate to be either true or false. Table 5-10 specifies expression condition.

Table 5-10 True and False Condition

Expression	Value	Mathematically
True	Any integer value other than 0	$-1 >= x >= 1$
False	Integer value of 0	$x = 0$

5.5.1   Expression and Null Statements

An expression statement is a valid C expression followed by a semicolon. The general form of an expression statement is

```
expression(optional);
```

Some valid expression statements are

```
x = y + z;   /* expression */
function(); /* function call */
;            /* null statement, performs no operation */
i < j        /* relational expression */
i && j || k /* logical expression */
```

5.5.2   Block or Compound Statement

Block statements are a set of related statements that are grouped into one
syntactic unit. A block usually begins with a left brace ({) and ends with a
right brace (}). The general form of a block statement is

```
block or statement
{
    declarations;
    statements
}
```

Example

```c
/* filename cex21.c */

#include <stdio.h>
#include <values.h>

main()
{
  /* block is a set of statements grouped together */
  /* First Block */
  {
    /* area of rectangle */
    int length = 3;
    int breadth = 4;

    int area;
    area = length * breadth;
    printf ("area of rectangle=%d\n", area);
  }
  /* Second Block */
  {
    /* area of a circle */
    float area, radius;
    radius = 10;

    /* Pi is defined in values.h */
    area = M_PI * (radius * radius);
    printf ("area of circle=%f\n", area);
  }
```

```
}
```

Output

```
area of rectangle=12
area of circle=314.159271
```

5.5.3   Selection Statements: if, else, switch

According to the value of the expression, the selection statement selects among a set of statements. The general syntax of a selection statement is

```
if (expression) statement

if (expression)
    statement
else
    statement
switch (expression)
        statement
```

- **if**

The `if` statement evaluates the expression to be true or false. If the expression is true (anything other than 0), it executes the statement associated with `if`. If the expression is false (0), the statement associated with `else` is executed.

```
if ( expression /= 0 ) execute statement
if ( expression = 0 ) else execute statement
```

Example

```
/* filename cex22.c */

#include <stdio.h>
#include <values.h>

main()
{
  int penny = 1, dime = 10;
```

```
    int length = 20, breadth = 40;

    /* expression associated with if evaluates to true */
    /* then execute statement associated with if */
    /* otherwise execute statement associated with else */
    if(dime > penny)
      printf("True:dime is greater than a penny\n");
    if(length == breadth)
      printf("True:length is equal to breadth\n");
    else
      printf("False:length is not equal to breadth\n");
}
```

Output

```
True:dime is greater than a penny
False:length is not equal to breadth
```

- **switch**

The switch statement successively tests the value of the expression against a list of integer or character constants. The controlling expression of a switch statement should be integral type. The general syntax of a switch statement is

```
switch (expression) {
    case constant1:    statement
                       break;
    case constant2:    statement
                       break;
    .          .        .
    default:           statement
}
```

Example

```
/* filename cex23.c */

#include <stdio.h>
```

```
main()
{
  int c;
  c = 2;

  /* switch statement tests value of the expression */
  /* successively against integer or character constant */
  switch (c) {
    case 1: printf("integer 1\n");
            break;
    case 2: printf("integer 2\n");
            break;
    default: printf("integer=%d\n", c);
  }
  c = 'b';
  switch (c) {
    case 'a': printf("character a\n");
              break;
    case 'b': printf("character b\n");
              break;
    default: printf("character=%c\n", c);
  }
}
```

Output

```
integer 2
character b
```

5.5.4   Iteration Statements: for, while, do

The iteration statement allows a set of instructions to be executed repeatedly until a certain condition is reached and the controlling expression compares equal to 0. The general form of iteration statements are;

```
for ( expression1;  expression2;  expression3 )
   statement

while ( expression )
   statement
```

```
do
   statement
while (expression)
```

• **for**

The for loop first initializes the variable and then compares the test condition that controls the loop. If the condition is true (anything other than 0), it executes the statement and increments or reinitializes the variable. If the condition is false (0), it falls through.

```
for ( initialization;  condition ;  increment )
   statement
```

Example

```
/* filename cex24.c */

#include <stdio.h>

main()
{
  int i, j;

  /* for statement initializes variable */
  /* tests the variable */
  /* if true executes body statements and */
  /* increments variable */
  /* otherwise exits loop */
  /* print character set */
  for(i = 0;  i < 0177;  i++)
     if ( isalpha(i) )
        printf("%c", i);
  printf("\n");
  /* infinite loop */
  i = 0;
  for(;;) {
    if(i >= 5)
      break;
    else
      printf("%d ",i);
```

```
      i++;
   }
   printf("\n");
   /* comma seperator */
   for(i=0, j=0; (i>=5)||(j<3); i++, j++)
      printf("[i, j]=[%d, %d]\n", i, j);
}
```

Output

```
ABCDEFGHIJKLMNOPQRSTUVWXYZabcdefghijklmnopqrstuvwxyz
0 1 2 3 4
[i, j]=[0, 0]
[i, j]=[1, 1]
[i, j]=[2, 2]
```

- **while**

In the while loop the expression is tested; if it evaluates to be true, the statement is executed, otherwise, it falls through. The while loop is the equivalent of the for loop, as follows

```
expression1;
while ( expression2 ) {
   statement
   expression3;
}
```

Example

```
/* filename cex25.c */

#include <stdio.h>

main()
{
   int i;

   /* while statement tests variable */
   /* if true executes body statements till it is false */
   /* otherwise exits loop */
```

```
/* print character set */
i = 0;
while(i < 0177) {
  if(isalpha(i))
    printf("%c", i);
  i++;
}
printf("\n");
/* infinite loop */
i = 0;
while(1) {
  if(i >= 5)
    break;
  else
    printf("%d ",i);
  i++;
}
printf("\n");
}
```

Output

```
ABCDEFGHIJKLMNOPQRSTUVWXYZabcdefghijklmnopqrstuvwxyz
0 1 2 3 4
```

- **do**

The do statement executes the statement first before evaluating the control expression. The test condition is evaluated at the bottom. First, the statement is executed. The expression is evaluated by `while`. If the expression is true, it loops back; otherwise, the loop terminates.

```
do
    statement
while (condition)
```

Example

/* filename cex26.c */

#include <stdio.h>

```
main()
{
  int i;

  /* do statement executes body statements */
  /* tests the expression in while */
  /* if true executes body statements again */
  /* otherwise exits loop */
  /* print character set */
  i = 0;
  do {
    if(isalpha(i))
      printf("%c", i);
    i++;
  } while(i < 0177);
  printf("\n");
}
```

Output

ABCDEFGHIJKLMNOPQRSTUVWXYZabcdefghijklmnopqrstuvwxyz

5.5.5 Jump Statements: break, continue, return, goto

The jump statement performs an unconditional branch. The general form of a jump statement is

```
break;
continue;
goto identifier;
return ( expression );
```

• **break**

The break statement can be used in two cases. First, in the loop body, if the test condition evaluates to be true and the break statement is encountered after it, the loop terminates. Second, it terminates a case statement.

Example

```
/* filename cex27.c */

#include <stdio.h>

main()
{
   int i;

   /* break statement terminates loop */
   for(i = 0; i <= 10; i++) {
      if (i == 5)
         break;
      printf("%d ", i);
   }
   printf("\n", i);
}
```

Output

```
0 1 2 3 4
```

- **continue**

The continue statement forces the next iteration of the loop to take place, skipping any code in between, that is, to the end of the loop body.

Example

```
/* filename cex28.c */

#include <stdio.h>

main()
{
  int i, j;
  /* continue statement forces next iteration of loop */
  for(i = 0, j = -1; i <= 10; i++) {
     j++;
     if ( (j == 3) || (j == 6) )
```

```
        continue;
     printf("%d ", i);
  }
  printf("\n");
}
```

Output

```
0 1 2 4 5 7 8 9
```

- **goto**

A goto statement allows an unconditional jump to the designated label. Since C has a rich set of statements like break, continue, and switch, a goto statement is rarely used in a C program. Using goto statements is taboo and is not good programming practice.

Example

```
/* filename cex29.c */

#include <stdio.h>

main()
{
  int i;

  /* goto statement allows unconditional jump */
  /* avoid using goto */
  for(i = 0; i <= 10; i++) {
     if( i == 4 )
       goto label;
     printf("%d ", i);
  }
  printf("\n");

label: printf("unconditional jump\n");

}
```

Output

```
0 1 2 3 unconditional jump
```

- **return**

A `return` statement terminates execution of the current function. It returns from a current function and returns control to its caller. The general form of a return statement is

```
return (expression)
```

If the expression has a type different from that of the function in which it appears, it is converted as if it were assigned to a variable of that type. If no return value is specified, the value returned is implementation dependent. If the function does not have a `return` statement on reaching right brace }, the function terminates by executing a `return` statement with an expression.

Example

```c
/* filename cex30.c */

#include <stdio.h>
#include <math.h>

char *strfunc(string)
char string[];
{
   strcat(string, " world");

   /* return terminates execution of current function */
   return(string);
}

/* pythagoras theorem */
double dblfunc(b, p)
double b, p;
{
   return(hypot(b,p));
}
```

```
main()
{
  int i;
  double ret_dbl;
  char *ret_str;
  char *strarg = "hello";

  ret_str = strfunc(strarg);
  printf("%s\n", ret_str);
  ret_dbl = dblfunc(3.00, 4.00);
  printf("hypotenuse=%f\n", ret_dbl);
}
```

Output

```
hello world
hypotenuse=5.000000
```

5.5.6   Labeled Statements: case, default

Label statements do not alter the flow of control. The general form of a labeled statement is
identifier: statement
case constant_expression: statement
default: statement

- **case and default**

The labeled statements case and default appear only in a switch statement. The expression of each case should be an integral constant. For a given switch statement, no two of the case shall have the same integral constant value.

The default statement is executed if no match is found within the switch statement (it is optional within a switch statement).

Example

```
/*   filename cex31.c   */

#include <stdio.h>
```

```
#include <math.h>

int matherr(x)
struct exception *x;
{
  switch (x->type) {
  /* print error type and function name */
  /* case expression should be an integral constant */
  case SING:
       printf("SING error in %s\n", x->name);
       break;
  case DOMAIN:
       printf("DOMAIN error in %s\n", x->name);
       break;
  case OVERFLOW:
       printf("OVERFLOW error in %s\n", x->name);
       break;
  case UNDERFLOW:
       printf("UNDERFLOW error in %s\n", x->name);
       break;
  case TLOSS:
       printf("TLOSS error in %s\n", x->name);
       break;
  case PLOSS:
       printf("PLOSS error in %s\n", x->name);
       break;
  /* default statement is executed if no match is found */
  default:
       printf("UNKNOWN math error\n");
  }
  return(x->retval);
}

main()
{
  double  matherr_value;
  double  log_value;
  struct  exception *err;

  /* generate SING error */
  log_value = log (0.0);
  matherr_value = matherr (err);
```

```
    printf("matherr return value is %d\n", matherr_value);

}
```

Output

```
SING error in log
matherr return value is 0
```

5.6　Functions

Almost all C programs consist of function calls. They can be library function calls from any of the libraries such as libc, libm, and libX11, or user-defined function or procedure calls. They are essentially the building blocks of any C program. A larger computing task can be broken into smaller ones. The program is easy to read and follow. The general form of a function is

```
data_type function_name(parameter_list)
{
   statements
}
```

The data type can be `int`, `char`, `long`, `float`, `double`, `void`, or other.. The statements could be any of the statements discussed in previous sections.

Example

```
/*  filename cex32.c  */

#include <stdio.h>
#include <math.h>

/* function definition */
int ap(a, d, count)
int a, d, count;
{
   int n, t;

   for(n = 1; n <= count; n++) {
      t = a + (n - 1) * d;
      printf("%d ", t);
```

```
    }
    printf("%\n", t);
    return (1);
}

/* function definition */
int gp(a, r, count)
int a, r, count;
{
    int n, t;

    for(n = 1; n <= count; n++) {
        t = a * pow (r, (n-1));
        printf("%d ", t);
    }
    printf("%\n", t);
    return (1);
}

main()
{
    int first = 1;
    int diff = 2;
    int ratio = 2;
    int number = 10;
    int ret_value;

    /* arithmetic progression */
    ret_value = ap(first, diff, number);
    if (ret_value != 1)
        printf("error: function ap failed\n");
    /* geometric progression */
    ret_value = gp(first, ratio, number);
    if (ret_value != 1)
        printf("error: function gp failed\n");
}
```

Output

```
1 3 5 7 9 11 13 15 17 19
1 2 4 8 16 32 64 128 256 512
```

5.6.1 Special main Function Arguments: argc, argv, envp

The main is a special function with two arguments: argc and argv. It allows the user to pass information through the command line while invoking the application and also allows access to the environment variables.

• **Accessing Command Line Arguments**

The arguments argc and argv can be used to retrieve command line information. The general form of the main function to access command line information is

```
main(argc, argv)
int argc;
char *argv[];
{
    statements;
}
```

The argument argv is a pointer to an array whose elements are pointers to arrays of characters each terminated by \0, so they can be treated as strings. The strings are passed to the application program. The argument argc gets the count of the number of strings specified in the command line, which are also contained in argv array. The argv[0] is the command or the application name itself, so argc is always greater than 0. Since argv is not NULL terminated, argc should be used when traversing it. The argc and argv are arguments to main and as such should be copied to external variables if they need to be used by other routines. The local copy of arguments can also be passed as arguments to other routines.

Example

```
/*  filename cex33.c  */

#include <stdio.h>

/* argc, argv are arguments to main function */
main(argc, argv)
int argc;
char *argv[];
{
  printf("argc=%d\n", argc);
```

```
    while (argc--) {
      printf("argv[%d]=%s\n", argc, argv[argc]);
    }
}
```

Output

```
argc=1
argv[0]=./cex31
```

- **Accessing Environment Variables**

The environment variable can also be accessed through the main() function.
The general form to access the program environment is

```
main(argc, argv, envp)
int argc;
char *argv[];
char *envp[];
{
    statements;
}
```

The environment argument envp contains an array of null terminated strings of the form
name=value that can be accessed. Unlike argv, the argument envp is null terminated.
The environment variable can also be obtained by the getenv() library function call. The
setenv() library function can be used to set the environment variables.

Example

```
/*  filename cex34.c  */

#include <stdio.h>

/* environment variables can be accessed */
/* through argument envp */
main(argc, argv, envp)
int argc;
char *argv[];
char *envp[];
{
```

```
  int i;

  /* execute cex32 -a hello */
  printf("argc=%d\n", argc);
  while (argc--) {
    printf("argv[%d]=%s\n", argc, argv[argc]);
  }
  i = 0;
  while(envp[i] != NULL) {
    printf("envp[%d]=%s\n", i, envp[i]);
    i++;
  }
}
```

Output

```
argc=1
argv[0]=./cex32
envp[0]=COUNTRY=1
envp[1]=HZ=100
envp[2]=KEYB=us
envp[3]=LANG=C
```

5.6.2 Call by Value

In call by value the calling function passes the actual values of the variables, the called function makes its own copy, and any changes in the variable value in the called function do not affect the calling function variable values.

Example

```
/*   filename cex35.c   */

#include <stdio.h>

/* call by value */
/* calling function passes actual value */
int callbyval(m, c)
int m, c;
{
  int E;
```

```
    int mo = 4, co = 2;

    m = mo + m;
    c = co + c;
    /* e = mc² */
    E = m * c * c;
    return (E);
}

main()
{
    int mass = 2;
    int velocity = 8;
    int energy;

    /* call by value */
    energy = callbyval(mass, velocity);
    printf("Energy=%d\n", energy);
    /* no change in value of mass and velocity */
    printf("mass=%d velocity=%d\n", mass, velocity);
}
```

Output

```
Energy=600
mass=2 velocity=8
```

5.6.3 Call by Reference

In call by reference the calling function passes the address of the variable, the called function makes a copy of the address, and any changes made to the variable pointed to by the parameter *do* affect the variable.

Example

```
/* filename cex36.c */

#include <stdio.h>

/* call by reference */
/* calling function passes address of the variable */
```

```
void callbyref(a, b)
int *a, *b;
{
   *a = 8;
   *b = 9;
}

main()
{
   int i = 1, j = 2;

   printf("Before [%d, %d]\n", i, j);
   callbyref(&i, &j);
   printf("After [%d, %d]\n", i, j);
}
```

Output

```
Before [1, 2]
After [8, 9]
```

5.6.4   Return Values

The function can return any data-type value. If no return value is specified, the return value is implementation dependent. If the function does not have a return statement, on reaching the right brace }, the function terminates by executing an implicit return statement with an expression.

Example

```
/* filename cex37.c */

#include <stdio.h>
#include <string.h>

/* function can return any data-type value */
/* depending on definition */
char *strfunc(string)
char string[];
{
```

```
   strcat(string, " Bye!");
   return(string);
}

main()
{
   char *ret_str;
   ret_str = strfunc("Good");
   printf("return string=%s\n", ret_str);
}
```

Output

```
return string=Good Bye!
```

5.6.5 Recursive Functions

The C function can call itself. A function is called recursive if within the body of the function it calls itself. The recursive function can be used to avoid duplication of code. The general form of a recursive function is

```
data_type func_name()
{
   statements;
   func_name();
}
```

Example

```
/* filename cex38.c */

#include <stdio.h>

int factorial(n)
int n;
{
   int nf;
   if ( n == 1 )
      return(1);
   /* In C language function can call itself */
   nf = factorial(n -1) * n;
```

```
  return (nf);
}

main()
{
  int number;
  int nfactorial;
  number = 4;

  nfactorial = factorial(4);
  printf("%d!=%d\n", number, nfactorial);
}
```

Output

```
4!=24
```

5.6.6 Function Prototypes

The ANSI C standard enforces strong argument-type checking in the C language. The argument-type checking allows compilers to report any illegal-type conversions between the types of arguments used to call a function and the type definition of its parameters. The compiler also reports the difference between the number of arguments used to call a function and the number of parameters in the function, if any. The general syntax is

```
data_type function_name(data_type arg1, data_type arg2, ...,
data_type argn);
```

5.6.7 Variable-length Parameter Lists

The C language allows variable-length parameter lists. The argument list should end with three periods (...) and should have at least one argument. The variable-length parameter is useful when the number of parameters is not known in advance. The general form is

```
data_type function_name (int i, char c, char * string, ...);
```

5.7 Arrays

In the C language, an array is a collection of variables of the same type that is referenced by a common name. An index is used to access a specific element in an array. All arrays consist of contiguous memory locations. In short, an array is a set of ordered data items of the same type. An array can have one or many dimensions. Strings or arrays of null terminated characters are the most common arrays in C. The amount of memory required to hold an array is directly related to its data type and size. This section covers the array operators and arrays of different dimensions.

5.7.1 Array Operator

The array operator is denoted by [ ]. In C, all arrays have zero as the index of their first element. The general form of array declaration is
data_type array_name[size1]...[sizeN];

Example

```
int i[3]; /* variables are i[0], i[1], i[2] */
int i[5]; char c[10][5]; double d[8][9][10];
```

5.7.2 Array Initialization

Arrays can be initialized at the time of declaration. The general form of array initialization is

```
data_type array_name[size1]...[sizeN] = {initializer list};
```

Example

The strings can be intialized in following two ways
```
char array_name[size] = "string";
char array_name[7] = { 's', 't', 'r', 'i', 'n', 'g', '\0' };
```

5.7.3 Single-dimensional Arrays

The general form of single-dimensional arrays is

```
data_type array_name[size];
```

The array_name is an array of size integers. For example, i[10] is an array of 10 integers.

Example

```
/* filename cex39.c */

#include <stdio.h>

main()
{
  int i;

  /* single dimensional arrays */
  int a[] = { 0, 1, 2, 3, };
  char c[] = { 'a', 'b', 'c', 'd', '\0', };

  for(i = 0; i < 4; i++)
     printf("a[%d]=%d\n", i, a[i]);
  for(i = 0; i < 4; i++)
     printf("c[%d]=%c\n", i, c[i]);
}
```

Output

```
a[0]=0
a[1]=1
a[2]=2
a[3]=3
c[0]=a
c[1]=b
c[2]=c
c[3]=d
```

5.7.4 Two-dimensional Arrays

The storage of two-dimensional arrays is in the row-column form in which the first index indicates the row and the second index indicates the column. The general form of two-dimensional arrays is

```
data_type array_name[size1][size2];
```

For instance in char c[4][8]; c is an array of 4 arrays of 8 characters each.

Example

```
/* filename cex40.c */

#include <stdio.h>

main()
{
  int r, c;

  /* two-dimensional array */
  int i[2][2] = {
      { 1, 2, },
      { 3, 4, },
  };
  for(r = 0; r < 2; r++ )
     for(c = 0; c < 2; c++ )
         printf("i[%d,%d]=%d\n", r, c, i[r][c]);
}
```

Output

```
i[0,0]=1
i[0,1]=2
i[1,0]=3
i[1,1]=4
```

5.7.5 Multidimensional Arrays

C language supports multidimensional arrays. Multidimensional arrays are rarely used because of the memory required. For example, a three-dimensional character array such as c[10][11][12] requires 1,320 bytes of memory.

Example

```
/* filename cex41.c */

#include <stdio.h>
```

```
main()
{
  int i, j, k;
  /* three dimensional array */
  int m[2][2][2] = {
      { 1, 2, 3, 4, },
      { 5, 6, 7, 8, },
  };
  for(i = 0; i < 2; i++ )
   for(j = 0; j < 2; j++ )
    for(k = 0; k < 2; k++ )
      printf("m[%d,%d,%d]=%d\n", i,j,k, m[i][j][k]);
}
```

Output

```
m[0,0,0]=1
m[0,0,1]=2
m[0,1,0]=3
m[0,1,1]=4
m[1,0,0]=5
m[1,0,1]=6
m[1,1,0]=7
m[1,1,1]=8
```

5.8   Pointers

A pointer is a variable that contains the memory address. The memory address is usually the location of another variable or pointer. In comparison with arrays, the pointers are easier to handle and allow faster access to elements. Using pointers, one can create excellent and efficient C programs. Pointers can also be easily misused in a program; such programs are difficult to debug.

5.8.1   Pointer Operators

A pointer operator is denoted by the signs * and &. The operator * retrieves the contents of the variable located at the address that follows. The unary operator & returns the memory address of the operator.

The operator * is always before the variable name and should not be confused with a * b where it implies multiplication of two variables.

```
int i, j;
int *p;
i = 2;
p = &i;
j = *p;
```

In this example, the unary operator & in p = &i retrieves the memory address of the variable i, and the variable p is now a pointer to variable i. The *p in j = *p gets the contents of variable i, a value of 2.

5.8.2 Pointer Assignment Rule (P Rule)

The following mathematical approach can be used to assign a pointer to a memory address. Hence-forth it will be referred to as the P rule.

```
int i, *p , **pp;

*p = i ;
```

Move pointer operator * to right hand side denominator
```
p = i/*;
p = (1/*) i;
```
replace (1/*) by pointer operator &
```
p = &i;
```

Using the above rule
```
**pp = *p;
```
Cancel out extra * operator on both sides
```
*pp = p;
```
replace (1/*) by operator & as above
```
pp = &p;
```

Here pp points to p; and p points to the address of variable i. The *p and **p both retrieve the contents of variable i.

Thus, to assign a pointer to a memory address, cancel out the extra * operator from lvalue and the operand side and replace (1/*) on operand side by address operator &.

5.8.3   Integer Pointer

The integer pointers are of data type int. For example,

int *p; int **pp; int ***ppp;

Here p is a pointer, pp is a pointer to the integer pointer, and so on.

Example

```
/* filename cex42.c */

#include <stdio.h>

main()
{
  int i, j;

  /* integer pointers are of data type int */
  int *p1, **p2, ***p3;
  int a[] = { 0, 1, 2 };
  i = 10;

  /* assigning pointer to memory address using P rule */
  p1 = &i;
  p2 = &p1;
  p3 = &p2;
  printf("i=%d, *p1=%d\n", i, *p1);
  printf("**p2=%d, ***p3=%d\n", **p2, ***p3);
  p1 = &a[0];
  for(j = 0; j <= 2; j++) {
    printf("p1+%d=%d\n", j, *p1);
    p1++;
  }
}
```

Output

i=10, *p1=10

```
**p2=10, ***p3=10
p1+0=0
p1+1=1
p1+2=2
```

5.8.4   Character Pointer

The character pointers are of data type char. For example,

char *c; char **cc; char ***cc;

Here c is a character pointer, cc is a pointer to a character pointer, and so on.

Example

```
/* filename cex43.c */

#include <stdio.h>

main()
{
  int j;
  / character pointers are of data type char */
  char c = 'a';
  char str[] = "string";
  char *p1, **p2, ***p3;

  /* assigning pointer to memory address using P Rule */
  p1 = &c;
  p2 = &p1;
  p3 = &p2;
  printf("c=%c *p1=%c\n", c, *p1);
  printf("**p2=%c ***p3=%c\n", **p2, ***p3);
  p1 = &str[0];
  printf("p1=%s\n", p1);
  for(j = 0; j <= 5; j++) {
    printf("p1+%d=%c\n", j, *p1);
    p1++;
  }
}
```

Output

```
c=a *p1=a
**p2=a ***p3=a
p1=string
p1+0=s
p1+1=t
p1+2=r
p1+3=i
p1+4=n
p1+5=g
```

5.8.5   Arrays of Pointers

The C language allows declaration of arrays of pointers. The declaration int
*i[5] is an array of integer pointers of size 5. Similarly, char *c[5] is an array
of character pointers of size 5.

Example

```
/* filename cex44.c */

#include <stdio.h>

main()
{
  int j;

  /* array of integer pointers */
  int *a[2];
  int i[2][2] = { { 1, 2, }, { 3, 4, },};

  /* array of character pointers */
  char *c[4] = { "This", "is" , "a", "String" };

  /* assigning pointer to memory address using P rule */
  a[0] = &i[0][0];
  a[1] = &i[1][0];
  for(j = 0; j < 2; j++ ){
     printf("%d\n", *a[0]); a[0]++;
     printf("%d\n", *a[1]); a[1]++;
```

```
    }
    for( j = 0; j < 4; j++ )
        printf("c[%d]=%s\n", j, c[j]);
}
```

Output

```
1
3
2
4
c[0]=This
c[1]=is
c[2]=a
c[3]=String
```

5.8.6 Pointers to Functions

The function is not a variable in C but it has a physical address in memory that can be assigned to a pointer. For example, the pointer assignment is of the form

```
int (*p)();
int func();
/* using P rule */
p = &func;
```

Example

```
/* filename cex45.c */

#include <stdio.h>
#include <string.h>

int force(m, a)
int m, a;
{
    int f;
    f = m * a;
    return(f);
}
```

```
main()
{
  int Force, ret_str;
  int mass = 100;
  int acceleration = 9;

  /* function pointer of data type int */
  int (*p)();

  /* assigning pointer to memory address using P rule */
  p = &force;
  Force = (*p)(mass, acceleration);
  printf("Force = mass * acceleration\n");
  printf("F = %d * %d = %d\n", mass, acceleration, Force);
  p = &strcmp;
  ret_str = (*p)("abc", "abc");
  printf("string comparison return value=%d\n", ret_str);
}
```

Output

```
Force = mass * acceleration
F = 100 * 9 = 900
string comparison return value=0
```

5.8.7 Pointer Arithmetic

Addition and subtraction are the only two arithmetic operations that can be performed on pointers. If the pointer is incremented by a value of 1, that is p++, it points to the next memory address, and similarly if the pointer is decremented by a value of 1, that is p--, it points to the previous memory address. The integer can be added or subtracted from the pointers. If the pointers point to the same data type but at a different location, they can be subtracted. The subtraction usually results in a number of elements between the two pointers. Two pointers pointing to the same object can be compared in a relational expression.

Example

/* filename cex46.c */

```
#include <stdio.h>

main()
{
  int a[] = { 0, 1, 2, 3, 4, };
  int *phead, *ptail;
  int total;
  phead = &a[0];
  ptail = &a[5];
  /* only addition and subtraction can be performed */
  /* on pointers */
  total = ptail - phead;
  printf("Total number of elements in array a[]\n");
  printf("%d\n", total);
}
```

Output

```
Total number of elements in array a[]
5
```

5.9   Structures, Unions, and Enumerations

The C language allows one to create a custom group of variables in a variety of ways using the keywords struct, union, enum, and typedef.

5.9.1   Structures

A structure is a set of one or more variables that is referenced under one name. Structure makes it easy to keep related information together. In the database and Pascal language domains, it is usually referred to as a record. The members of a structure can have different object types (unlike arrays, whose members are all of the same data type). The general form of the structure declaration is

```
struct tag {
   data_type variable_name1;
   data_type variable_name2;
   ...
```

```
    data_type variable_nameN;
} struct_var_names
```

The `tag` is the name of the structure definition and is the name of a new data type. The `tag` can be used to declare actual structure variable names as `struct_var_names`. The structure members are referenced by the operator period (.). If the variable is a pointer to the structure, it is referenced by an arrow (->).

The structures can be easily assigned if they are of the same type. The variable values of one structure are copied to another structure variable, instead of copying individual elements.

Arrays of structures can be defined similarly to arrays of variables of data type `int, char` and the like.

The C language allows variable structures to be passed as call by value, as well as call by reference.

Example

/* filename cex47.c */

```
#include <stdio.h>

main()
{
  /* struct is set of one or more variables */
  /* under same name */
  struct stag {
    char *name;
    char *make;
    char *color;
    int  year;
  };

  struct stag vehicle = { "car", "carmaker", "red" , 94 };
  struct stag *sp;

  printf("vehicle.name=%s\n", vehicle.name);
  printf("vehicle.make=%s\n", vehicle.make);
```

```
    printf("vehicle.color=%s\n", vehicle.color);
    printf("vehicle.year=%d\n", vehicle.year);

    sp = &vehicle;
    printf("sp->name=%s\n", sp->name);
    printf("sp->make=%s\n", sp->make);
    printf("sp->color=%s\n", sp->color);
    printf("sp->year=%d\n", sp->year);
}
```

Output

```
vehicle.name=car
vehicle.make=carmaker
vehicle.color=red
vehicle.year=94
sp->name=car
sp->make=carmaker
sp->color=red
sp->year=94
```

5.9.2   Unions

In C , a union is a variable that is shared by two or more variables of different
types and sizes. The union definition is analogous to that of a `struct`. Unlike
a structure, a union stores the value of only one member at a given time. The
union reserves enough storage to hold its largest member. The general form is

```
union tag {
    data_type variable_name1;
    data_type variable_name2;
    ...
    data_type variable_nameN;
} union_var_names
```

Unions are generally used for machine independent portable code, because the
compiler keeps track of the size and alignment requirements of variables that
make up a union. A union is accessed the same way as a structure.

Example

```
/* filename cex48.c */

#include <stdio.h>

main()
{
  /* union is a variable shared by two or more variables */
  /* of different types and sizes */
  union utag {
    char c[2];
    short s;
    long l;
  };

  union utag data, *up;
  data.c[0] = 'a';

  printf("data.c[0]=%c\n", data.c[0]);
  up = &data;
  printf("up->c[0]=%c\n", up->c[0]);
}
```

Output

```
data.c[0]=a
up->c[0]=a
```

5.9.3 Enumerations

An enumeration enum is a data type supported by C that consists of a set of constants called enumerators. The enumerators are declared as constants of type int. Consider the enum declaration

```
enum colors { red, blue, green };
```

In this enumeration type, each symbol red, blue, and green stands for an integer value. They can be used anywhere that an integer may be used. The value of the first enumeration type is assigned zero, and the next symbol is given a value one greater than the symbol it precedes.

```
enum element { silver=10, gold, platinum };
```

Here silver is assigned a value of 10, gold is 11, and platinum is 12.

Example

```
/* filename cex49.c */

#include <stdio.h>

main()
{
  /* enum assigns integer value 0, 1, ... */
  /* to symbols by default */
  enum money { dollar, pound, franc, deutchemark };
  enum money currency;

  currency = franc;
  printf("currency=%d\n", currency);
}
```

Output

```
currency=2
```

5.10 The C Preprocessor

The C preprocessor contains the following directives:

#if
#else
#elif
#endif
#include
#define
#undef
#ifdef
#ifndef
#line
#error
 # and ## Preprocessor Operators

All C preprocessor directives have the # sign at the beginning. The preprocessor directives are used in a program to include files, define identifiers, and conditions and so on.

- **#if, #else, #elif, and #endif**

The directives listed previously allow a portion of source code to be compiled selectively. The conditional compilation is used to include or exclude part of the source code ported to a particular architecture. The general form is

```
#if expression
    statement
#endif
```

Example

```
/* filename cex50.c */

#include <stdio.h>

#define BUFFER 1024

main()
{
#if BUFFER > 1023
   printf("Buffer size greater than 1K byte\n");
#endif
}
```

Output

```
Buffer size greater than 1K byte
```

To execute the false part, the general form is

```
#if expression
    statement
#else
    statement
#endif
```

Example

```
/* filename cex51.c */

#include <stdio.h>

#define BUFFER 1000

main()
{
#if BUFFER > 1023
   printf("Buffer size greater than 1K byte\n");
#else
   printf("Buffer size less than 1K byte\n");
#endif
}
```

Output

Buffer size less than 1K byte

If multiple constant expressions are to be evaluated, the following form can be used

```
#if expression1
    statement
#elif expression2
    statement
#elif expression3
    statement
#elif expressionN
    statement
#endif
```

Example

```
/* filename cex52.c */

#include <stdio.h>

#define NICKEL   5
```

```
#define DIME    10
#define QUARTER 25
#define CENT DIME

main()
{
#if CENT==NICKEL
  printf("selected NICKEL\n");
#elif CENT==DIME
  printf("selected DIME\n");
#else
  printf("selected QUARTER\n");
#endif
}
```

Output

```
selected DIME
```

- **#include**

The #include directive allows one to read a source file enclosed by angle brackets or quotes. The general form is

```
#include <filename.h>
#include "filename.h"
```

Example

```
#include <abc.h>
#include "abc.h"

#include <stdio.h>
#include "stdio.h"
```

If the filename is enclosed by angle brackets, the compiler looks for the file in a special directory set aside for include files. If the filename is enclosed by quotes, usually the file is searched for in the current working directory; if it does not find the file in that directory, it searches for, file as if the filename has been enclosed by angle brackets.

Example

```
/* filename cex53.h */

int i = 1;
char c = 'a';
char *str = "This is defined in header file";

struct record {
  char *name;
  int id;
  char grade;
};

/* filename cex53.c */

#include <stdio.h>
#include "cex53.h"

main()
{
  struct record student = { "Bill", 1234, 'A' };
  /* The C preprocessor will include the header file */
  /* and its content */
  printf("main program has access to\n");
  printf("contents of header file cex53.h\n");
  printf("integer i=%d\n", i);
  printf("character c=%c\n", c);
  printf("string=%s\n", str);
  printf("student name =%s\n", student.name);
  printf("student id   =%d\n", student.id);
  printf("student grade=%c\n", student.grade);
}
```

Output

```
main program has access to
contents of header file cex53.h
integer i=1
character c=a
string=This is defined in header file
```

```
student name =Bill
student id   =1234
student grade=A
```

- **#define**

The #define is used to define an identifier or macro and a character sequence that will be substituted for the identifier every time it is encountered in the source code. The general form is

```
#define macro_name character sequence
```

Example

```
/* filename cex54.c */

#include <stdio.h>

#define HYDROGEN  1
#define NUMBER "atomic number"
#define MAXIMUM(a,b)    ((a > b) ? a : b)

main()
{
  int h = HYDROGEN;
  int max;
  printf("%s of hydrogen = %d\n", NUMBER, h);
  max = MAXIMUM(1,99);
  printf("maximum of two numbers=%d\n", max);
}
```

Output

```
atomic number of hydrogen = 1
maximum of two numbers=99
```

- **#undef**

The #undef directive removes previously defined macro definitions through the #define directive. The general form of declaration is

```
#undef macro_name
```

Example

```
/* filename cex55.c */

#include <stdio.h>

#define URANIUM 238
#define NUMBER  "atomic number"
#define ABSOLUTE(x) ((x) < 0 ? -(x) : (x))

main()
{
  int u = URANIUM;
  int absolute;

  printf("%s of uranium = %d\n", NUMBER, u);
  absolute = ABSOLUTE(-100);
  printf("absolute value of -100 = %d\n", absolute);

#undef URANIUM

#ifndef URANIUM
  printf("Identifier URANIUM is not defined\n");
#endif

#undef ABSOLUTE

#ifndef ABSOLUTE
  printf("Identifier ABSOLUTE(x) is not defined\n");
#endif
}
```

Output

```
atomic number of uranium = 238
absolute value of -100 = 100
Identifier URANIUM is not defined
Identifier ABSOLUTE(x) is not defined
```

- **#ifdef and #ifndef**

The #ifdef directive can be used to do conditional compilation if the macro has been previously defined by the #define directive. If the macro is defined, the #ifdef evaluates to be true, and the statements are compiled; otherwise, they are skipped. The general form is

```
#ifdef macro_name
    statements
#endif
```

The #ifndef directive can be used to check if the macro has been previously defined or not defined by #define directive. If the macro is not defined, the #ifundef evaluates to be True, and the statements are compiled, otherwise they are skipped. The general form is

```
#ifndef macro_name
    statements
#endif
```

Example

```
/* filename cex56.c */

#include <stdio.h>

#define SIZE 100

main()
{

#ifdef SIZE
  printf("SIZE is defined = %d\n");
#endif

#ifndef BUF
  printf("BUF is not defined\n");
#endif

}
```

Output

```
SIZE is defined = 284
BUF is not defined
```

- **#line and #error**

The #line directive is used to change the predefined identifiers __LINE__ and __FILE__ contents in the compiler. The general form is

```
#line line_number "filename"
```

The line_number should be integral constant. The directive is used for debugging purposes in the program. The line_number becomes the current line number of the source file.

Example

```
/* filename cex57.c */

#include <stdio.h>

#line 10

main()
{
  printf("executing application\n");
  printf("reached line %d\n",__LINE__);
}
```

Output

```
executing application
reached line 14
```

- **#error**

During compilation the #error directive forces the compiler to stop compilation when it is encountered. Like #line, this is also used for debugging purposes.

The general form is

```
#error "error_string"
```

Example

```
/* filename cex58.c */

#include <stdio.h>

main()
{
  printf("executing application\n");
#error "debugging application"
  printf("compiler will never reach this statement\n");
}
```

Output

```
cc  compiler  error:"cex58.c",  line  9:  #error:  "debugging
application"
```

- **The Preprocessor Operators # and ##**

C supports two preprocessor operators: # and ##. The operators are used with the #define directive. The # operator is used as a prefix to the argument and causes it to be turned into a quoted string. The ## operator concatenates two tokens.

Example

```
/* filename cex59.c */

#include <stdio.h>

#define ADD_QUOTE(str) # str
#define CONCATENATE(x, y) x ## y

main()
{
```

```
/* The C preprocessor will add quotes as below */
/* printf("C is an excellent programming language\n"); */
printf(ADD_QUOTE(C is an excellent progamming
                    language\n));

/* The C preprocessor transforms above into */
/* following statements */
/* printf("CONCATENATE(1,9)=%d\n", xy); */
/* printf("CONCATENATE(Good,Bye)=%s\n", xy); */
printf("CONCATENATE(1,9)=%d\n", CONCATENATE(1,9));
printf("CONCATENATE(Good,Bye!)=%s\n",
                    CONCATENATE("Good", "Bye!"));
}
```

Output

```
C is an excellent programming language
CONCATENATE(1,9)=19
CONCATENATE(Good,Bye!)=GoodBye!
```

5.11 Linked Lists and Trees

C pointers allow us to create self-referential data structures, such as single linked lists, doubly link list, circular list, queues, stack, trees etc.

- **Single Link List**

In single link list each structure consists of data members and a member structure of the same type which acts as a pointer to the next structure in the list. Consider example:

```
struct container {
  int value;
  struct container *next;
};
```

Here the struct container consists of data member value and a member next, which is a pointer to a container structure. If two variables of data type struct container are declared as

```
struct container head, body;
```

and if the next pointer of structure head is set to point to structure body by the statement

```
head.next = &body;
```

it makes a link between head and body. Figure 5-3 represents singly link list with three items.

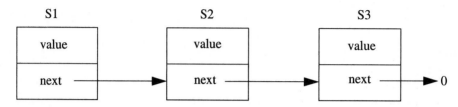

Figure 5-3
Single link list

Example

```
/* filename  cex60.c */

#include <stdio.h>

main()
{
  struct container {
      int value;
      struct container *next;
  };
  struct container head, body, tail;
  struct container *start;

  head.value  =  1;
  body.value  =  2;
  tail.value  =  3;

  /* make links */
  head.next = &body;
```

```
    body.next = &tail;
    tail.next = (struct container *)0;
    start = &head;
    printf("head value=  %d\n", head.value);
    printf("body value=  %d\n", head.next->value);
    printf("tail value=  %d\n", body.next->value);
    while (start != (struct container *)0)
    {
        printf("%d\n", start->value);
        start = start->next;
    }
}
```

Output

```
head value= 1
body value= 2
tail value= 3
1
2
3
```

```
/* filename cex61.c */

#include  <stdio.h>

struct container {
  int i;
  char c;
  char str[5];
  struct container *next;
};

struct container *salloc()
{
  struct container *bytes;
  /* allocate memory for struct container */
  bytes = (struct container *)malloc(sizeof
          (struct container));
  return(bytes);
}
```

```c
struct container *create_list(p, c)
struct container *p;
char c;
{
  if(p == NULL) {
    /* allocate memory and assign values */
    p = salloc();
    p->i = c;
    p->c = c;
    /* save decimal and ASCII value in the form of string */
    sprintf(p->str, "%d %c", p->i, p->c);
    p->next = NULL;
  }
  else
    p->next = create_list(p->next, c);
  return(p);
}

print_list(p)
struct container *p;
{
  if(p != NULL) {
    printf("0%o %c\n", p->i, p->c);
    print_list(p->next);
  }
}

struct container *delete_item(p, c)
struct container *p;
char c;
{
  static struct container *current;

  if(p != NULL) {
    if(p->c == c) {
      /* save address of the current structure */
      current = p;
      /* assign to p address of next structure */
      p = p->next;
      /* deallocate current structure */
      free(current);
    } /* end if p->c */
```

```
    else
      p->next = delete_item(p->next, c);
  }
  return(p);
}

struct container *insert_item(p, c)
struct container *p;
char c;
{
  static struct container *current;

  if(p != NULL) {
    if ( c <= p->c) {
        /* save address of the current structure */
        current = p;
        /* create new structure and allocate memory */
        p = salloc();
        p->i = c;
        p->c = c;
        sprintf(p->str, "%d %c", p->i, p->c);
        /* assign address of the current structure */
        p->next = current;
    } /* end if p->c */
    else
      p->next = insert_item(p->next, c);
  } else /* no match add to the tail end */
      p = create_list(p,c);
  return(p);
}

main()
{
  int i;
  struct container *head;

  head = NULL;
  printf("creating list\n");
  for(i = 'a'; i <= 'e'; i++)
     head = create_list(head, i);
  print_list(head);
  printf("\ndelete character d from the list\n");
```

```
    head = delete_item(head, 'd');
    print_list(head);
    printf("\ninsert character d to the list\n");
    head = insert_item(head, 'd');
    print_list(head);
}
```

Output

```
creating list
0141 a
0142 b
0143 c
0144 d
0145 e
delete character d from the list
0141 a
0142 b
0143 c
0145 e
insert character d to the list
0141 a
0142 b
0143 c
0144 d
0145 e
```

- **Doubly Link List**

In doubly link list each structure consists of data members and two member structure of the same type which act as a pointer to the next structure and previous structure in the list. Consider example

```
struct container {
  int value;
  struct container *prev;
  struct container *next;
};
```

Here the struct container consists data member value and members prev and next which are pointers to a container structure. If two variables of data type `struct container` are declared as:

```
struct container head, body;
```

and if the `next` pointer of structure head is set to point to structure body by the statement

```
head.next = &body;
```

it makes a link between head and body. Similarly if the `prev` pointer of structure body is set to point to structure head by the statement

```
body.prev = &head;
```

it makes a link from body to head. The preceding two statements in effect creates link doubly link list. Figure 5-4 represents doubly link list with three items.

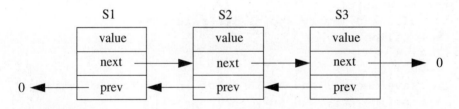

Figure 5-4
Doubly link list

Example

```
/* filename cex62.c */

#include  <stdio.h>

struct container {
   int i;
   char c;
   char str[5];
   struct container *prev;
```

```
    struct container *next;
};

static struct container *tail;

struct container *salloc()
{
  struct container *bytes;

  /* allocate memory for struct container */
  bytes = (struct container *)malloc(
              sizeof(struct container));
  return(bytes);
}

struct container *create_list(p, c)
struct container *p;
char c;
{
  if(p == NULL) {
    /* allocate memory and assign values */
    p = salloc();
    p->i = c;
    p->c = c;
    /* save decimal and ASCII value in the form of string */
    sprintf(p->str, "%d %c", p->i, p->c);
    p->next = NULL;
    p->prev = tail;
    tail = p;
  }
  else
    p->next = create_list(p->next, c);
  return(p);
}

print_next(p)
struct container *p;
{
  if(p != NULL) {
    printf("0%o %c\n", p->i, p->c);
    print_next(p->next);
  }
```

```
}

print_prev(p)
struct container *p;
{
  if(p != NULL) {
    printf("0%o %c\n", p->i, p->c);
    print_prev(p->prev);
  }
}

/* delete an item within the list */
struct container *delete_item(p, c)
struct container *p;
char c;
{
  static struct container *current;

  if(p != NULL) {
    if(p->c == c) {
      /* save address of the current structure */
      current = p;
      /* assign to p address of next structure */
      p = p->next;
      p->prev = current->prev;
      /* deallocate current structure */
      free(current);
    } /* end if p->c */
    else
      p->next = delete_item(p->next, c);
  }
  return(p);
}

/* insert character within the list */
struct container *insert_item(p, c)
struct container *p;
char c;
{
  static struct container *current;

  if(p != NULL) {
```

```
      if ( c <= p->c) {
         /* save address of the current structure */
         current = p;
         /* create new structure and allocate memory */
         p = salloc();
         p->i = c;
         p->c = c;
         sprintf(p->str, "%d %c", p->i, p->c);
         /* assign address of the current structure */
         p->next = current;
         current->prev = p;
      } /* end if p->c */
      else
         p->next = insert_item(p->next, c);
   }
   return(p);
}

main()
{
   int i;
   struct container *head;
   head = tail = NULL;

   for(i = 'a'; i <= 'c'; i++)
      head = create_list(head, i);

   printf("forward traverse\n");
   print_next(head);

   printf("reverse traverse\n");
   print_prev(tail);

   printf("\ndelete character b from the list\n");
   head = delete_item(head, 'b');
   printf("forward traverse\n");
   print_next(head);
   printf("reverse traverse\n");
   print_prev(tail);
   printf("\ninsert character b to the list\n");
   head = insert_item(head, 'b');
   printf("forward traverse\n");
```

```
    print_next(head);
    printf("reverse traverse\n");
    print_prev(tail);
}
```

Output

```
forward traverse
0141 a
0142 b
0143 c
reverse traverse
0143 c
0142 b
0141 a
delete character b from the list
forward traverse
0141 a
0143 c
reverse traverse
0143 c
0141 a

insert character b to the list
forward traverse
0141 a
0142 b
0143 c
reverse traverse
0143 c
0142 b
0141 a
```

• **Tree**

A tree is a data structure with exactly one vertex, called root with every vertex
except root having one entering edge. There is a unique path from root to each
vertex. A binary tree is a tree where every vertex has no more than one left
node nor more than one right node. Figure 5-5 depicts binary tree.

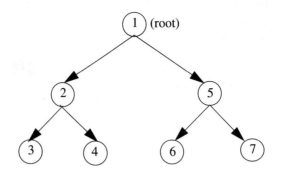

Figure 5-5
Binary tree

Example

```
/* filename cex63.c */

#include   <stdio.h>

struct container {
  char ch;
  struct container *left;
  struct container *right;
};

struct container *salloc()
{
  struct container *bytes;

  /* allocate memory for struct container */
    bytes = (struct  container  *)malloc(sizeof(struct  con-
tainer));
  return(bytes);
}

struct container *create_tree(p, c)
struct container *p;
char c;
{
  if(p == NULL) {
```

```
    /* allocate memory and assign values */
    p = salloc();
    p->ch = c;
    p->left = p->right = NULL;
  } else if ( c < p->ch )
      /* create left node */
      p->left = create_tree(p->left, c);
    else
      /* create right node */
      p->right = create_tree(p->right, c);
  return(p);
}

print_tree(p)
struct container *p;
{
  if(p != NULL) {
    print_tree(p->left);
    printf("%c\n", p->ch);
    print_tree(p->right);
  }
}

main()
{
  int i;
  struct container *head;
  head = NULL;
  head = create_tree(head, 'c');
  for(i = 'a'; i <= 'e'; i++)
    if(i != 'c')
      head = create_tree(head, i);
  print_tree(head);
}
```

Output

```
a
b
c
d
e
```

5.12   The C Input/Output

5.12.1 Terminal I/O

The input and output mechanism in its simplest form reads a character from the terminal and writes a character back. This can be achieved with the get-char() and putchar() functions. The scanf() and printf() functions allow format-ted input and output of the data from the terminal. The following example explains the usage of C library functions and system calls to read from the ter-minal and write to the terminal.

Example

```
/* filename cex64.c */

#include <stdio.h>

main()
{
  int number;
  char string[80];

  /* screen input and output */
  printf("implicit use of stdin and stdout\n");
  printf("type an integral number\n");

  /* to get any integer value from standard input */
  /* use an address operator & */
  scanf("%d", &number);
  printf("input number=%d\n", number);
  printf("type a string\n");
  scanf("%s", string);
  printf("input string=%s\n", string);

  /* stdin - standard input file stream attached */
  /* to screen file descriptor 0 */
  /* stdout - standard output file stream attached */
  /* to screen file descriptor 1 */
  /* stderr - standard output file stream attached */
  /* to screen file descriptor 2 */
  fprintf(stdout,"explicit use of stdin and stdout\n");
```

```
    fprintf(stdout,"type an integral number\n");
    fscanf(stdin,"%d", &number);
    fprintf(stdout,"input number=%d\n", number);
    fprintf(stdout,"type a string\n");
    fscanf(stdin,"%s", string);
    fprintf(stdout,"input string=%s\n", string);
    fprintf(stderr, "this is a test error message\n");
}
```

Output

```
implicit use of stdin and stdout
type an integral number
10
input number=10
type a string
hello
input string=hello
explicit use of stdin and stdout
type an integral number
20
input number=20
type a string
world
input string=world
this is a test error message
```

```
/* filename cex65.c */

#include <stdio.h>
#include <fcntl.h>
#include <errno.h>
#include <string.h>
#include <sys/stat.h>

#define PERM_ALL (S_IRWXU | S_IRWXG | S_IRWXO)
extern int errno;

main()
{
    int bytes;
    char *buf;
```

```
    char *out = "type a string\n";

    /* write to stdout file descriptor 1 */
    /* i.e to screen */

    write (1, out, strlen(out));

    /* read from stdin file descriptor 0 */
    /* i.e from screen */
    buf = (char *)malloc(80);
    bytes = read(0, buf, 80);
    if (bytes != strlen(buf))
    printf("error:%s\n",strerror(errno));
    printf("string in buf=%s", buf);
    write(1,buf,80);
}
```

Output

```
type a string
Good Morning
string in buf=Good Morning
Good Morning
```

5.12.2 File I/O

A file in C can be anything: a text file, executable file, disk file, terminal, and so on. The files are accessed by either the file descriptor or stream associated with a filename. The files can be seeked to any position. This allows random access and writing at a desired position in a file. The following example explains file I/O.

Example

```
/* filename cex66.c */

#include <stdio.h>
#include <fcntl.h>
#include <errno.h>
#include <string.h>
#include <sys/stat.h>
```

```
#define PERM_ALL (S_IRWXU | S_IRWXG | S_IRWXO)
extern int errno;

main()
{
  int buflen, fildes;
  int length, bytes;
  char *buf;
  char *string = "hello world";

  /* create testfile write and read the string */
  /* using file descriptor */
  length = strlen(string);
  fildes = creat("testfile", PERM_ALL);
  buflen = write(fildes, string, length);
  if(buflen != length)
     printf("error:%s\n",strerror(errno));
  close(fildes);
  fildes = open("testfile", O_RDONLY);
  buf = (char *)malloc (length);
  bytes = read(fildes, buf, length);
  if(bytes == length) {
     printf("string in buf=%s\n", buf);
     printf("number of bytes read=%d\n", bytes);
  }
  else
     printf("error:%s\n",strerror(errno));
  close(fildes);
  remove("testfile");
}
```

Output

```
string in buf=hello world
number of bytes read=11
```

/* filename cex67.c */

```
#include <stdio.h>
#include <errno.h>
```

```
extern int errno;

main()
{
  FILE *stream;
  int  length;
  int  value;
  char str1[10], str2[10];
  char string[] = "Good Morning";

  length = strlen (string);
  stream = fopen("testfile", "w+r");
  fwrite(string, sizeof(char), length, stream);
  fflush(stream);
  fseek(stream,0,SEEK_SET);
  value = fscanf(stream, "%s %s", str1, str2);
  if (value != 2)
     printf("error: %s\n", strerror(errno));
  fprintf(stdout, "%s %s\n", str1, str2);
  remove("testfile");
}
```

Output

```
Good Morning
```

5.12.3 Format States

The scanf(), printf(), fscanf(), and fprintf() functions allow the numbers and strings to read and write strings in a controlled fashion. The format commands in the argument field allow formatted printing. The following examples explain some of the formats.

Example

```
/* filename cex68.c */

#include <stdio.h>

main()
{
```

```
int     integer = 1;
long    longval = 12L;
float   floating = 1.2345;
double  doubleval = 1.234E3;
char    character = 'a';
char    *string = "hello world";

/* print controls for different data types */
printf("integer=%d\n", integer);
printf("longval=%ld\n", longval);
printf("float=%f\n", floating);
printf("doubleval=%f\n", doubleval);
printf("character=%c\n", character);
printf("string=%s\n", string);
}
```

Output

```
integer=1
longval=12
float=1.234500
doubleval=1234.000000
character=a
string=hello world
```

/* filename cex69.c */

```
#include <stdio.h>

main()
{
  unsigned int integer = 1;
  unsigned int octal = 03;
  unsigned int hex = 0xab;
  unsigned int HEX = 0XCD;
  double sci = 1.234e5;
  double SCI = 1.234E5;

  /* print controls for different data types */
  printf("integer=%u\n", integer);
  printf("octal=0%o\n", octal);
  printf("hex=0x%x\n", hex);
```

```
    printf("hex=%#x\n", hex);
    printf("HEX=0X%X\n", HEX);
    printf("HEX=%#X\n", HEX);
    printf("sci=%e\n", sci);
    printf("SCI=%E\n", SCI);
}
```

Output

```
integer=1
octal=03
hex=0xab
hex=0xab
HEX=0XCD
HEX=0XCD
sci=1.234000e+05
SCI=1.234000E+05
```

/* filename cex70.c */

```
#include <stdio.h>

main()
{
    double number = 12.3456;
    char *string = "Good Bye!";

    /* print within field width specifier */
    printf("%f\n", number);
    printf("%12f\n", number);

    /* pad begining with zeros */
    printf("%012f\n", number);

    /* print within precision specifier */
    printf("%2.6f\n", number);
    /* the statement below is equivalent of */
    /* printf("%1.3f\n",number); */
    printf("%*.*f\n", 1,3,number);

    /* right justified */
```

```
    printf("%15s\n", string);

    /* left justified */
    printf("%-15s\n", string);
}
```

Output

```
12.345600
    12.345600
00012.345600
12.345600
12.346
        Good Bye!
Good Bye!
```

5.13 Exercises

5.1   Enter the following text lines into a file called ctest.c; then execute make
      ctest to create the ctest binary file. Run ctest. What output do you see at
      the terminal?

```
#include <stdio.h>
#include <stdlib.h>

main()
{
    printf("Introduction to C programming language\n");
    fprintf(stdout, "Course number 100\n");
}
```

5.2   Write a program that prints the following text at the standard output:
      a) C is a high-level programming language.
      b) Many applications can be written using C.

5.3   List 10 reserved C keywords. What are the restrictions on the use of
      these keywords?

5.4   What is the general form of a C program?

5.5   What is an object and a binary file? From the source file ctest.c of Exer-
      cise 5.1 create an object file. What compiler option is needed to create an

object file?

5.6 What is a C library? Compare static and dynamic libraries.

5.7 Which of the following are invalid variable names?
int   Char   Long   float $int   ?ret_val   No#1

5.8 What effect do the keywords const and volatile have on variables?

5.9 What type of modifiers are typdef, extern, and static?

5.10 What action does a cast operator have on a given expression? List five examples.

5.11 List the precedence of all the C operators, including their associativity.

5.12 Evaluate the following expressions
2 + 3 - 1   4 / 5 + 6   4.0/5.0 + 2   3 + 5 * 2.2   10 % 2 * 1.23
add = 1;   result = ++add ;
sub = 2;   result = sub--;
(1 >= 1)   (2 <= 3)   (100 < 99)   (-9 > -8)
(0 && 1)   (1 && 2)   (0 || 1)   (1 || 2)
i = 01, j = 02;   result = i & j;   result = i | j;   result = j << 1;
j = 2; k = 4; j +=k; j = 10; j -= k; k = 2; j *= k;

5.13 Write a program to find the maximum or minimum of two numbers using the selection statements if and else, and print to the terminal the maximum of the two numbers.

5.14 Implement programs using iteration statements for, while and do to calculate the area of circles with radii 1 through 9 and print them on the terminal.

5.15 Write a program to print ASCII uppercase characters A through Z using the jump statements break and continue.

5.16 Implement a program using switch and labeled statements case and default that executes statements associated with integer constants -9, -5, 0, 5, 10 and any other constant.

5.17 Write a program that accepts command line option -h help and prints usage messages on the screen. Modify this program to print the value of the environment variable HOME.

5.18 What is call by reference and call by value?

5.19 Write a program that has a function called energy() that takes mass (m) and velocity (v) of data type float as an argument to function and returns energy of data type float. The function should calculate energy using Einstein's equation $e = m * c^2$. Assume values for mass and velocity.

5.20 Implement the function of Exercise 5.19 using call by reference and call by value.

5.21 Write a program having a recursive function rap() to print the first 10 numbers of an arithmetic progression whose first term is 1 (a) and common difference is 2 (d). *Hint*: Use $t = a + (n-1) * d$ (here t is the value of the nth term).

5.22 Write a program having a recursive function rgp() to print the first ten numbers of a geometric progression whose first term is 1 (a) and common ratio is 2 (r). *Hint*: Use $t = a * r^{(n-1)}$ (here t is the value of the nth term).

5.23 Write a program that has a single dimensional character and integer array of size 26 that stores the English alphabet in the character array and corresponding sequence number in the integer array. Print the stored array values on the terminal.

5.24 What is a pointer? Compare pointers and arrays.

5.25 Implement a pointer version of a program by having the function hypot() take as a pointer arguments to base (b) and perpendicular (p), and return a value of hypotenuse. *Hint*: Use $h = sqrt(b^2 + p^2)$.

5.26 What is the difference between struct and union?

5.27 Write a program having the data type struct with members as

```
struct cdata {
    int i;
    char c;
    char *string;
};
```

Initialize the members with some assumed values and display those values on the terminal.

5.28 Write unit test program to test the examples of section 5.11. The test should cover all possible boundary values. Document the test results.

5.29 What is an enumeration? Write a program that contains enumerators enum fruit {apple, oranges, banana};

Print the default integer value and new assigned values apple=1, oranges=50, banana=100 on the terminal.

5.30 Implement a program containing the C preprocessor statement

```
#include <stdio.h>

main()
{
    fprintf(stdout, invoking application...\n");
#ifdef DEBUG
    fprintf(stdout, "debugging application...\n");
#else
    fprintf(stdout, "DEBUG is not defined\n");
#endif
}
```

Compile and execute this program. What output do you see on the terminal? Now compile this program with -DDEBUG option. What output do you see now?

Add the statement #define DEBUG 1 after #include line and recompile program without the compiler -DDEBUG option. What output do you see on the terminal?

5.31 Write a program that reads an integer and string from the terminal. Print these values on the terminal.

5.32 Write a program that reads a line width of 80 characters from a file and prints it on the terminal.

6

The C++ Language

6.1   Introduction

The C++ programming language is a superset of the C language; all the features of C are retained in C++. The C++ language was introduced by Bjarne Stroustrup in 1980 at Bell Laboratories in Murray Hill, New Jersey. The language was initially known as "C with Classes." In 1983 it was changed to C++. The C++ language introduced the notion of objects, polymorphism, and inheritance. These new features allowed one to write large, complex programs. Although C is adequate for most programs, if the program is large and complex, it is difficult to write and understand in C. Since C++ is a superset of C any program, large or small, can be written in C++. The C++ language incorporates object-oriented programming (OOP) features as in the programming language Simula67. Currently, the ANSI C++ committee X3J16 and ISO's C++ standards group WG21 are closely working together to standardize C++. Object oriented programming revolves around a logical entity-the object. In addition to object-oriented programming features, C++ offers better type checking, modular programming, abstract data types, and the overloading of operators and functions. This chapter covers all C++ and OOP features with examples. The reader is advised to go through the chapter on C to fully understand and grasp the features of C++.

6.2   C++ Reserved Keywords

In addition to reserved keywords in C, Table 6-1 gives additional keywords reserved for use with C++.

Table 6-1 C++ Reserved Keywords

catch	class	delete	friend	inline	new
operator	overload	private	protected	public	template
this	throw	try	virtual		

The keywords catch, throw, and try deal with exception handling and are reserved also. The keyword overload is obsolete, a carry-over from the first release.

6.3   C++ Program Structure

The C++ program structure is similar to C with minor differences. It consists of include files at the beginning, followed by global, base class, and derived class declarations, as well as user-defined functions and the main() function, as shown in Figure 6-1.

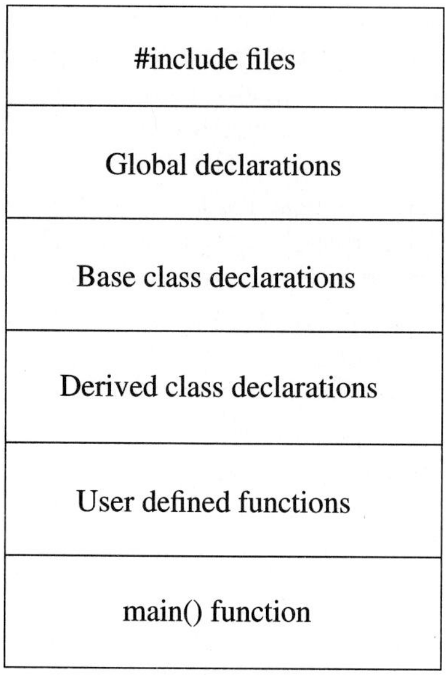

#include files
Global declarations
Base class declarations
Derived class declarations
User defined functions
main() function

Figure 6-1
C++ program structure diagram

The general form of the C++ program is

```
/* include files */
#include <some.h>
#include <headers.h>
...

/* global declarations */
int integer;
char character;...

/* base class declaration */
class class_name {
   private data
   private function
   ...
   private:
      data and functions
   protected:
      data and functions
   public:
      data and functions
   ...
} class_list
...

/* derived class declarations */
class Derived : public class_name {
   private data
   ...
}

/* user-defined functions */
date_type function1(parm1, parm2, ...)
data_type parm1;
audiotape parm2;
{
   declarations
   statements
   return(data_type x);
}
...
```

```
main()
{
   declarations
   data_type value1;
   data_type arg1, arg2;
   class_name nuclease;
   ...

   value1 = function1(arg1, arg2, ... );
   ...
   /* process the return values */
   ...
   statements
}
```

Example

// filename cpex1.c

```
#include <stdlib.h>
#include <stream.h>

main()
{
  // comment line in C++
  cout << "Programming in C++ UNIX\n";
  cout << "C++ Source Code File\n";
}
```

Output

```
Programming in C++ UNIX
C++ Source Code File
```

// filename cpex2.c

```
#include <stdlib.h>
#include <string.h>
#include <stream.h>
```

```
// class declaration
class vehicle {
  private:
    int license; // license number
    int registration; // registration number
  protected:
    int doors; // number of doors
  public:
    char name[20];   // vehicle name
    char color[20]; // vehicle color
    int year;       // vehicle make year
    // constructor
    vehicle(char *n, char *c, int d, int l, int y);
    // destructor
    ~vehicle();
    int getlicense();
    int getdoors();
};

// constructor -- no return type
vehicle::vehicle(char *n, char *c, int d, int l, int y)
{
  cout << "initializing object" "\n";
  license = l; doors = d; year = y;
  strcpy(name, n); strcpy(color, c);
}

// destructor -- no arg, no return type
vehicle::~vehicle()
{
  cout << "destructing object" << "\n";
  license = 0; doors = 0; year = 0;
  strcpy(name, "\0"); strcpy(color, "\0");
}

/* class function definition */
int vehicle::getlicense()
{
  return(license);
}
```

```
/* class function definition */
int vehicle::getdoors()
{
  return(doors);
}

// User-defined function
int carusage(int parm1, int parm2)
{
  // local declaration
  int yearold;

  /* statements */
  yearold = parm2 - parm1;
  return(yearold);
}

main()
{
  // local declarations
  int license, doors, yearused;
  int current = 1994;

  vehicle car("race car", "red", 2, 123456, 1989);

  // statements
  license = car.getlicense();
  doors = car.getdoors();
  cout << "name of the car=" << car.name << "\n";
  cout << "color of the car=" << car.color << "\n";
  cout << "number of doors=" << doors<< "\n";
  cout << "license number=" << license << "\n";
  cout << "make year=" << car.year << "\n";

  yearused = carusage(car.year, current);
  cout << "number of years old=" << yearused << "\n";
}
```

Output

```
initializing object
name of the car=race car
```

```
color of the car=red
number of doors=2
license number=123456
make year=1989
number of years old=5
destructing object
```

// filename cpex3.c

```
#include <stdlib.h>
#include <stream.h>

main()
{
  int number;
  char string[40];

  // cin -  standard input, cout - standard output
  // cerr - standard error, clog - buffered standard error
  cout << "type an integral number\n";
  cin >> number;
  cout << "input number is=" << number << "\n";

  cout << "type a string\n";
  cin >> string;
  cout << "input string is=" << string << "\n";

  cerr << "error: this is error message\n";
  clog << "error: this is buffered error message\n";
}
```

Output

```
type an integral number
input number is=9
type a string
input string is=hello
error: this is error message
error: this is buffered error message
```

6.4   Object-oriented Programming (OOP)

Object-oriented programming is based on the concept of objects, encapsulation, polymorphism, and inheritance. OOP is a new approach to writing large,
complex programs by dividing the task into smaller modules. Object-oriented
programming is based on the principle of structured and modular programming, unlike conventional procedural programming.

The object-oriented programming technique revolves around a logical entity
called an object that contains both data and code. In geometrical space the
object could be something like a point, line, rectangle, circle, or ellipse. In alge-
braic space it could be any polynomial equation. In trigonometric space it
could be any trigonometric function. In short, it could be any user-defined logical entity with certain basic common properties. For a given object, it can
define some of the code and/or data to be private to the object and inaccessible
to anything outside the object. This offers protection against changes by some
other part of the program.

Object-oriented analysis (OOA) analyzes the problem domain in terms of
objects and classes, while object-oriented design (OOD) reflects the system to
be built in the same term. The usual progression is from OOA -> OOD -> OOP
in an implementation. OOA and OOD differ from OOP in that the notations
are graphical instead of the usual textual declarative form. This allows easier
visualization and makes dependencies more explicit. For example, an association is an annotated and labeled line connecting classes in an OOA or an OOD
diagram, but is often a pointer declaration or an instance of other calls in
OOP.

6.4.1   Encapsulation

The linkage of code and data is referred to as encapsulation. In C++, encapsulation is provided by the `class` keywords, which allows one to combine the
data and functions into a `class` entity. The keywords `struct` and `union` also
allow loosely coupled encapsulation. The data and code of an object are pack-
aged into a capsule (class). Following is an example of the `class` keyword
providing encapsulation of object `rectangle`.

```
class rectangle {
  private:
    int length;
    int height;
```

```
  protected:
    int diagonal;
    int area;
  public:
    rectangle(int l, int h) // contructor
    ~rectangle() // destructor
    int DrawRectangle(int length, int height);
    int DeleteRectangle(int length, int height);
};
```

The `length`, `height`, `diagonal`, and `area` are data members of the class. `rectangle`, `~rectangle`, `DrawRectangle`, and `DeleteRectangle` are member functions of the class. The properties of the object rectangle type cannot be accessed from outside the object. The object of type rectangle can be initialized by the function `rectangle` and destroyed by the function `~rectangle`. The behavior of the object can be manipulated by the `DrawRectangle` and `DeleteRectangle` functions. Thus, by defining the object in this way, the details of the object are not visible to or accessible by the outside. This is encapsulation, which leads to modular programming with reusable code.

6.4.2 Polymorphism

Poly means "many" and morph means "form". In OOP polymorphism is one name or interface with multiple purposes. The C++ language allows the use of certain operators and functions for many slightly differing tasks. The operators are called overloaded operators and the functions are overloaded functions. For instance, the cube of a number for a given type could be found in some of these ways:

1. `short cube (short number);`

2. `long cube (long number);`

3. `double cube (double number);`

In each case the function name `cube()` or interface is the same, but it returns data of multiple types. The function `cube()` is overloaded. In C this is not allowed, but in C++ it is legal and, depending on the data type of the number, the function `cube()` will be called [that is, if the `cube()` with data type `long` is called, then function "2" will be called]. Similarly, operator `<<` is overloaded; it is used for two purposes: (1) for left shift operation and (2) as output stream.

Example

```
// filename cpex4.c

#include <stdlib.h>
#include <stream.h>

short cube(short n)
{
  short value;
  value = n * n * n;
  cout << "invoked function cube with data type short\n";
  return (value);
}

long cube(long n)
{
  long value;
  value = n * n * n;
  cout << "invoked function cube with data type long\n";
  return (value);
}

double cube(double n)
{
  double value;
  value = n * n * n;
  cout << "invoking function cube with data type double\n";
  return (value);
}

main()
{
  // Polymorphism - many forms
  // one function name multiple purposes
  short s, scube;
  long l, lcube;
  double d, dcube;

  scube = 2; lcube = 3; dcube = 1.1;

  s = cube(scube);
```

```
  cout << "cube of a 2 short=" << s << "\n";

  l = cube(lcube);
  cout << "cube of a 3 long=" << l << "\n";

  d = cube(dcube);
  cout << "cube of a 1.1 double=" << d << "\n";
}
```

Output

```
invoked function cube with data type short
cube of a 2 short=8
invoked function cube with data type long
cube of a 3 long=27
invoking function cube with data type double
cube of a 1.1 double=1.331
```

6.4.3   Inheritance

Inheritance is the process by which a child object inherits certain properties from the parent object. The parent object is usually referred to as the base class and the child object is referred to as the derived class. Inheritance, in short, is the ability to create a class that has the properties and behaviors of another class. Consider the class `rectangle` with properties length and height; from this class one can define the derived class `square`, for which the length and height are equal.

Example

// filename cpex5.c

```
#include <stdlib.h>
#include <stream.h>
```

// base class declaration
```
class base {
  private:
    int i;
  protected:
```

```
      char c;
  public:
    // base constructors
    base() {};
    base(int i, char c) { i = 0; c = 0; };
    void setic(int bi, char bc) { i = bi; c = bc; };
    void display() {
      cout << "i=" << i << " c=" << c << "\n";
    };
};

// derived class declaration
// inherits base class members
class derived:public base {
  private:
    int j;
    char *string;
  public:
    int k;
    // derived constructor
    derived(int, int, int);
};

derived::derived(int dk, int bi, int bc)
:base(bi,bc)
{
  k = dk;
}

main()
{
  derived Dobj(4,0,0);

  // set members of base
  Dobj.setic(9,'z');
  cout << "derived class can access base class members\n";
  Dobj.display();
  cout << "value of derived class member\n";
  cout << "k=" << Dobj.k << "\n";
}
```

Output

```
derived class can access base class members
i=9 c=z
value of derived class member
k=4
```

6.5 Classes

A class in C++ defines a data type, much like `struct` and union in C. The difference being by default that the members of `struct` and union are public, whereas a `class` has private default member access. An object is a region of storage with associated semantics. After the declaration of class shape, shape is an object of type class. A class declaration for a given object links code and data. The data members of several types are combined along with methods of manipulating stored data into one object. Objects of an empty class have a nonzero size. Class objects can be passed as arguments to functions and returned by functions and can also be assigned to a pointer. Classes can be used as array types, nested. The memory can also be allocated dynamically for class objects.

6.5.1 Declaration

The declaration of `class` introduces a new data type with data members and data functions with access permissions of `private`, `protected`, and `public`. The data and function members by default have `private` values. The keywords `private`, `protected`, and `public` are optional. The general form of class declaration is

```
class class_name {
   private data
   private function
   ...
   private:
      data and functions
   protected:
      data and functions
   public:
      data and functions
   ...
```

```
} class_list
```

Access permissions for members of classes are:

- **Private:** A private member can be accessed only by members and friends of its own class.
- **Protected:** A protected member is accessible by member functions of its own class and also to members of classes derived from it.
- **Public:** A public member can be accessed by anyone.

Table 6-2 tabulates the access permissions for class members.

Table 6-2 Class Members Access Permissions

Class Members	Access Permissions
private	Members and friends
protected	Members and derived class members
public	Anyone

Example

// filename cpex6.c

```
#include <stdlib.h>
#include <string.h>
#include <stream.h>
```

// class declaration
```
class person {
  private:
    int salary;
    int id;
  protected:
    char *birthdate;
    char hiredate[20];
  public:
    int department;
    char name[20];
    char address[100];
```

```
      // constructors
      person() { salary = 0; id = 0; };
      person(char *n, int i, int d, char *h);
      // destructor
      ~person();
      int getid() { return id; };
      char *gethiredate();
};

// constructor function -- no return type
person::person(char *n, int i, int d, char *h)
{
   cout << "initializing object" << "\n";
   strcpy(name, n); id = i;
   department = d; strcpy(hiredate, h);
}

// destructor function -- no arg, no return type
person::~person()
{
   cout << "destructing object" << "\n";
   strcpy(name, "\0"); id = 0;
   department = 0; strcpy(hiredate, "\0");
}

char *person::gethiredate()
{
   return(hiredate);
}

main()
{
   char *hiredate;
   person employee("John", 1234, 12, "01/01/94");

   hiredate = employee.gethiredate();
   cout << "employee name=" << employee.name << "\n";
   cout << "employee number=" << employee.getid() << "\n";
   cout << "department number=" << employee.department <<
           "\n";
   cout << "hire date=" << hiredate << "\n";
}
```

Output

```
initializing object
employee name=John
employee number=1234
department number=12
hire date=01/01/94
destructing object
```

6.5.2 Data Members

Data members declaration is analogous to declarations of data variables outside a class. Class data members cannot be explicitly initialized; they should be initialized only by member or friend functions. The data members can be in the private, protected, or public parts of a class.

Example

```
// filename cpex7.c

#include <stdlib.h>
#include <string.h>
#include <stream.h>

// class declaration

class C {
  private:
    int i; // data member
  protected:
    char c; // data member
  public:
    char s[10]; // data member
    // constructor
    C(int ci, char cc, char *cs);
    // destructor
    ~C();
    int geti();
    char getch();
    void getic(int *ci, char *cc);
```

```
};

// constructor function -- no return type
C::C(int ci, char cc, char *cs)
{
  cout << "initializing object" << "\n";
  i = ci; c = cc; strcpy(s, cs);
}

// destructor function -- no arg, no return type
C::~C()
{
  cout << "destructing object" << "\n";
  i = 0; c = '\0'; strcpy(s, "\0");
}

int C::geti()
{
  return(i);
}

char C::getch()
{
  return(c);
}

void C::getic(int *ci, char *cc)
{
  *ci = i; *cc = c;
}

main()
{
  int mi; char mc; char *ms;
  int pmi; char pmc;
  C obj(1, 'a', "hello");

  // access to private and protected members
  // limited via member function
  mi = obj.geti();
  mc = obj.getch();
```

```
  // public members can be accessed directly
  obj.getic(&pmi, &pmc);
  cout << "private data member i=" << mi << "\n";
  cout << "protected data member c=" << mc << "\n";
  cout << "public data member s=" << obj.s << "\n";
  cout << "private data member i=" << pmi << "\n";
  cout << "protected data member c=" << pmc << "\n";
}
```

Output

```
initializing object
private data member i=1
protected data member c=a
public data member s=hello
private data member i=1
protected data member c=a
destructing object
```

6.5.2.1   Static Data Members

If a data member is declared `static`, it is shared by all objects of a class. A `static` data member can also be referred to by the qualification to the class name and not necessarily via any specific object of that class. The definition of a `static` data member in its class declaration is not actually a definition. The `static` data members can be initialized; otherwise, they are initialized to zero when the first object is created.

Example

```
// filename cpex8.c

#include <stdlib.h>
#include <string.h>
#include <stream.h>

// class declaration
class C {
  private:
    int i;
    static int si;
```

```
  protected:
    char c;
    static char sc;
  public:
    static char *sstr;
    C(int ci, char cc);
    ~C();
    void getic(int *ci, char *cc);
    void getsic(int *csi, char *csc);
};

// Initialize static members via class
int C::si = 1;
char C::sc = 'a';
char *C::sstr = "hello";

// constructor
C::C(int ci, char cc)
{
  i = ci; c = cc;
}

// destructor
C::~C()
{
  i = c = 0;
}

void C::getic(int *ci, char *cc)
{
  *ci = i; *cc = c;
}

void C::getsic(int *csi, char *csc)
{
  *csi = si; *csc = sc;
}

main()
{
  int mi; char mc;
  int msi; char msc;
```

```
C obj1(2, 'b');
C obj2(3, 'c');

obj1.getic(&mi, &mc);
obj1.getsic(&msi, &msc);
cout << "private obj1 member i=" << mi << "\n";
cout << "protected obj1 member c=" << mc << "\n";
cout << "static private obj1 member si=" << msi << "\n";
cout << "static protected obj1 member sc=" << msc << "\n";
cout << "static public obj1 member sstr=" <<
        obj1.sstr << "\n";

obj2.getic(&mi, &mc);
obj2.getsic(&msi, &msc);
cout << "private obj2 member i=" << mi << "\n";
cout << "protected obj2 member c=" << mc << "\n";
cout << "static private obj2 member si=" << msi << "\n";
cout << "static protected obj2 member sc=" << msc << "\n";
cout << "static public obj2 member sstr=" <<
        obj2.sstr << "\n";
}
```

Output

```
private obj1 member i=2
protected obj1 member c=b
static private obj1 member si=1
static protected obj1 member sc=a
static public obj1 member sstr=hello
private obj2 member i=3
protected obj2 member c=c
static private obj2 member si=1
static protected obj2 member sc=a
static public obj2 member sstr=hello
```

6.5.2.2   Const Data Members

If a data member is declared const, it should be initialized in every constructor's definition. The const data member name and its initial value are enclosed in parentheses, separated from the constructor's argument list by a colon. The data members can also be variables of another class.

Example

```
// filename cpex9.c

#include <stdlib.h>
#include <string.h>
#include <stream.h>

// class declaration
class C {
  private:
    int i;
    const int permi;
  protected:
    char c;
    const char permc;
  public:
    const char *perms;
    C(int ci, char cc, int cpi, char cpc, char *cps);
    void getic(int *ci, char *cc);
    void getcic(int *cpi, char *cpc);
};

// constructor should initialize const data members
C::C(int ci, char cc, int cpi, char cpc, char *cps)
:permi(cpi), permc(cpc), perms(cps)
{
  i = ci; c = cc;
}

void C::getic(int *ci, char *cc)
{
  *ci = i; *cc = c;
}

void C::getcic(int *cpi, char *cpc)
{
  *cpi = permi; *cpc = permc;
}

main()
```

```
{
  int mi; char mc;
  int mci; char mcc;
  C obj(1, 'a', 9, 'z', "hello");

  obj.getic(&mi, &mc);
  cout << "private obj member i=" << mi << "\n";
  cout << "protected obj member c=" << mc << "\n";

  obj.getcic(&mci, &mcc);
  cout << "const private obj member permi=" << mci << "\n";
  cout << "const protected obj member permc=" << mcc << "\n";
  cout << "const public obj member perms=" <<
          obj.perms << "\n";
}
```

Output

```
private obj member i=1
protected obj member c=a
const private obj member permi=9
const protected obj member permc=z
const public obj member perms=hello
```

6.5.3   Member Functions

In C++ a function declared in the private, protected, or public parts of a class is called a member function. These functions manipulate the data members of a class and have access to all members in the private, protected, or public access regions of a class. The definition of a member function is considered to be within the scope of its class. This implies that it can use the names of members of its class directly.

Example

// filename cpex10.c

```
#include <stdlib.h>
#include <string.h>
#include <stream.h>
```

```
// class declaration
class person {
  private:
    int id;
    char grade;
    // private member function
    char getgrade();
  protected:
    char *birthdate;
  public:
    char name[20];
    int course_number;
    char course_name[50];
    // constructor function
    person(char *cn, int ci, char *ccn, char cg);
    // destructor function
    ~person();
    // public member function
    void getinfo(char *cn, int *ci, char *ccn, char *cg);
};

// constructor function -- no return type
person::person(char *cn, int ci, char *ccn, char cg)
{
  strcpy(name, cn); id = ci;
  strcpy(course_name, ccn); grade = cg;
}

// destructor function -- no arg, no return type
person::~person()
{
  strcpy(name, "\0"); id = 0;
  strcpy(course_name, "\0"); grade = 0;
}

char person::getgrade()
{
  return(grade);
}

void person::getinfo(char *cn, int *ci, char *ccn, char *cg)
{
```

```
    strcpy(cn, name); *ci = id;
    strcpy(ccn, course_name); *cg = getgrade();
}

main()
{
  int mid;
  char mn[20], mcn[50], mg;

  person student("Bill", 9876,
          "Introduction to C++ Language", 'A');
  student.getinfo(mn, &mid, mcn, &mg);
  cout << "student name=" << mn << "\n";
  cout << "student number=" << mid << "\n";
  cout << "course name=" << mcn << "\n";
  cout << "grade=" << mg << "\n";
}
```

Output

```
student name=Bill
student number=9876
course name=Introduction to C++ Language
grade=A
```

6.5.3.1   static Member Functions

A static member function does not have a this pointer, so it can access nostatic members of its class only by using . or ->. There cannot be a static and a nonstatic member function with the same name and the same argument types. A static member function can use only the names of static members, enumerators, and nested types directly. static member functions cannot be const or virtual.

Example

// filename cpex11.c

```
#include <stdlib.h>
#include <string.h>
#include <stream.h>
```

```
// class declaration
class C {
  private:
    int i;
    static int si;
  protected:
    char c;
    static char sc;
  public:
    static char *sstr;
    C(int ci, char cc);
    ~C();
    // static member function
    // cannot be virtual or const
    static int geti_si_sc(int *ci, int *csi, char *csc);
};

// Initialize static members via class
int C::si = 1;
char C::sc = 'a';
char *C::sstr = "hello";

// constructor
C::C(int ci, char cc)
{
  i = ci; c = cc;
}

// destructor
C::~C()
{
  i = c = 0;
}

// define object
C obj(2, 'b');
int C::geti_si_sc(int *ci, int *csi, char *csc)
{
  *ci = obj.i;
  *csi = si; *csc = sc;
  return (99);
```

```
}

main()
{
  int mi, msi; char msc;
  int qi, qsi; char qsc;
  int svalue;
  C obj(2, 'b');

  svalue = obj.geti_si_sc(&mi, &msi, &msc);
  cout << "private obj member i=" << mi << "\n";
  cout << "static private obj member si=" << msi << "\n";
  cout << "static protected obj member sc=" << msc << "\n";
  cout << "static public obj member sstr=" <<
          obj.sstr << "\n";
  cout << "static function return value=" << svalue << "\n";

  // get values using class as qualifier
  C::geti_si_sc(&qi, &qsi, &qsc);
  cout << "private obj member i=" << qi << "\n";
  cout << "static private obj member si=" << qsi << "\n";
  cout << "static protected obj member sc=" << qsc << "\n";
}
```

Output

```
private obj member i=2
static private obj member si=1
static protected obj member sc=a
static public obj member sstr=hello
static function return value=99
private obj member i=2
static private obj member si=1
static protected obj member sc=a
```

6.5.3.2   const Member Functions

Member functions can be declared const, which does not permit them to change their value nor allow them to return a non-const reference or pointer to any data member. A const member function can be created by placing the keyword const after the argument list and before the opening brace of the function. A const member function may be called for const and non-const objects. const member functions cannot be static, and viceversa.

Example

```
// filename cpex12.c

#include <stdlib.h>
#include <string.h>
#include <stream.h>

// class declaration
class C {
  private:
    int i;
    const int permi;
  protected:
    char c;
    const char permc;
  public:
    const char *perms;
    C(int ci, int cpi, char cpc, char *cps);
    // const member function
    // cannot be static
    int getcic(int *ci ,int *cpi, char *cpc) const;
};

// constructor should initialize const data members
C::C(int ci, int cpi, char cpc, char *cps)
:permi(cpi), permc(cpc), perms(cps)
{
  i = ci;
}

int C::getcic(int *ci, int *cpi, char *cpc) const
{
  *ci = i;
  *cpi = permi; *cpc = permc;
  return (67);
}

main()
```

```
{
  int mi, mci, cvalue;
  char mcc;
  const char *ms;
  C obj(1, 9, 'z', "hello");

  cvalue = obj.getcic(&mi, &mci, &mcc);
  cout << "private obj member i=" << mi << "\n";
  cout << "const private obj member permi=" << mci << "\n";
  cout << "const protected obj member permc=" << mcc << "\n";
  cout << "const public obj member str=" <<
          obj.perms << "\n";
  cout << "return value of getcic=" << cvalue << "\n";
}
```

Output

```
private obj member i=1
const private obj member permi=9
const protected obj member permc=z
const public obj member str=hello
return value of getcic=67
```

6.5.3.3   inline Member Functions

The C++ language allows one to create functions that are not actually called, but their code is expanded in line at the point of each invocation. The is the equivalent of the C parameterized macro. The inline expansion of the function can be achieved by preceding the name of the function with the inline keyword.

Example

```
int i ;
class A {
  char *str;
  char *func() { return (str) };
};
```

is equivalent to

```
int i ;
class A {
  char *str;
  char *func();
}

inline char *A::func() { return (str); }
```

A member function defined in the class declaration is an implicit inline function. Thus, defining a function within a class declaration is equivalent to declaring it inline. If the definition of a member function is outside the class declaration, it can be made inline. In this case, a member function declaration should have keyword inline followed by the class name, a :: operator, and a function name.

Example

// filename cpex13.c

```
#include <stdlib.h>
#include <stream.h>
// class declaration
class C {
  private:
    int i;
  protected:
    char j;
  public:
    C(int ci, char cj) { i = ci; j = cj; };
    ~C() { i = 0; j = 0; };
    int getmax();
};

// equivalent of C parameterized macro
// i.e.expand the code at the point of invocation
inline int C::getmax()
{
  if ( i >= j )
   return(i);
  else
   return (j);
};
```

```
main()
{
  int ret_val;
  C obj(-9, 5);

  ret_val = obj.getmax();
  cout << "max(-9,5)=" << ret_val << "\n";
}
```

Output

```
max(-9,5)=5
```

6.5.3.4   The this pointer

The keyword `this` is an implicit pointer to the object for which the function is called in a nonstatic member function. The `this` pointer contains the address of a class object. The `this` pointer is not needed explicitly most of the time in a program. The address of a class object is useful in linked list types of programs with self-referential class objects.

Example

// filename cpex14.c

```
#include <stdlib.h>
#include <stream.h>

// class declaration
class divide {
  private:
    double num;
    long den;
    double result;
  public:
    divide(double cn, long cd);
    double getdiv() { return (result);};
};
```

```
divide::divide(double cn, long cd)
{
  // this, an implicit pointer to an object
  this->num = cn;
  this->den = cd;
  // equivalent of
  // num = cn; den = cd;
  result = this->num/this->den;
}

main()
{
  double ret_val;
  divide obj1(4.0, 2);
  divide obj2(13.2, 4);

  ret_val = obj1.getdiv();
  cout << "4.0/2=" << ret_val << "\n";
  ret_val = obj2.getdiv();
  cout << "13.2/4=" << ret_val << "\n";
}
```

Output

```
4.0/2=2
13.2/4=3.3
```

// filename cpex15.c

```
#include <stdlib.h>
#include <stream.h>

class C {
  public:
    int i;
    char c;
    char *s;
    C(int ci, char cc, char *cs) {
      // implicit this pointer can be used
      // to access members
      this->i = ci; this->c = cc; this->s = cs;
    };
```

```
    ~C() { this->i = this->c = 0; };
    // overloaded () operator
    C *operator->() { return (this); };
};

main()
{
  C object(9,'z',"Bye!");

  cout << "object->i=" << object->i << "\n";
  cout << "object->c=" << object->c << "\n";
  cout << "object->s=" << object->s << "\n";
}
```

Output

```
object->i=9
object->c=z
object->s=Bye!
```

6.5.4   Pointers to Members

A pointer can point to data members, member functions, and objects. The C++ language has two types of pointers: regular C pointers, which are the addresses of data variables, and member pointers, which are relative offsets into objects of a class. The member pointer operators are .* and ->*. The static members are referred to in a different way since the program contains only one copy for that class.

Example

// filename cpex16.c

```
#include <stdlib.h>
#include <stream.h>

// class declaration
class C {
  public:
    int i , j;
    C(int ci, int cj) { i = ci; j = cj; };
```

```
      int add() { return (i + j); }; };
};

main()
{
  // class data member pointer declaration
  int C::*pi; int C::*pj;
  // class function member pointer declaration
  int (C::*func)();
  C obj(2, 3);
  // get address of class members
  pi = &C::i; pj = &C::j; func = &C::add;
  // access members of object using .*
  cout << "obj.*pi=" << obj.*pi << "\n";
  cout << "obj.*pj=" << obj.*pj << "\n";
  cout << "obj.*func=" << (obj.*func)() << "\n";
}
```

Output

```
obj.*pi=2
obj.*pj=3
obj.*func=5
```

// filename cpex17.c

```
#include <stdlib.h>
#include <stream.h>

// class declaration
class C {
  public:
    int i , j;
    C(int ci, int cj) { i = ci ; j = cj ; };
    int add() { return (i + j); };
};

main()
{
  // class data member pointers declaration
  int C::*pi;
  int C::*pj;
```

```
    // class function member pointer declaration
    int (C::*func)();
    C *pobj;
    C obj(2, 3);

    // get address of specific object
    pobj = &obj;
    // get address of class members
    pi = &C::i; pj = &C::j; func = &C::add;
    // access members of object using ->*
    cout << "pobj->*pi=" << pobj->*pi << "\n";
    cout << "pobj->*pj=" << pobj->*pj << "\n";
    cout << "(pobj->*func)()=" << (pobj->*func)() << "\n";
}
```

Output

```
pobj->*pi=2
pobj->*pj=3
(pobj->*func)()=5
```

// filename cpex18.c

```
#include <stdlib.h>
#include <stream.h>

// class declaration
class C {
  public:
    int i , j;
    C(int ci, int cj) { i = ci; j = cj; };
    int add() { return (i + j); };
};

main()
{
  // data member pointers
  int *pi, *pj;
  C obj(1, 2);

  // get address of a specific object member
  pi = &obj.i; pj = &obj.j;
```

```
    cout << "*pi=" << *pi << "\n";
    cout << "*pj=" << *pj << "\n";
    cout << "obj.add=" << obj.add() << "\n";
}
```

Output

```
*pi=1
*pj=2
obj.add=3
```

6.5.5   Constructors and Destructors

6.5.5.1   Constructors

A member function with the same name as its class is called a constructor. A constructor is a function that is automatically called while creating an object of a class. Constructors are also invoked when the new operator is called. Constructors can be in the `private`, `protected`, or `public` parts of a class. A constructor often has parameters that receive information needed to initialize data fields. Classes do not have to have constructor functions. Constructor functions are needed only if objects need to be initialized. Constructors are not inherited.

For a constructor in the `private` part of a class, only `friend` functions can create objects of that class. For a constructor in the `protected` part, only `friend` functions or member functions of a derived class can create objects.

A default constructor is called for a class implicitly if no constructor has been declared and defined when a new object is created.

A copy constructor for a class is a constructor that can be used to copy an object of a class. A copy constructor for a class C is not allowed to take an argument of type C.

Constructors for elements of an array are called in the order of increasing addresses.

An object of a `class` with a constructor cannot be member of a union. Constructors cannot be declared `static`, `const`, `volatile`, `virtual`, or `void` (that is, no return type can be specified). A return statement in the body of a constructor may not specify a return value. One cannot take the address of a constructor. A constructor function can be overloaded. Member functions may be called in constructors.

Example

```
// filename cpex19.c

#include <stdlib.h>
#include <stream.h>

// class declaration
class C {
  private:
    int i;
  protected:
    int j;
  public:
    int k;
    // multiple constructor
    // constructor - no return type
    C(int ci, int cj);
    C(int ci, int cj, int ck);
    // destructor - no arguments and return type
    ~C();
    // sum of data members
    int getsij() { return (i+j); };
    int getsijk();
};

// constructor definition
C::C(int ci, int cj)
{
  cout << "Constructor 1 Initializing Members\n";
  i = ci; j = cj;
}

// constructor definition
C::C(int ci, int cj, int ck)
{
  cout << "Constructor 2 Initializing Members\n";
```

```
  i = ci; j = cj; k = ck;
}

// destructor definition
C::~C()
{
  cout << "Destructor Destroying Contents\n";
  i = j = k = 0;
}

int C::getsijk()
{
  return(i+j+k);
}

main()
{
  // object creation automatically invokes constructor
  C obj1(1,2);
  cout << "1+2=" << obj1.getsij() << "\n";

  C obj2(1,2,3);
  cout << "1+2+3=" << obj2.getsijk() << "\n";
}
```

Output

```
Constructor 1 Initializing Members
1+2=3
Constructor 2 Initializing Members
1+2+3=6
Destructor Destroying Contents
Destructor Destroying Contents
```

// filename cpex20.c

```
#include <stdlib.h>
#include <stream.h>

// class declaration
class C {
  private:
```

```
      int i;
      // constructor in private part
      // only friend function can create objects
      C(int ci, int cj, int ck);
    protected:
      int j;
    public:
      int k;
      // destructor
      ~C();
      friend void func();
      int getsum();
};

C::C(int ci, int cj, int ck)
{
  cout << "Constructor Initializing Members\n";
  i = ci; j = cj; k = ck;
}

C::~C()
{
  cout << "Destructor Destroying Contents\n";
  i = j = k = 0;
}

int C::getsum()
{
  return(i+j+k);
}

// constructor in private part
// friend function can create objects
void func()
{
  C obj(1,2,3);
  cout << "1+2+3=" << obj.getsum() << "\n";
}

main()
{
  func();
```

```
}
```

Output

```
Constructor Initializing Members
1+2+3=6
Destructor Destroying Contents
```

// filename cpex21.c

```
#include <stdlib.h>
#include <stream.h>

// class declaration
class base {
  protected:
    int i,j;
    // constructor in protected part
    // only friend or member function of
    // derived class can create objects
    base(int ci, int cj, int ck);
  public:
    int k;
    // destructor
    ~base();
    friend void func();
    int getsum();
};

base::base(int ci, int cj, int ck)
{
  cout << "Base Constructor Intializing Members\n";
  i = ci; j = cj; k = ck;
}

base::~base()
{
  cout << "Base Destructor Destroying Contents\n";
  i = j = k = 0;
}
```

```cpp
int base::getsum()
{
  return(i+j+k);
}

// friend function
void func()
{
  // constructor in protected part
  // friend can create objects
  base Bobj1(1,2,3);
  cout << "1+2+3=" << Bobj1.getsum() << "\n";
}

class derived: public base {
  private:
    int l;
  public:
    // contains derived member and base constructor
    // member arguments for initialization
    derived(int, int, int, int);
    void newsum();
};

// derived constructor members followed by
// base constructor arguments
derived::derived(int cl, int ci, int cj, int ck)
:base(ci, cj, ck)
{
  cout << "Derived Constructor Initializing Members\n";
  i = ci; j = cj; k = ck; l = cl;
}

void derived::newsum()
{
  // constructor in protected part
  // member function of derived class
  // can create objects
  base Bobj2(5,6,7);
  cout << "5+6+7=" << Bobj2.getsum() << "\n";
}
```

```
main()
{
  // constructor function automatic invocation
  func();
  derived Dobj(1,2,3,4);

  cout << "1+2+3+4=" << Dobj.getsum() << "\n";
}
```

Output

```
Base Constructor Initializing Members
1+2+3=6
Base Destructor Destroying Contents
Base Constructor Initializing Members
Derived Constructor Initializing Members
1+2+3+4=9
Base Destructor Destroying Contents
```

// filename cpex22.c

```
#include <stdlib.h>
#include <values.h>
#include <stream.h>

class C {
  private:
    static int count;
    int num;
  public:
    // overloaded constructors have different argument type
    // and argument numbers
    C(int n) {
      num = ++count;
      cout << "Created Object" << count << "(" << n << ")\n";
    }
    C() {
      num = ++count;
      cout << "Created Object" << count << "\n";
    }
```

```
        // destructor
        ~C() {
          cout << "Deleted Object" << num << "\n";
        }
};

int C::count = 0;

main()
{
  C Object1(99);
  C Object2;
  C *Object3;

  // allocate Object3 using new
  // operator new invokes constructor
  Object3 = new(C);
  // deallocate Object3 using delete
  delete(Object3);
}
```

Output

```
Created Object1(99)
Created Object2
Created Object3
Deleted Object3
Deleted Object2
Deleted Object1
```

6.5.5.2 Destructors

A member function of a class C with a tilde (~) before the name of the class (for example. ~C) is called a destructor. Destructors are used to release any resources allocated by the object's constructor. The usual resource being acquired in a constructor is dynamically allocated memory. Destructors are invoked automatically to clean up the resources before an object is to be destroyed. They can also be invoked by the delete operator to free the resources.

The constructor for a class is not called during assignment; however, the destructor is called for the assigned object.

A destructor cannot have any arguments, nor can any return type be specified. Like constructor, it is not possible to take the address of a destructor. A destructor can be invoked for a const or volatile object.

A destructor cannot be declared static, const, or volatile; it can be virtual, however. Destructors cannot be inherited. Member functions can be called from within a destructor. An object of a class with a destructor cannot be a member of a union. Destructors for element arrays are called in reverse order of their construction.

If the object is automatic, the destructor is invoked when the scope of the object exits. If the object is static, the destructor is invoked when the program exits. If the object is dynamic, the destructor is invoked when operation delete is performed on the object.

Example

```
// filename cpex23.c

#include <stdlib.h>
#include <stream.h>

// class declaration
class C {
  private:
    int i;
  protected:
    int j;
  public:
    int k;

    // constructor - no return type
    C(int ci, int cj, int ck);
    // destructor - no arguments and return type
    ~C();
    int getsum();
};
```

```
C::C(int ci, int cj, int ck)
{
  cout << "Constructor Initializing Members\n";
  i = ci; j = cj; k = ck;
}

C::~C()
{
  cout << "Destructor Destroying Contents\n";
  i = j = k = 0;
}

int C::getsum()
{
  return (i+j+k);
}

void CreateObj()
{
  C obj(1, 2, 3);
  cout << "1+2+3=" << obj.getsum() << "\n";
  cout << "Destroy Object\n";
  // invoke destructor after return from function
  // scope of object exits
}

main()
{
  cout << "Create Object\n";
  CreateObj();
  cout << "Object Destroyed\n";
}
```

Output

```
Create Object
Constructor Initializing Members
1+2+3=6
Destroy Object
Destructor Destroying Contents
Object Destroyed
```

```
// filename cpex24.c

#include <stdlib.h>
#include <stream.h>

class C {
  private:
    int   n;
    static int count;
    public :
      C() {
        n = ++count;
        cout << "Constructor for Object#" << n << "\n";
      }
      ~C() {
      cout << "Destructor for Object#" << n << "\n";
      }
};

int C::count = 0;

void func()
{
  // The constructor for a class is not called during
  // assignment; however, the destructor is called for the
  // assigned object.
  C obj1, obj2 = obj1;
}

main()
{
  func();
}
```

Output

```
Constructor for Object#1
Destructor for Object#1
Destructor for Object#1
```

```
// filename cpex25.c

#include <stdlib.h>
#include <stream.h>

class C {
  private:
    int  n;
    static int count;
    public :
      C() {
        n = ++count;
        cout << "Constructor for Object#" << n << "\n";
      }
      ~C() {
      cout << "Destructor for Object#" << n << "\n";
      }
};

int C::count = 0;
void func()
{
  C obj1;
}

main()
{
  C *obj2;
  func();
  obj2 = new(C);
  // operator delete invokes destructor
  delete(obj2);
}
```

Output

```
Constructor for Object#1
Destructor for Object#1
Constructor for Object#2
Destructor for Object#2
```

6.5.6 Friends of a Class

A friend is a class or function that is not a member of a class, but is given permission to access private and protected members of that class. Friendship is declared using the C++ keyword friend before the name. Friends are not class members. Strictly speaking, they violate the encapsulation barrier of class members by their mere existence. On the other hand, friends could be considered a syntactic variant of class public members.

The advantage of friends is syntactic; that is, both member and friend are equally privileged. Friends have three disadvantages.

1. Friends add to the global namespace, in contrast to member functions and member classes, whose namespace is buried within a class, reducing the chance for namespace collisions.

2. Friendship is neither inherited nor transitive.

3. Friends do not bind dynamically; that is, they do not respond to polymorphism.

Example

```
// filename cpex26.c

#include <stdlib.h>
#include <stream.h>

// class declaration
class A {
  private:
    int i;
  protected:
    int j;
  public:
    int k;
    enum { e = 5 };
    A(int ci, int cj) { i = ci; j = cj; };
    // friend function
    friend int subtract(A X);
    // friend class
    friend class B;
};
```

```cpp
class B {
  private:
    // access class A member
    int a[A::e];
  public:
    void seta();
    void display() {
      int n;
      for(n = 0; n < A::e; n++)
        cout << "a[" << n << "]=" << a[n] << "\n";
    }
};

void B::seta()
{
  int n;
  for (n = 0; n < A::e; n++)
          a[n] = 2*n;
}

int subtract(A X)
{
  // friend function can access private and
  // protected members directly
  return(X.i - X.j);
}

main()
{
  int diff;
  A Aobj(9,1);
  B Bobj;

  diff = subtract(Aobj);
  cout << "9-1=" << diff << "\n";
  Bobj.seta();
  Bobj.display();
}
```

Output

```
9-1=8
```

```
a[0]=0
a[1]=2
a[2]=4
a[3]=6
a[4]=8
```

6.5.6.1   Friend Classes

A class B that is a friend of class A is known as a friend class. The class B has permission to access private, protected data and function members of class A. All the functions of class B are friends of class A. Here, class B is not automatically a friend of class A. A friend class cannot access private or protected members of a class derived from the class for which it is a friend.

Example

```
// filename cpex27.c

#include <stdlib.h>
#include <stream.h>

// class declaration
class A {
  private:
    int i;
  protected:
    int j;
  public:
    int k;
    enum { e = 5 };
    A(int ci, int cj, int ck) {
      i = ci; j = cj; k = ck;
    };
    // friend class
    friend class B;
};

class B {
  private:
    // friend class B can access class A member
    int a[A::e];
```

```
  public:
    void seta();
    void getsum(A X, int& res);
    void display() {
      int n;
      for(n = 0; n < A::e; n++)
        cout << "a[" << n << "]=" << a[n] << "\n";
    }
};


void B::getsum(A X, int& res){
  res = X.i + X.j + X.k;
}

void B::seta(){
  int n;
  for (n = 0; n < A::e; n++)
        a[n] = 2*n;
}

main()
{
  int sum;
  A Aobj(1,2,3);
  B Bobj;

  Bobj.getsum(Aobj,sum);
  cout << "1+2+3=" << sum << "\n";
  Bobj.seta();
  Bobj.display();
}
```

Output

```
1+2+3=6
a[0]=0
a[1]=2
a[2]=4
a[3]=6
a[4]=8
```

6.5.6.2 Friend Functions

A friend function of a class is a function that is not a member of the class but is permitted to use the `private` and `protected` member names from the class. A friend function first declared in a friend declaration is equivalent to an extern declaration. A friend function defined in a class declaration is `inline` and is in the scope of the class in which it is defined. A friend function can be a friend to more that one class.

Example

```
// filename cpex28.c

#include <stdlib.h>
#include <stream.h>

// class declaration
class A {
  private:
    int i;
  protected:
    int j;
  public:
    A(int ci, int cj) { i = ci; j = cj; };
    ~A() { i = j = 0; };
    // friend function
    friend int mod(A X);
};

// friend function mod
int mod(A X)
{
  // friend can access private and protected
  // members of a class
  int result;
  result = X.i/X.j;
  return(result);
}

main()
{
  int modvalue;
```

```
    A obj(113,5);

    modvalue = mod(obj);

    cout << "113 mod 5=" << modvalue << "\n";
}
```

Output

```
113 mod 5=22
```

6.5.7   Structure and Union Classes

The structure and union classes are alternative ways to specify a class. A struct is identical to a class, with the only difference being that all members of struct are public by default and private in a class. The union can be used to define a class. Like struct, all the members of union are public by default. The union classes cannot be used as base classes nor can they have base classes.

Example

```
// filename cpex29.c

#include <stdlib.h>
#include <stream.h>

// class declaration
class Class1 {
    // default declaration is private
    int i;
  protected:
    int j;
  public:
    Class1(int ci, int cj) { i = ci; j = cj; };
    ~Class1() { i = j = 0; };
    int subtract();
};

// equivalent struct declaration
struct Struct1 {
```

```
    // defualt declaration is public
    Struct1(int ci, int cj) { i = ci; j = cj; };
    ~Struct1() { i = j = 0; };
    int subtract();
  private:
    int i;
  protected:
    int j;
};

int Class1::subtract()
{
  return(i-j);
}

int Struct1::subtract()
{
  return(i-j);
}

main()
{
  Class1 Cobj(9,1);
  Struct1 Sobj(9,1);

  cout << "Cobj.subtract=9-1=" << Cobj.subtract() << "\n";
  cout << "Sobj.subtract=9-1=" << Sobj.subtract() << "\n";
}
```

Output

```
Cobj.subtract=9-1=8
Sobj.subtract=9-1=8
```

6.5.8 Nested Classes

A class declared within another class is called a nested class. The nested class is in the scope of its enclosing class. Member functions of a nested class have no special access to members of an enclosing class; they obey the usual access rules and vice versa. Static data members and member functions of a nested class can be defined in the global scope.

Example

```
// filename cpex30.c

#include <stdlib.h>
#include <stream.h>

// global variables

int i = 1, j = 2;

// class declaration
class enclose {
    int i;
  public:
    static int s;
    enclose(int ei) { i = ei; };
    ~enclose() { i = 0; };
    int abs();
    // nested class declaration
    class inner {
      public:
        int j;
        inner(int ij) { j = ij; };
        void ifunc(int x);
    };
    int addij(inner *Iobj) {
        return (i + Iobj->j);
    }
};

int enclose::abs()
{
  if (i < 0)
    return(-i);
  else
    return(i);
}
```

```
int enclose::s = 3;

// inner class function definition
void enclose::inner::ifunc(int x)
{
  // i = x; // error: cannot assign enclose i
  enclose::s = x;     // assign to static

  // global assignment can be in two ways
  ::i = x;   // assign to global i
  j = x;     // assign to global j

  cout << "global i=" << i << "\n";
  cout << "global ::i=" << ::i << "\n";
  cout << "global j=" << j << "\n";
  cout << "enclose s=" << enclose::s << "\n";
}

main()
{
  enclose OuterObj(-9);

  // inner nested class object declaration
  enclose::inner InnerObj(10);
  cout << "abs(-9)=" << OuterObj.abs() << "\n";

  InnerObj.ifunc(4);
  cout << "-9+4=";
  cout << OuterObj.addij(&InnerObj) << "\n";
}
```

Output

```
abs(-9)=9
global i=4
global ::i=4
global j=4
enclose s=4
-9+4=-5
```

6.6   Derived Classes

A derived class is a class that contains at least one base class. A derived class inherits the member functions and member data fields of its base class. Unless redefined in the derived class, members of `public` and `protected` parts of a base class can be referred to as if they were members of the derived class. There can be any number of levels of derivation; a base class can itself be derived from another class. A pointer to a derived class can be implicitly converted to a pointer to a public base class. Like a pointer, a reference to a derived class can be implicitly converted to a reference to a public base class.

6.6.1   Declaration

The declaration of a derived class introduces a new data type with data members, data functions, and base classes with access permissions of `private`, `protected`, and `public`. By default, all have `private` access permissions. The general form of a derived class is

```
class derived_class_name : access base_class_name
{
    derived class members
}
```

The permission of the base class members inside the derived class is determined by access modifier values. The access modifier values can be private, protected, and public. If the access permission for the base class is not specified, it is private by default, although public access for the base class is more common and useful. For a struct derived class, the access permission is public by default. The access permission of private, protected, and public to a base class in a derived class has the following effects:

- **`private`:** All the `protected` and `public` members of a base class become `private` members of a derived class.
- **`protected`:** All the `protected` and `public` members of a base class become `protected` members of a derived class.
- **`public`:** All the `protected` and `public` members of a base class become `public` members of a derived class.

These inheritances can be represented as in Figure 6-2.

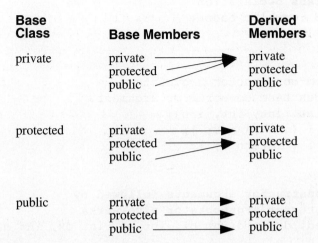

Figure 6-2
Derived class member access inheritance from base class

Example

```
// filename cpex31.c

#include <stdlib.h>
#include <stream.h>

// class declaration
class base {
    int i;
  public:
    int j;
    base(int, int);
    ~base() { i = j = 0; };
    int geti() { return i; };
};

base::base(int bi, int bj)
{
  i = bi; j = bj;
}
```

```
// derived class declaration
class derived : public base {
    int k;
  public:
    int l;
    // derived constructor arguments
    // includes base constructor arguments
    derived(int, int, int, int);
    ~derived() { k = l = 0; };
    int getk() { return k; };
};

// derived constructor arguments followed by
// base constructor arguments or vice-versa
// i.e derived::derived(int bi, int bj, int dk, int dl)
//      :base(bi, bj)
derived::derived(int dk, int dl, int bi, int bj)
:base(bi, bj)
{
    k = dk; l = dl;
};

main()
{
    // 8,9 initialized by derived constructor
    // 1,2 initialized by base constructor
    derived Dobj(8,9,1,2);

    cout << "base class members\n";
    cout << "i=" << Dobj.geti() << " ";
    cout << "j=" << Dobj.j << "\n";

    cout << "derived class members\n";
    cout << "k=" << Dobj.getk() << " ";
    cout << "l=" << Dobj.l << "\n";
}
```

Output

```
base class members
i=1 j=2
```

```
derived class members
k=8 l=9
```

// filename cpex32.c

```
#include <stdlib.h>
#include <stream.h>

// class declaration
class base {
  public:
    int i, j;
    base(int, int);
    ~base() { i = j = 0; };
};

base::base(int bi, int bj)
{
  i = bi; j = bj;
}

// derived class declaration
class derived : public base {
  public:
    int j, k;
    derived(int, int, int, int);
    ~derived() { j = k = 0; };
};

derived::derived(int dj, int dk, int bi, int bj)
:base(bi, bj)
{
    j = dj; k = dk;
};

main()
{
  derived Dobj(8,9,1,2);
  cout << "base i=" << Dobj.i << "\n";

  // derived class can access base class members
  cout << "derived object accessing base member j" << "\n";
```

```
  cout << "base j=" << Dobj.base::j << "\n";
  cout << "derived j=" << Dobj.j << "\n";
  cout << "derived k=" << Dobj.k << "\n";
}
```

Output

```
base i=1
derived object accessing base member j
base j=2
derived j=8
derived k=9
```

6.6.2 Access Declarations

Once the base class has been declared private, public, or protected in a
derived class, its member access can again be changed within the body of the
derived class. The general form for changing the access of a base member
within a derived class is

```
base_class::base_member
```

In private base class, protected and public members can be made protected or public again in a derived class. public base class protected
members of a base class can be made public again in a derived class.

Example

```
// filename cpex33.c

#include <stdlib.h>
#include <stream.h>

// class declaration
class base {
  private:
    int i;
  protected:
    int j;
  public:
    int k;
```

```
     base(int, int, int);
     ~base() { i = j = k = 0; };
     int geti() { return i; };
     int getj() { return j; };
};

base::base(int bi, int bj, int bk)
{
  i = bi; j = bj; k = bk;
}

// derived class declaration
class derived : private base {
  protected:
     // make base class protected member protected
     // in derived class
     base::j; // make j protected member
  public:
     // make base class public member public
     // in derived class
     base::k; // make k public member
     base::geti;
     base::getj;
     int l;
     derived(int, int, int, int);
     ~derived() { l = 0; };
};

derived::derived(int dl, int bi, int bj, int bk)

:base(bi, bj, bk)
{
    l = dl;
};

main()
{
  derived Dobj(4,3,2,1);

  cout << "base i=" << Dobj.geti() << "\n";
  cout << "base j=" << Dobj.getj() << "\n";
  cout << "base k=" << Dobj.k << "\n";
```

```
    cout << "derived l=" << Dobj.l << "\n";
}
```

Output

```
base i=3
base j=2
base k=1
derived l=4
```

6.6.3   Member Functions

A base class member function can be overridden by the derived class member function of the same name. The argument number, argument types, and return type of the member function of a derived class can be different from that of a base class.

Example

// filename cpex34.c

```
#include <stdlib.h>
#include <iostream.h>
// class declaration

class base {
  public:
    int i, j;
    base(int, int);
    ~base() { i = j = 0; };
    int rotate(char a);
};

base::base(int bi, int bj)
{
  i = bi; j = bj;
}

int base::rotate(char a)
{
  int tmp;
```

```
    tmp = i; i = j; j = tmp;
    cout << "base rotate function a=" << a << "\n";
    return(tmp);
}

// derived class declaration
class derived : public base {
  public:
    int k;
    derived(int, int, int);
    ~derived() { k = 0; };
    // derived declaration can override
    // base function declaration
    char rotate(int a);
};

derived::derived(int dk, int bi, int bj)
:base(bi, bj)
{
    k = dk;
};

char derived::rotate(int a)
{
  int tmp;

  tmp = i; i = j; j = k; k = tmp;
  cout << "derived rotate function a=" << a << "\n";
  return('a');
}

main()
{
  char c;
  derived Dobj(1,2,3);

  cout << "base i=" << Dobj.i << "\n";
  cout << "base j=" << Dobj.j << "\n";
  cout << "derived k=" << Dobj.k << "\n";

  // invoke derived class function
  c = Dobj.rotate(9);
```

```
    cout << "base i=" << Dobj.i << "\n";
    cout << "base j=" << Dobj.j << "\n";
    cout << "derived k=" << Dobj.k << "\n";
    cout << "rotate function return value=" << c << "\n";
}
```

Output

```
base i=2
base j=3
derived k=1
derived rotate function a=9
base i=3
base j=1
derived k=2
rotate function return value=a
```

6.6.4   Virtual Member Functions

One very important feature of C++ is to allow us to defer determination of what functions are called at run time. This ability is provided through the use of virtual functions. If a base class contains a virtual function func(), and a class derived from it also contains a function func() of the same return type, number, and types of arguments, then a call of func() for an object of class derived invokes derived::func. The derived class function overrides the base class function. If the function types are different, the virtual mechanism is suppressed.

The keyword virtual specifies membership, so a virtual function cannot be a global function or a static member, but can be a declared friend in another class. A virtual function can have default implementation. If a derived class does not implement the function, the default base class virtual function is invoked. The keyword virtual on a member function of a base class has the effect of allowing derived classes to replace the implementation of the function. The replacement is always called whenever the object in question is actually of the derived class. The impact is that the algorithm in the base class can be replaced in the derived class without affecting the operation of the base class. The replacement can be either full or partial, since the derived class operation can invoke the base class version if desired. The invocation of the member function is based on the type of class object pointed to and not the type of the pointer.

Example

```
// filename cpex35.c

#include <stdlib.h>
#include <stream.h>

// class declaration
class base {
  public:
    int i, j;
    base(int, int);
    // class with virtual function should have
    // virtual destructor
    virtual ~base() { i = j = 0; };
    // virtual function rotate, the derived class
    // has same return type and argument
    virtual int rotate(char a);
};

base::base(int bi, int bj)
{
  i = bi; j = bj;
}

int base::rotate(char a)
{
  int tmp;
  tmp = i; i = j; j = tmp;
  cout << "base rotate function arg=" << a << "\n";
  return(tmp);
}

// derived class declaration
class derived : public base {
  public:
    int k;
    derived(int, int, int);
    virtual ~derived() { k = 0; };
    // same declaration as in base class
    int rotate(char a);
```

```
};

derived::derived(int dk, int bi, int bj)
:base(bi, bj)
{
   k = dk;
};

int derived::rotate(char a)
{
  int tmp;

  tmp = i; i = j; j = k; k = tmp;
  cout << "derived rotate function arg=" << a << "\n";
  return(tmp);
}

main()
{
  int ret;
  derived Dobj(1,2,3);

  cout << "base i=" << Dobj.i << "\n";
  cout << "base j=" << Dobj.j << "\n";
  cout << "derived k=" << Dobj.k << "\n";

  // derived class function overrides
  // base class virtual function declaration
  // invoke derived class function
  ret = Dobj.rotate('z');
  cout << "ret=" << ret << "\n";
}
```

Output

```
base i=2
base j=3
derived k=1
derived rotate function arg=z
ret=2
```

```
// filename cpex36.c

#include <stdlib.h>
#include <stream.h>

// class declaration
class base {
  public:
    int i, j;
    base(int, int);
    virtual ~base() { i = j = 0;};
    // derived class has same function return type
    // and argument
    virtual int rotate(char a);
};

base::base(int bi, int bj)
{
  i = bi;j = bj;
}

int base::rotate(char a)
{
  int tmp;
  tmp = i;i = j;j = tmp;
  cout << "base rotate function arg=" << a << "\n";
  return(tmp);
}

// derived class declaration
class derived : public base {
  public:
    int k;
    derived(int, int, int);
    virtual ~derived() { k = 0;};
    int rotate(char a);
};

derived::derived(int dk, int bi, int bj)
:base(bi, bj)
{
    k = dk;
```

```
};

int derived::rotate(char a)
{
  int tmp;

  tmp = i; i = j; j = k; k = tmp;
  cout << "derived rotate function arg=" << a << "\n";
  return(tmp);
}

main()
{
  int ret;
  base Bobj(8,9);
  derived Dobj(1,2,3);
  base *p;

  // invoke base class function
  p = &Bobj;
  ret = p->rotate('a');
  cout << "base i=" << p->i << "\n";
  cout << "base j=" << p->j << "\n";
  cout << "ret=" << ret << "\n";

  // invoke derived class function
  p = &Dobj;
  ret = p->rotate('z');
  cout << "base i=" << p->i << "\n";
  cout << "base j=" << p->j << "\n";
  cout << "base k=" << Dobj.k << "\n";
  cout << "ret=" << ret << "\n";
}
```

Output

```
base rotate function arg=a
base i=9
base j=8
ret=8
derived rotate function arg=z
base i=3
```

```
base j=1
base k=2
ret=2
```

6.6.5   Constructors and Destructors

The constructor and destructor functions can be in the base class, derived class, or both. When an object is created, first the base class and then the derived class constructors are executed. The constructor functions are responsible for the initialization of objects. The destructor functions are invoked at the time of object deletion to free up memory or to perform other cleanup tasks. The derived class constructor is executed before the base class.

6.6.5.1   Constructors

If a derived class and base class both have constructors, the base class constructors are invoked before the derived class constructors. In the derived class, the name of the derived class constructor, base class constructor, and its arguments are separated by a colon. If a derived class has multiple base classes, they are separated by a comma. The general form of the derived class constructor is

```
derived_constructor(arg_list):base1_constructor(arg_list),
base2_constructor(arg_list),..
```

The derived class constructor should never call a pure `virtual` member function directly or indirectly, but it can invoke nonpure virtual member functions.

Example

```
// filename cpex37.c

#include <stdlib.h>
#include <stream.h>

class Class1 {
  public:
    Class1() { cout << "Class1 constructor\n"; }
    ~Class1() { cout << "Class1 destructor\n"; }
};
```

```cpp
class Class2 :  public Class1 {
  public:
    Class2() { cout << "Class2 constructor\n"; }
    ~Class2() { cout << "Class2 destructor\n"; }
};

class Class3 : public Class2 {
  public:
    Class3() { cout << "Class3 constructor\n"; }
    ~Class3() { cout << "Class3 destructor\n"; }
};

class Createmsg {
  public:
    Createmsg( int i ) {
    cout << "\nCreating object of Class" << i << "\n";
    }
};

class Destroymsg {
  public:
    Destroymsg( int i ) {
    cout << "Destroying object of Class" << i << "\n";
    }
};

main()
{
  Class1 *Obj1; Class2 *Obj2; Class3 *Obj3;

  Createmsg C1(1);  Obj1 = new(Class1);
  Destroymsg D1(1); delete (Obj1);

  // base class constructors are invoked before
  // derived class constructors
  Createmsg C2(2);  Obj2 = new(Class2);

  // derived class destructors are invoked before
  // base class destructors
  Destroymsg D2(2); delete (Obj2);
  Createmsg C3(3);  Obj3 = new(Class3);
```

```
   Destroymsg D3(3); delete (Obj3);
}
```

Output

```
Creating object of Class1
Class1 constructor
Destroying object of Class1
Class1 destructor
Creating object of Class2
Class1 constructor
Class2 constructor
Destroying object of Class2
Class2 destructor
Class1 destructor
Creating object of Class3
Class1 constructor
Class2 constructor
Class3 constructor
Destroying object of Class3
Class3 destructor
Class2 destructor
Class1 destructor
```

```
// filename cpex38.c

#include <stdlib.h>
#include <stream.h>

// class declaration
class base {
  protected:
    int i;
  public:
    base(int);
    ~base() { i = 0; };
    int negate() { return -i; };
};

base::base(int bi)
{
  i = bi;
```

```
}

// derived class declaration
class derived : public base {
    double j;
  public:
    // function declaration has
    // derived constructor argument list followed by
    // base constructor argument list
    derived(double, int);
    ~derived() { j = 0; };
    void getij(int *bi, double *dj);
};

// derived constructor argument list followed by
// base constructor argument list or vice-versa
// base variable bi is passed to base constructor
derived::derived(double dj, int bi)
:base(bi)
{
    j = dj;
};

void derived::getij(int *bi, double *dj)
{
  *bi = i; *dj = j;
}

main()
{
  int bx;
  double dy;

  derived Dobj(1.21,5);

  Dobj.getij(&bx, &dy);
  cout << "i=" << bx << " ";
  cout << "j=" << dy << "\n";
  cout << "-i=" << Dobj.negate() << "\n";
}
```

Output

```
i=5  j=1.21
-i=-5
```

6.6.5.2   Destructors

If a derived class and base class both have destructors, the derived class destructors are invoked before the base class destructors. When there is a chain of destructors, they are called in the opposite order used for the constructors. Thus, the destructor for a derived class is always called before the destructor for its base class. Destructors are not inherited. If a base or a member has a destructor and a derived class has no destructor, a default destructor is generated. This generated destructor calls the destructors for bases and members of the derived class. Generated destructors are `public`.

If there are multiple base classes for all non virtual base classes, destructors are called in reverse order by which the constructors for the classes were called. If the classes have no constructors, the destructors are called in the reverse order to the way they appear in the program.

Example

// filename cpex39.c

```
#include <stdlib.h>
#include <stream.h>

class Class1 {
  public :
    Class1() { cout << "Class1 constructor\n"; }
    ~Class1() { cout << "Class1 destructor\n"; }
};

class Class2 :  public Class1 {
  public:
    Class2() { cout << "Class2 constructor\n"; }
    ~Class2() { cout << "Class2 destructor\n"; }
};
```

```cpp
class Class3 : public Class2 {
  public:
    Class3() { cout << "Class3 constructor\n"; }
    ~Class3() { cout << "Class3 destructor\n"; }
};

class Createmsg {
  public:
    Createmsg( int i ) {
    cout << "\nCreating object of Class" << i << "\n";
    }
};

class Destroymsg {
  public:
    Destroymsg( int i ) {
    cout << "Destroying object of Class" << i << "\n";
    }
};

// object is within the scope of function func1
// destructor is invoked when returning from function
void func1()
{
  Createmsg C1(1);
  Class1 Obj1;
  Destroymsg D1(1);
}

// object is within the scope of function func2
// destructors are invoked by delete
void func2()
{
  Class2 *Obj2;
  Createmsg C2(2);  Obj2 = new(Class2);
  Destroymsg D2(2); delete (Obj2);
}

main()
{
  func1(); func2();
```

```
    // destructors are also invoked when exiting program
    Createmsg C3(3);
    Class3 Obj3;
    Destroymsg D3(3);
}
```

Output

```
Creating object of Class1
Class1 constructor
Destroying object of Class1
Class1 destructor
Creating object of Class2
Class1 constructor
Class2 constructor
Destroying object of Class2
Class2 destructor
Class1 destructor
Creating object of Class3
Class1 constructor
Class2 constructor
Class3 constructor
Destroying object of Class3
Class3 destructor
Class2 destructor
Class1 destructor
```

```
// filename cpex40.c

#include <stdlib.h>
#include <stream.h>

// class declaration
class abstract {
  protected:
    int i,j;
  public:
    abstract(int, int);
    // destructor for abstract class
    // is always virtual
    virtual ~abstract() { i = j = 0; };
    virtual double add() = 0;
```

```
};

abstract::abstract(int ci, int cj) {
  i = ci; j = cj;
}

// sum class declaration
class sum : public abstract {
    double k;
  public:
    // sum arg list followed by abstract arg list
    sum(double, int, int);
    ~sum() { k = 0; };
    double add() { return (i+j+k); };
};

// sum constructor argument list followed by
// abstract constructor argument list or vice-versa
sum::sum(double dk, int ci, int cj)
:abstract(ci, cj)
{
    k = dk; i = ci; j = cj;
}

main()
{
  sum Dobj(1.66,2,3);
  cout << "1.66+2+3=" << Dobj.add() << "\n";
}
```

Output

```
1.66+2+3=6.66
```

6.6.6 Abstract Classes

A class is called an abstract class if it has at least one pure `virtual` function.
A pure `virtual` function is a `virtual` function that has only the declaration,
of the function but no definition within the base class. This is usually achieved
by setting the member function declaration to zero. The general form of declaration is

```
virtual data_type function_name(arg_list) = 0;
```

Since an abstract class contains pure `virtual` functions for which there is no definition, no objects can be created by using a base class; thus the abstract class constitutes the incomplete class data type. Pointers to an abstract class can be created to support run-time polymorphism. Conceptually, the abstract class mechanism supports the notion of general concepts. Consider an abstract base class shape that has a `drawshape` member function. From the abstract class shape one can have concrete derived class variants, like rectangle, circle, or ellipse. Each of these derived classes reimplements the function `drawshape` overriding the action of shape::drawshape and drawing the particular shape represented by the class.

The abstract base class allows one to express the idea that any actual object created from a concrete class derived from the abstract base class will have the indicated member function, but there is not enough information to define it yet. Abstract base classes allow separation of the interface from implementation.

Figure 6-3 depicts a complete base class and an incomplete, or abstract, base class:

(a) Complete base class   (b) Abstract base class
(incomplete)

Figure 6-3
Complete and abstract base class

Example

// filename cpex41.c

```
#include <stdlib.h>
#include <stream.h>
#include <values.h>
```

```
// class declaration
class shape {
  public:
    int i, j;
    shape(int, int);
    virtual ~shape() { i = j = 0; };

    // definition creates abstract class which is an
    // incomplete class, no object of class can be created
    virtual int area() = 0;
    // virtual int draw() = 0;
};

shape::shape(int si, int sj)
{
  i = si; j = sj;
}

// complete class description
// using abstract class
class triangle : public shape {
  public:
    int a;
    int area();
};

int triangle::area()
{
  a = (i * j)/2;
  return (a);
}

// complete class description
// using abstract class
class rectangle : public shape {
  public:
    int a;
    int area();
};
```

```
int rectangle::area()
{
  a = i * j;
  return (a);
}

main()
{
  int area;
  triangle trig(5,10);
  rectangle rect(2,3);

  cout << "base of triangle=" << trig.i << "\n";
  cout << "height of triangle=" << trig.j << "\n";
  cout << "area of triangle(bxh/2)=" << trig.area() << "\n";
  cout << "length of rectangle=" << rect.i << "\n";
  cout << "breadth of rectangle=" << rect.j << "\n";
  cout << "area of rectangle(lxb)=" << rect.area() << "\n";
}
```

Output

```
base of triangle=5
height of triangle=10
area of triangle(bxh/2)=25
length of rectangle=2
breadth of rectangle=3
area of rectangle(lxb)=6
```

6.6.7 Multiple Base Classes

A derived class can contain more than one base class. The use of more than one base class is referred to as multiple inheritance or derived classes with multiple base classes. The order of multiple base classes in a derived class is not significant, except for default initialization by the constructors, cleanup by destructors, and for memory allocation.

Members of multiple base classes in a derived class can have the same names. Access to members with the same name should be nonambiguous with base qualification. A class can appear as a base class more than once as a parent of a derived class. This inheritance can be represented as shown in Figure 6-4.

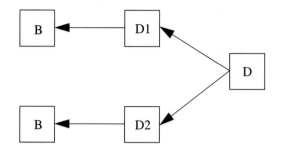

Figure 6-4
Multiple base classes

Example

```
// filename cpex42.c

#include <stdlib.h>
#include <stream.h>

// class declaration
class base1 {
  protected:
    int i;
  public:
    int j;
    base1(int, int);
    virtual ~base1() { i = j = 0; };
    int geti() { return i; };
};

base1::base1(int b1i, int b2j)
{
  i = b1i; j = b2j;
}

// class declaration
class base2 {
  protected:
```

```
      int k;
  public:
    base2(int);
    virtual ~base2() { k = 0; };
    int getk() { return k; };
};

base2::base2(int b2k)
{
  k = b2k;
}

// derived class declaration can have two base classes
class derived : public base1, public base2 {
  protected:
    int l;
  public:
    derived(int, int, int, int);
    ~derived() { l = 0; };
    int getl() { return l; };
};

// derived destructor arguments followed by base
// destructor aruguments
derived::derived(int dl, int b1i, int b1j, int b2k)
:base1(b1i, b1j), base2(b2k)
{
  l = dl;
};

main()
{
  derived Dobj(1,2,3,4);

  cout << "i=" << Dobj.geti() << " ";
  cout << "j=" << Dobj.j << " ";
  cout << "k=" << Dobj.getk() << " ";
  cout << "l=" << Dobj.getl() << "\n";
}
```

Output

```
i=2 j=3 k=4 l=1
```

6.6.8 Virtual Base Classes

A base class can be declared `virtual`. This is done when the derived classes have the same name base class, and only an instance of the base class is needed. The quality of being a `virtual` base class only applies to the use of a class as a base class. The class itself is not declared `virtual`.

The effect of the `virtual` keyword is that there is only one instance of the common base in a given derived class. Members of the common base class can be accessed directly since there is only one instance, as shown in Figure 6-5.

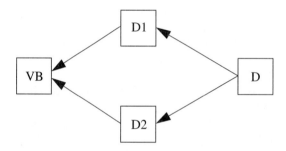

Figure 6-5
Virtual base classes

Example

```
// filename cpex43.c

#include <stdlib.h>
#include <stream.h>

class base {
  public:
    int i;
    base(int);
```

```
         virtual ~base() { i = 0; };
};

base::base(int bi)
{
   i = bi;
}

// derived1 contains virtual base class
class derived1 : virtual public base {
  public:
     int j;
     derived1(int, int);
     virtual ~derived1() { j = 0; };
};

derived1::derived1(int d1j, int bi)
:base(bi)
{
   j = d1j;
}

class derived2 : virtual public base {
  public:
     int k;
     derived2(int, int);
     ~derived2() { k = 0; };
};

derived2::derived2(int d2k, int bi)
:base(bi)
{
   k = d2k;
}

// derived class declaration
class derived3 : public derived1, public derived2 {
  public:
     int l;
     derived3(int, int, int, int);
     ~derived3() { l = 0; };
```

```
    int addall() { return (i+j+k+l); };
};
```

```
// virtual declaration of base class allows
// derived3 class to contain only one instance of base class
derived3::derived3(int d3l, int d1j, int d2k, int bi)
:base(bi), derived1(d1j, bi), derived2(d2k, bi)
{
   l = d3l;
};
```

```
main()
{
  derived3 Dobj(1,2,3,4);

  cout << "1+2+3+4=" << Dobj.addall() << "\n";
}
```

Output

```
1+2+3+4=10
```

6.7   Operator Overloading

The C++ language allows all operators to be overloaded except ::, sizeof, ., ?:, .*, and the preprocessing symbols # and ##. Most overloaded operators perform special operations relative to classes. This is done by declaring a function with a name consisting of the C++ keyword operator followed by one of the built-in operators, also known as operator functions.

An operator function defines the specific operations that the overloaded operator will perform relative to the class it is designed to work on. For example, a class compute that does mathematical operations might overload + to perform addition, - to perform subtraction, * to perform multiplication, and / to perform division, and so on. Table 6-3 lists the operators that can be overloaded.

The general form for member operator overloading function declarations is

```
operator_func_name operator#(arg_list)
```

Table 6-3 Operators That Can Be Overloaded

+	-	*	/	%	--
++	>	>=	<	<=	==
!=	&&	||	!	&	|
^	~	>>	<<	=	+=
-=	*=	/=	%=	^=	&=
|=	>>=	<<=	,	->	->*
()	[]	new	delete		

The name of the function name `operator_func_name` and data type of `arg_list` are usually the `class` name on which the operation needs to be performed. The `operator` is the C++ keyword, and # can be substituted for any of the operators in Table 6-3. Examples of operator overloading function declarations to perform mathematical operations are

```
compute operator+(compute a);
compute operator-(compute s);
compute operator*(compute m);
compute operator/(compute d);
```

The general form forthe member operator function definition is

```
data_type class_name::operator#(arg_list)
{
    statements
}
```

The functions `data_type` and `class_name` and data type of `arg_list` usually have that same name as that of `class` and # can be substituted for any of the operators from Table 6-3. For unary operators the argument list `arg_list` is empty; for binary operators it contains one parameter. Here is an example for overloaded operator +:

```
compute compute::operator+(compute a)
{
    addition statements
}
```

6.7.1   Unary Operators

A unary operator can be declared by a nonstatic member function taking no arguments. Thus, for unary operator #, x# is interpreted as x.operator#().

A unary operator can also be declared for a non member function by taking one argument that must be a class variable or reference to one. Thus, for any unary operator #, x# is interpreted as operator#(x).

6.7.1.1   Arithmetic, Address, Logical, and Bitwise Unary Operators

The unary operators +, -, &, *, !, and ~ can all be overloaded. The declarations for member and non member functions follow the unary operator rules.

Example

```
// filename cpex44.c

#include <stdlib.h>
#include <stream.h>

class unary {
  private:
    int *i;
  public:
    unary() {};
    unary(int *ci) { i = ci; };
    // overloaded member functions
    // no arguments
    void operator+();
    void operator-();
    void operator&();
    void operator*();
    void operator!();
    void operator~();
    void display() {
      cout << "*i=" << *i << "\n";
    }
};
```

```
void unary::operator+(){
  *i = +(*i);
}

void unary::operator-(){
  *i = -(*i);
}

void unary::operator&(){
  int j = 2;
  i = &j;
}

void unary::operator*(){
  *i = 3;
}

void unary::operator!(){
  *i = !(*i);
}

void unary::operator~(){
  *i = ~(*i);
}

main()
{
  int i = 01; int j = 01;
  unary Uobj1(&i), Uobj2(&j);
  unary plus, minus, address, derefer;
  unary lognot, bitnot;

  cout << "Implicit operator function invocation\n";
  plus = minus = address = derefer = lognot = bitnot = Uobj1;
  +plus; plus.display();
  -minus; minus.display();
  &address; address.display();
  *derefer; derefer.display();
  !lognot; lognot.display();
  ~bitnot; bitnot.display();
```

```
    // The operation below is identical to one above
    cout << "Explicit operator function invocation\n";
    plus = minus = address = derefer = Uobj2;
    plus.operator+(); plus.display();
    minus.operator-(); minus.display();
    address.operator&(); address.display();
    derefer.operator*(); derefer.display();
    lognot.operator!(); lognot.display();
    bitnot.operator~(); bitnot.display();
}
```

Output

```
Implicit operator function invocation
*i=1
*i=-1
*i=137475004
*i=3
*i=0
*i=-1
Explicit operator function invocation
*i=1
*i=-1
*i=137475004
*i=3
*i=0
*i=-1
```

// filename cpex45.c

```
#include <stdlib.h>
#include <stream.h>

// classobj declaration
class unary {
  private:
    int *i;
  public:
    unary() { i = 0; };
    unary(int *ci) { i = ci; };
    // friend member function has class
    // or class reference argument
```

```
      friend unary operator+(unary& x);
      friend unary operator-(unary& x);
      friend unary operator&(unary& x);
      friend unary operator*(unary& x);
      friend unary operator!(unary& x);
      friend unary operator~(unary& x);
      void display() {
        cout << "*i=" << *i << "\n";
      }
};

unary operator+(unary& x)
{
  *x.i = +(*x.i);
  return(x);
}

unary operator-(unary& x)
{
  *x.i = -(*x.i);
  return(x);
}

unary operator&(unary& x)
{
  int j = 2;
  x.i = &j;
  return(x);
}

unary operator*(unary& x){
  *x.i = 3;
  return(x);
}

unary operator!(unary& x){
  *x.i = !(*x.i);
  return(x);
}

unary operator~(unary& x)
{
```

```
    *x.i = ~(*x.i);
    return(x);
}

main()
{
    int i = 01; int j = 01;
    int z = 0;

    unary Uobj1(&i), Uobj2(&j);
    unary plus(&z), minus, address, derefer;
    unary lognot, bitnot;

    cout << "Implicit operator function invocation\n";
    plus = minus = address = derefer = lognot = bitnot = Uobj1;
    plus = +plus; plus.display();
    minus = -minus; minus.display();
    address = &address; address.display();
    derefer = *derefer; derefer.display();
    lognot = !lognot; lognot.display();
    bitnot = ~bitnot; bitnot.display();
}
```

Output

```
Implicit operator function invocation
*i=1
*i=-1
*i=137447348
*i=3
*i=0
*i=-1
```

6.7.1.2   Increment and Decrement Operators

Increment and decrement operators (++, --) can be overloaded in both prefix
and postfix mode. In prefix mode a member operator function is declared having no arguments or a friend operator function having one class or class reference argument. In postfix mode a member operator function is declared
having at least one int argument or a friend operator function having one
class or class reference argument and one int argument.

Example

```
// filename cpex46.c

#include <stdlib.h>
#include <stream.h>

// classobj declaration
class unary {
  private:
    int i, j;
  public:
    unary() {};
    unary(int ci, int cj) { i = ci; j = cj; };
    // prefix usage has no arguments
    void operator++();
    void operator--();
    // postfix usage needs int as an argument
    void operator++(int);
    void operator--(int);
    void display() {
      cout << "i=" << i << " ";
      cout << "j=" << j << "\n";
    }
};

void unary::operator++(){
  i = ++i; j = ++j;
}

void unary::operator--(){
  i = --i; j = --j;
}

void unary::operator++(int){
  i = i++; j = j++;
}

void unary::operator--(int){
  i = i--; j = j--;
}
```

```
main()
{
  unary Uobj(2,8);
  unary pre_plus, pre_minus;
  unary post_plus, post_minus;

  cout << "Implicit operator function invocation\n";
  pre_plus = pre_minus = post_plus = post_minus = Uobj;
  ++pre_plus; pre_plus.display();
  --pre_minus; pre_minus.display();
  post_plus++; post_plus.display();
  post_minus--; post_minus.display();

  // The operation below is identical to the one above
  cout << "Explicit operator function invocation\n";
  pre_plus = pre_minus = post_plus = post_minus = Uobj;
  pre_plus.operator++(); pre_plus.display();
  pre_minus.operator--(); pre_minus.display();
  post_plus.operator++(); post_plus.display();
  post_minus.operator--(); post_minus.display();
}
```

Output

```
Implicit operator function invocation
i=3 j=9
i=1 j=7
i=3 j=9
i=1 j=7
Explicit operator function invocation
i=3 j=9
i=1 j=7
i=3 j=9
i=1 j=7
```

// filename cpex47.c

```
#include <stdlib.h>
#include <stream.h>
```

```
class unary {
  private:
    int i, j;
  public:
    unary() {};
    unary(int ci, int cj) { i = ci; j = cj; };
    // friend member function prefix usage
    // has class argument
    friend unary operator++(unary x);
    friend unary operator--(unary x);
    // friend member function postfix usage
    // has class and int as arguments
    friend unary operator++(unary x,int);
    friend unary operator--(unary x,int);
    void display() {
      cout << "i=" << i << " ";
      cout << "j=" << j << "\n";
    }
};

unary operator++(unary x){
  unary res;
  res.i = ++x.i; res.j = ++x.j;
  return res;
}

unary operator--(unary x){
  unary res;
  res.i = --x.i; res.j = --x.j;
  return res;
}

unary operator++(unary x,int){
  unary res;
  res.i = x.i++; res.j = x.j++;
  return res;
}

unary operator--(unary x,int){
  unary res;
  res.i = x.i--; res.j = x.j--;
  return res;
```

```
}

main()
{
  unary Uobj(2,8);
  unary pre_plus, pre_minus;
  unary post_plus, post_minus;

  cout << "Implicit operator function invocation\n";
  pre_plus = pre_minus = post_plus = post_minus = Uobj;
  pre_plus = ++Uobj; pre_plus.display();
  pre_minus = --Uobj; pre_minus.display();
  post_plus = Uobj++; post_plus.display();
  post_minus = Uobj--; post_minus.display();
}
```

Output

```
Implicit operator function invocation
i=3 j=9
i=1 j=7
i=2 j=8
i=2 j=8
```

6.7.2   Binary Operators

A binary operator can be declared by a non static member function taking one argument. Thus, for any operator #, x#y is interpreted as x.operator#(y).

A binary operator can also be declared for a nonmember function taking two arguments, one of which should be a class variable or class reference argument. Thus, for any operator #, x#y is interpreted as operator#(x,y).

6.7.2.1   Arithmetic Operators

The arithmetic operators +, -, *, /, and % can all be overloaded. Since arithmetic operators are binary operators, the argument list to a non static member operator function declaration and general form contains one parameter. A nonmember or friend operator function can have two arguments having one class or class reference argument.

Example

```
// filename cpex48.c

#include <stdlib.h>
#include <math.h>
#include <stream.h>
#include <streambuf.h>

// class declaration
class complex {
  private:
    double real, imag;
  public:
    complex() { real = 0; imag = 0; };
    complex(double r, double i) {
      real = r; imag = i;
    };

    // overloaded binary arithmetic operators + - * /
    // have at least one class argument
    complex operator+(complex x);
    complex operator-(complex x);
    complex operator*(complex x);
    complex operator/(complex x);

    void display() {
      if(imag > 0)
        cout << real << "+" << imag << "i" << "\n";
      else
        cout << real << imag << "i" << "\n";
    }
};

complex complex::operator+(complex x)
{
  complex result;
  result.real = real + x.real;
  result.imag = imag + x.imag;
  return (result);
}
```

```
complex complex::operator-(complex x)
{
  complex result;
  result.real = real - x.real;
  result.imag = imag - x.imag;
  return (result);
}

complex complex::operator*(complex x)
{
  complex result;
  result.real = (real * x.real) - (imag * x.imag);
  result.imag = (imag * x.real) + (real * x.imag);
  return (result);
}

complex complex::operator/(complex x)
{
  double denom;
  complex result;
  denom = pow(x.real, 2.00) + pow(x.imag, 2.00);
  result.real = (real * x.real) + (imag * x.imag);
  result.imag = (imag * x.real) - (real * x.imag);
  result.real = result.real/denom;
  result.imag = result.imag/denom;
  return (result);
}

main()
{
  complex comp1(1.2, 3.4), comp2(5.6, 7.8);
  complex add, subtract, multiply, divide;

  cout << "Implicit overloaded operator function
           invocation\n";
  add = comp1 + comp2; add.display();
  subtract = comp1 - comp2; subtract.display();
  multiply = comp1 * comp2; multiply.display();
  divide = comp1 / comp2; divide.display();

  // The operation below is identical to the one above
```

```
   cout << "Explicit overloaded operator function
          invocation\n";
   add = comp1.operator+(comp2); add.display();
   subtract = comp1.operator-(comp2); subtract.display();
   multiply = comp1.operator*(comp2); multiply.display();
   divide = comp1.operator/(comp2); divide.display();
}
```

Output

```
Implicit overloaded operator function invocation
6.8+11.2i
-4.4-4.4i
-19.8+28.4i
0.360521+0.104989i
Explicit overloaded operator function invocation
6.8+11.2i
-4.4-4.4i
-19.8+28.4i
0.360521+0.104989i
```

// filename cpex49.c

```
#include <stdlib.h>
#include <math.h>
#include <stream.h>

// class declaration
class complex {
  private:
    double real, imag;
  public:
    complex() { real = 0; imag = 0; };
    complex(double r, double i) {
      real = r; imag = i;
    };
    // overloaded binary arithmetic operators + - * /
    // using class reference as an argument
    complex operator+(complex&);
    complex operator-(complex&);
    complex operator*(complex&);
    complex operator/(complex&);
```

```
    void display() {
      if(imag > 0)
        cout << real << "+" << imag << "i" << "\n";
      else
        cout << real << imag << "i" << "\n";
    }
};

complex complex::operator+(complex& x)
{
  complex result;
  result.real = real + x.real;
  result.imag = imag + x.imag;
  return (result);
}

complex complex::operator-(complex& x)
{
  complex result;
  result.real = real - x.real;
  result.imag = imag - x.imag;
  return (result);
}

complex complex::operator*(complex& x)
{
  complex result;
  result.real = (real * x.real) - (imag * x.imag);
  result.imag = (imag * x.real) + (real * x.imag);
  return (result);
}

complex complex::operator/(complex& x)
{
  double denom;
  complex result;
  denom = pow(x.real, 2.00) + pow(x.imag, 2.00);
  result.real = (real * x.real) + (imag * x.imag);
  result.imag = (imag * x.real) - (real * x.imag);
  result.real = result.real/denom;
  result.imag = result.imag/denom;
  return (result);
```

```
}

main()
{
  complex comp1(1.2, 3.4), comp2(5.6, 7.8);
  complex add, subtract, multiply, divide;

  cout << "Implicit overloaded operator function
           invocation\n";
  add = comp1 + comp2; add.display();
  subtract = comp1 - comp2; subtract.display();
  multiply = comp1 * comp2; multiply.display();
  divide = comp1 / comp2; divide.display();

  // The operation below is identical to the one above
  cout << "Explicit overloaded operator function
           invocation\n";
  add = comp1.operator+(comp2); add.display();
  subtract = comp1.operator-(comp2); subtract.display();
  multiply = comp1.operator*(comp2); multiply.display();
  divide = comp1.operator/(comp2); divide.display();
}
```

Output

```
Implicit overloaded operator function invocation
6.8+11.2i
-4.4-4.4i
-19.8+28.4i
0.360521+0.104989i
Explicit overloaded operator function invocation
6.8+11.2i
-4.4-4.4i
-19.8+28.4i
0.360521+0.104989i
```

// filename cpex50.c

```
#include <stdlib.h>
#include <math.h>
#include <stream.h>
```

```
// class declaration
class complex {
  private:
    double real, imag;
  public:
    complex() { real = 0; imag = 0; };
    complex(double r, double i) {
      real = r; imag = i;
    };
    // friend functions can have two arguments
    // having one class or class reference argument
    friend complex operator+(complex x, complex y);
    friend complex operator-(complex x, complex y);
    friend complex operator*(complex x, complex y);
    friend complex operator/(complex x, complex y);
    void display() {
      if(imag > 0)
        cout << real << "+" << imag << "i" << "\n";
      else
        cout << real << imag << "i" << "\n";
    }
};

complex operator+(complex x, complex y)
{
  complex result;
  result.real = x.real + y.real;
  result.imag = x.imag + y.imag;
  return (result);
}

complex operator-(complex x, complex y)
{
  complex result;
  result.real = x.real - y.real;
  result.imag = x.imag - y.imag;
  return (result);
}

complex operator*(complex x, complex y)
{
  complex result;
```

```
    result.real = (x.real * y.real) - (x.imag * y.imag);
    result.imag = (x.imag * y.real) + (x.real * y.imag);
    return (result);
}

complex operator/(complex x, complex y)
{
    double denom;
    complex result;
    denom = pow(y.real, 2.00) + pow(y.imag, 2.00);
    result.real = (x.real * y.real) + (x.imag * y.imag);
    result.imag = (x.imag * y.real) - (x.real * y.imag);
    result.real = result.real/denom;
    result.imag = result.imag/denom;
    return (result);
}

main()
{
    complex comp1(1.2, 3.4), comp2(5.6, 7.8);
    complex add, subtract, multiply, divide;

    add = comp1 + comp2; add.display();
    subtract = comp1 - comp2; subtract.display();
    multiply = comp1 * comp2; multiply.display();
    divide = comp1 / comp2; divide.display();
}
```

Output

```
6.8+11.2i
-4.4-4.4i
-19.8+28.4i
0.360521+0.104989i
```

6.7.2.2 Assignment Operators

The assignment operators =, +=, -=, *=, /=, %=, ^=, &=, |=, <<=, and >>= can all be used with the class objects to perform member wise assignment. If two objects are of the same type, each data member value of one object is assigned to the corresponding data member of the other object.

Example

```
// filename cpex51.c

#include <stdlib.h>
#include <stream.h>

// class declaration
class assign {
  private:
    int i, j;
  public:
    assign() { i = 0; j = 0; };
    assign(int ci, int cj) {
      i = ci; j = cj;
    };

    // overloaded binary assignment operators = += *= /= %=
    // have at least one class argument
    assign operator+=(assign x);
    assign operator-=(assign x);
    assign operator*=(assign x);
    assign operator/=(assign x);
    assign operator%=(assign x);
    void display() {
      cout << "i=" << i << " j=" << j << "\n";
    }
};


assign assign::operator+=(assign x)
{
  i += x.i;
  j += x.j;
  return (x);
}
assign assign::operator-=(assign x)
{
  i -= x.i;
  j -= x.j;
  return (x);
```

```
}

assign assign::operator*=(assign x)
{
  i *=  x.i;
  j *=  x.j;
  return (x);
}

assign assign::operator/=(assign x)
{
  i /= x.i;
  j /= x.j;
  return (x);
}

assign assign::operator%=(assign x)
{
  i %= x.i;
  j %= x.j;
  return (x);
}

main()
{
  assign obj1(4,12), obj2(2,4), obj3(3,7);
  assign add, subtract, multiply, divide, mod;

  cout << "Implicit operator function invocation\n";
  add = subtract = multiply = divide = mod = obj1;
  add += obj2; add.display();
  subtract -= obj2; subtract.display();
  multiply *= obj2; multiply.display();
  divide /= obj2; divide.display();
  mod %= obj3; mod.display();

  // The operation below is identical to the one above
  cout << "Explicit operator function invocation\n";
  add = subtract = multiply = divide = mod = obj1;
  add.operator+=(obj2); add.display();
  subtract.operator-=(obj2); subtract.display();
  multiply.operator*=(obj2); multiply.display();
```

```
    divide.operator/=(obj2); divide.display();
    mod.operator%=(obj3); mod.display();
}
```

Output

```
Implicit operator function invocation
i=6 j=16
i=2 j=8
i=8 j=48
i=2 j=3
i=1 j=5
Explicit operator function invocation
i=6 j=16
i=2 j=8
i=8 j=48
i=2 j=3
i=1 j=5
```

// filename cpex52.c

```
#include <stdlib.h>
#include <stream.h>

// class declaration
class assign {
  private:
    int i, j;
  public:
    assign() { i = 0; j = 0; };
    assign(int ci, int cj) {
      i = ci; j = cj;
    };
    // overloaded binary assignment operators = += *= /= %=
    // using class reference as an argument
    assign operator+=(assign&);
    assign operator-=(assign&);
    assign operator*=(assign&);
    assign operator/=(assign&);
    assign operator%=(assign&);
    void display() {
      cout << "i=" << i << " j=" << j << "\n";
```

```
      }
};

assign assign::operator+=(assign& x)
{
  i += x.i;
  j += x.j;
  return (x);
}

assign assign::operator-=(assign& x)
{
  i -= x.i;
  j -= x.j;
  return (x);
}

assign assign::operator*=(assign& x)
{
  i *=  x.i;
  j *=  x.j;
  return (x);
}

assign assign::operator/=(assign& x)
{
  i /= x.i;
  j /= x.j;
  return (x);
}

assign assign::operator%=(assign& x)
{
  i %= x.i;
  j %= x.j;
  return (x);
}

main()
{
  assign obj1(4,12), obj2(2,4), obj3(3,7);
  assign add, subtract, multiply, divide, mod;
```

```
cout << "Implicit operator function invocation\n";
add = subtract = multiply = divide = mod = obj1;
add += obj2; add.display();
subtract -= obj2; subtract.display();
multiply *= obj2; multiply.display();
divide /= obj2; divide.display();
mod %= obj3; mod.display();

// The operation below is identical to the one above
cout << "Explicit operator function invocation\n";
add = subtract = multiply = divide = mod = obj1;
add.operator+=(obj2); add.display();
subtract.operator-=(obj2); subtract.display();
multiply.operator*=(obj2); multiply.display();
divide.operator/=(obj2); divide.display();
mod.operator%=(obj3); mod.display();
}
```

Output

```
Implicit operator function invocation
i=6  j=16
i=2  j=8
i=8  j=48
i=2  j=3
i=1  j=5
Explicit operator function invocation
i=6  j=16
i=2  j=8
i=8  j=48
i=2  j=3
i=1  j=5
```

// filename cpex53.c

```
#include <stdlib.h>
#include <stream.h>

// class declaration
class assign {
  private:
```

```
      int i, j;
   public:
      assign() { i = 0; j = 0; };
      assign(int ci, int cj) {
         i = ci; j = cj;
      };
      // friend functions can have two arguments
      // having one class or class reference argument
      friend assign operator+=(assign& x, assign& y);
      friend assign operator-=(assign& x, assign& y);
      friend assign operator*=(assign& x, assign& y);
      friend assign operator/=(assign& x, assign& y);
      friend assign operator%=(assign& x, assign& y);
      void display() {
         cout << "i=" << i << " j=" << j << "\n";
      }
};

assign operator+=(assign& x, assign& y)
{
   x.i += y.i;
   x.j += y.j;
   return(x);
}

assign operator-=(assign& x, assign& y)
{
   x.i -= y.i;
   x.j -= y.j;
   return(x);
}

assign operator*=(assign& x, assign& y)
{
   x.i *= y.i;
   x.j *= y.j;
   return(x);
}

assign operator/=(assign& x, assign& y)
{
   x.i /= y.i;
```

```
    x.j /= y.j;
    return(x);
}

assign operator%=(assign& x, assign& y)
{
    x.i %= y.i;
    x.j %= y.j;
    return(x);
}

main()
{
    assign obj1(4,12), obj2(2,4), obj3(3,7);
    assign add, subtract, multiply, divide, mod;

    add = subtract =  multiply = divide = mod = obj1;
    add += obj2; add.display();
    subtract -= obj2; subtract.display();
    multiply *= obj2; multiply.display();
    divide /= obj2; divide.display();
    mod %= obj3; mod.display();
}
```

Output

```
i=6  j=16
i=2  j=8
i=8  j=48
i=2  j=3
i=1  j=5
```

// filename cpex54.c

```
#include <stdlib.h>
#include <stream.h>

// class declaration
class assign {
  private:
    int i, j;
  public:
```

```
    assign() { i = 0; j = 0; };
    assign(int ci, int cj) {
      i = ci; j = cj;
    };

    // overloaded binary assignment operators ^=  &= |=
    // <<= and >>= have at least one class argument
    assign operator^=(assign x);
    assign operator&=(assign x);
    assign operator|=(assign x);
    assign operator<<=(assign x);
    assign operator>>=(assign x);
    void display() {
      cout << "i=" << i << " j=" << j << "\n";
    }
};

assign assign::operator^=(assign x)
{
  i ^= x.i;
  j ^= x.j;
  return (x);
}

assign assign::operator&=(assign x)
{
  i &= x.i;
  j &= x.j;
  return (x);
}

assign assign::operator|=(assign x)
{
  i |=  x.i;
  j |=  x.j;
  return (x);
}

assign assign::operator<<=(assign x)
{
  i <<= x.i;
  j <<= x.j;
```

```
    return (x);
}

assign assign::operator>>=(assign x)
{
  i >>= x.i;
  j >>= x.j;
  return (x);
}

main()
{
  assign obj1(04,06), obj2(01,02);
  assign eor, and, or, shiftleft, shiftright;

  cout << "Implicit operator function invocation\n";
  eor = and = or = shiftleft = shiftright = obj1;
  eor ^= obj2; eor.display();
  and &= obj2; and.display();
  or |= obj2; or.display();
  shiftleft <<= obj2; shiftleft.display();
  shiftright >>= obj2; shiftright.display();

  // The operation below is identical to the one above
  cout << "Explicit operator function invocation\n";
  eor = and = or = shiftleft = shiftright = obj1;
  eor.operator^=(obj2); eor.display();
  and.operator&=(obj2); and.display();
  or.operator|=(obj2); or.display();
  shiftleft.operator<<=(obj2); shiftleft.display();
  shiftright.operator>>=(obj2); shiftright.display();
}
```

Output

```
Implicit operator function invocation
i=5 j=4
i=0 j=2
i=5 j=6
i=8 j=24
i=2 j=1
```

```
Explicit operator function invocation
i=5 j=4
i=0 j=
i=5 j=6
i=8 j=24
i=2 j=1
```

```
// filename cpex55.c

#include <stdlib.h>
#include <stream.h>

// class declaration
class assign {
  private:
    int i, j;
  public:
    assign() { i = 0; j = 0; };
    assign(int ci, int cj) {
      i = ci; j = cj;
    };
    // overloaded binary assignment operators ^= &= |=
    // <<= and >>= using class reference as an argument
    assign operator^=(assign&);
    assign operator&=(assign&);
    assign operator|=(assign&);
    assign operator<<=(assign&);
    assign operator>>=(assign&);
    void display() {
      cout << "i=" << i << " j=" << j << "\n";
    }
};

assign assign::operator^=(assign& x)
{
  i ^= x.i;
  j ^= x.j;
  return (x);
}

assign assign::operator&=(assign& x)
{
```

```
  i &= x.i;
  j &= x.j;
  return (x);
}

assign assign::operator|=(assign& x)
{
  i |=  x.i;
  j |=  x.j;
  return (x);
}

assign assign::operator<<=(assign& x)
{
  i <<= x.i;
  j <<= x.j;
  return (x);
}

assign assign::operator>>=(assign& x)
{
  i >>= x.i;
  j >>= x.j;
  return (x);
}

main()
{
  assign obj1(04,06), obj2(01,02);
  assign eor, and, or, shiftleft, shiftright;

  cout << "Implicit operator function invocation\n";
  eor = and = or = shiftleft = shiftright = obj1;
  eor ^= obj2; eor.display();
  and &= obj2; and.display();
  or |= obj2; or.display();
  shiftleft <<= obj2; shiftleft.display();
  shiftright >>= obj2; shiftright.display();

  // The operation below is identical to the one above
  cout << "Explicit operator function invocation\n";
  eor = and = or = shiftleft = shiftright = obj1;
```

```
   eor.operator^=(obj2); eor.display();
   and.operator&=(obj2); and.display();
   or.operator|=(obj2); or.display();
   shiftleft.operator<<=(obj2); shiftleft.display();
   shiftright.operator>>=(obj2); shiftright.display();
}
```

Output

```
Implicit operator function invocation
i=5 j=4
i=0 j=2
i=5 j=6
i=8 j=24
i=2 j=1
Explicit operator function invocation
i=5 j=4
i=0 j=2
i=5 j=6
i=8 j=24
i=2 j=1
```

```
// filename cpex56.c

#include <stdlib.h>
#include <stream.h>

// class declaration
class assign {
  private:
    int i, j;
  public:
    assign() { i = 0; j = 0; };
    assign(int ci, int cj) {
      i = ci; j = cj;
    };
    // friend functions can have two arguments
    // having one class or class reference argument
    friend assign operator^=(assign& x, assign& y);
    friend assign operator&=(assign& x, assign& y);
    friend assign operator|=(assign& x, assign& y);
    friend assign operator<<=(assign& x, assign& y);
```

```
      friend assign operator>>=(assign& x, assign& y);
      void display() {
        cout << "i=" << i << "j=" << j << "\n";
      }
};

assign operator^=(assign& x, assign& y)
{
  x.i ^= y.i;
  x.j ^= y.j;
  return (x);
}

assign operator&=(assign& x, assign& y)
{
  x.i &= y.i;
  x.j &= y.j;
  return (x);
}

assign operator|=(assign& x, assign& y)
{
  x.i |=  y.i;
  x.j |=  y.j;
  return (x);
}

assign operator<<=(assign& x, assign& y)
{
  x.i <<= y.i;
  x.j <<= y.j;
  return (x);
}

assign operator>>=(assign& x, assign& y)
{
  x.i >>= y.i;
  x.j >>= y.j;
  return (x);
}
```

```
main()
{
  assign obj1(04,06), obj2(01,02);
  assign eor, and, or, sleft, sright;

  cout << "Implicit operator function invocation\n";
  eor = and = or = sleft = sright = obj1;
  eor ^= obj2; eor.display();
  and &= obj2; and.display();
  or |= obj2; or.display();
  sleft <<= obj2; sleft.display();
  sright >>= obj2; sright.display();
}
```

Output

```
Implicit operator function invocation
i=5j=4
i=0j=2
i=5j=6
i=8j=2
i=2j=1
```

6.7.2.3   Bitwise Logical Operators

The binary operators &, |, ^, ~, >>, and << can be overloaded by passing member operator functions only one argument. Non member or friend operator functions have two arguments, with one argument that must be a class or class reference argument.

Example

```
// filename cpex57.c
```

```
#include <stdlib.h>
#include <stream.h>
```

```
// class declaration
class logical {
  private:
    int i, j;
```

```
  public:
    logical() { i = 0; j = 0; };
    logical(int ci, int cj) {
      i = ci; j = cj;
    };
    // overloaded binary logical operators & | ^ << >>
    // have at least one class argument
    logical operator&(logical x);
    logical operator|(logical x);
    logical operator^(logical x);
    logical operator<<(logical x);
    logical operator>>(logical x);
    void display(logical obj1, logical obj2, char *str) {
      cout << obj1.i << str << obj2.i << "=" << i << " ";
      cout << obj1.j << str << obj2.j << "=" << j << "\n";
    }
};

logical logical::operator&(logical x)
{
  logical result;
  result.i = (i & x.i);
  result.j = (j & x.j);
  return (result);
}

logical logical::operator|(logical x)
{
  logical result;
  result.i = (i | x.i);
  result.j = (j | x.j);
  return (result);
}

logical logical::operator^(logical x)
{
  logical result;
  result.i = (i ^ x.i);
  result.j = (j ^ x.j) ;
  return (result);
}
```

```
logical logical::operator>>(logical x)
{
  logical result;
  result.i = (i >> x.i);
  result.j = (j >> x.j);
  return (result);
}

logical logical::operator<<(logical x)
{
  logical result;
  result.i = (i << x.i);
  result.j = (j << x.j);
  return (result);
}

main()
{
  logical obj1(01, 02), obj2(03, 04);
  logical addr, or, eor;
  logical rshift, lshift;

  cout << "Implicit operator function invocation\n";
  addr = obj1 & obj2; addr.display(obj1, obj2, "&");
  or = obj1 | obj2; or.display(obj1, obj2, "|");
  eor = obj1 ^ obj2; eor.display(obj1, obj2, "^");
  rshift = obj1 >> obj2; rshift.display(obj1, obj2, ">>");
  lshift = obj1 << obj2; lshift.display(obj1, obj2, "<<");

  // The operation below is identical to the one above
  cout << "Explicit operator function invocation\n";
  addr = obj1.operator&(obj2); addr.display(obj1,
                    obj2, "&");
  or = obj1.operator|(obj2); or.display(obj1, obj2, "|");
  eor = obj1.operator^(obj2); eor.display(obj1, obj2, "^");
  rshift = obj1.operator>>(obj2); rshift.display(obj1, obj2,
                    ">>");
  lshift = obj1.operator<<(obj2); lshift.display(obj1, obj2,
                    "<<");
}
```

Output

```
Implicit operator function invocation
1&3=1  2&4=0
1|3=3  2|4=6
1^3=2  2^4=6
1>>3=0  2>>4=0
1<<3=8  2<<4=32
Explicit operator function invocation
1&3=1  2&4=0
1|3=3  2|4=6
1^3=2  2^4=6
1>>3=0  2>>4=0
1<<3=8  2<<4=32
```

// filename cpex58.c

```
#include <stdlib.h>
#include <stream.h>

// class declaration
class logical {
  private:
    int i, j;
  public:
    logical() { i = 0; j = 0; };
    logical(int ci, int cj) {
      i = ci; j = cj;
    };
    // overloaded binary logical operators & | ^ << >>
    // using class reference as an argument
    logical operator&(logical&);
    logical operator|(logical&);
    logical operator^(logical&);
    logical operator<<(logical&);
    logical operator>>(logical&);
    void display(logical obj1, logical obj2, char *str) {
      cout << obj1.i << str << obj2.i << "=" << i << " ";
      cout << obj1.j << str << obj2.j << "=" << j << "\n";
    }
};
```

```
logical logical::operator&(logical& x)
{
  logical result;
  result.i = (i & x.i);
  result.j = (j & x.j);
  return (result);
}

logical logical::operator|(logical& x)
{
  logical result;
  result.i = (i | x.i);
  result.j = (j | x.j);
  return (result);
}

logical logical::operator^(logical& x)
{
  logical result;
  result.i = (i ^ x.i);
  result.j = (j ^ x.j) ;
  return (result);
}

logical logical::operator>>(logical& x)
{
  logical result;
  result.i = (i >> x.i);
  result.j = (j >> x.j);
  return (result);
}

logical logical::operator<<(logical& x)
{
  logical result;
  result.i = (i << x.i);
  result.j = (j << x.j);
  return (result);
}
```

```
main()
{
  logical obj1(01, 02), obj2(03, 04);
  logical addr, or, eor;
  logical rshift, lshift;

  cout << "Implicit operator function invocation\n";
  addr = obj1 & obj2; addr.display(obj1, obj2, "&");
  or = obj1 | obj2; or.display(obj1, obj2, "|");
  eor = obj1 ^ obj2; eor.display(obj1, obj2, "^");
  rshift = obj1 >> obj2; rshift.display(obj1, obj2, ">>");
  lshift = obj1 << obj2; lshift.display(obj1, obj2, "<<");

  // The operation below is identical to one above
  cout << "Explicit operator function invocation\n";
  addr = obj1.operator&(obj2); addr.display(obj1, obj2,
                    "&");
  or = obj1.operator|(obj2); or.display(obj1, obj2, "|");
  eor = obj1.operator^(obj2); eor.display(obj1, obj2, "^");
  rshift = obj1.operator>>(obj2); rshift.display(obj1, obj2,
                    ">>");
  lshift = obj1.operator<<(obj2); lshift.display(obj1, obj2,
                    "<<");
}
```

Output

```
Implicit operator function invocation
1&3=1 2&4=0
1|3=3 2|4=6
1^3=2 2^4=6
1>>3=0 2>>4=0
1<<3=8 2<<4=32

Explicit operator function invocation
1&3=1 2&4=0
1|3=3 2|4=6
1^3=2 2^4=6
1>>3=0 2>>4=0
1<<3=8 2<<4=32
```

```
// filename cpex59.c

#include <stdlib.h>
#include <stream.h>

// class declaration
class logical {
  private:
    int i, j;
  public:
    logical() { i = 0; j = 0; };
    logical(int ci, int cj) {
      i = ci; j = cj;
    };
    // friend functions can have two arguments
    // having one class or class reference argument
    friend logical operator&(logical x, logical y);
    friend logical operator|(logical x, logical y);
    friend logical operator^(logical x, logical y);
    friend logical operator<<(logical x, logical y);
    friend logical operator>>(logical x, logical y);
    void display(logical obj1, logical obj2, char *str) {
      cout << obj1.i << str << obj2.i << "=" << i << " ";
      cout << obj1.j << str << obj2.j << "=" << j << "\n";
    }
};

logical operator&(logical x, logical y)
{
  logical result;
  result.i = (x.i & y.i);
  result.j = (x.j & y.j);
  return (result);
}

logical operator|(logical x, logical y)
{
  logical result;
  result.i = (x.i | y.i);
  result.j = (x.j | y.j);
  return (result);
}
```

```
logical operator^(logical x, logical y)
{
  logical result;
  result.i = (x.i ^ y.i);
  result.j = (x.j ^ y.j) ;
  return (result);
}

logical operator>>(logical x, logical y)
{
  logical result;
  result.i = (x.i >> y.i);
  result.j = (x.j >> y.j);
  return (result);
}

logical operator<<(logical x, logical y)
{
  logical result;
  result.i = (x.i << y.i);
  result.j = (x.j << y.j);
  return (result);
}

main()
{

  logical obj1(01, 02), obj2(03, 04);
  logical addr, or, eor;
  logical rshift, lshift;

  cout << "Implicit operator function invocation\n";
  addr = obj1 & obj2; addr.display(obj1, obj2, "&");
  or = obj1 | obj2; or.display(obj1, obj2, "|");
  eor = obj1 ^ obj2; eor.display(obj1, obj2, "^");
  rshift = obj1 >> obj2; rshift.display(obj1, obj2, ">>");
  lshift = obj1 << obj2; lshift.display(obj1, obj2, "<<");

}
```

Output

```
Implicit operator function invocation
1&3=1  2&4=0
1|3=3  2|4=6
1^3=2  2^4=6
1>>3=0 2>>4=0
1<<3=8 2<<4=32
```

6.7.2.4 Relational and Logical Operators

The operators <, <=. ==, !=, >, >= , &&, | |, and ! can all be overloaded. Except for !, all are binary operators and non static member operator functions that require at least one parameter to the argument list. A friend operator function or nonmembers can have two arguments having one class or class reference argument.

Example

```
// filename cpex60.c

#include <stdlib.h>
#include <stream.h>

// class declaration
class relation {
  private:
    int i, j;
  public:
    relation() { i = 0; j = 0; };
    relation(int ci, int cj) {
      i = ci; j = cj;
    };
    // overloaded binary relational operators < <= == != >
    // >= && || have at least one class argument
    relation operator<(relation x);
    relation operator<=(relation x);
    relation operator==(relation x);
    relation operator!=(relation x);
    relation operator>(relation x);
    relation operator>=(relation x);
```

```
    relation operator&&(relation x);
    relation operator||(relation x);
    void display(char *str) {
      if (i && j)
        cout << "True: obj1 " << str << " obj2" << "\n";
      else
        cout << "False: obj1 " << str << " obj2" << "\n";
    }
};

relation relation::operator<(relation x)
{
  relation result;
  result.i = (i < x.i);
  result.j = (j < x.j);
  return (result);
}

relation relation::operator<=(relation x)
{
  relation result;
  result.i = (i <= x.i);
  result.j = (j <= x.j);
  return (result);
}

relation relation::operator==(relation x)
{
  relation result;
  result.i = (i == x.i);
  result.j = (j == x.j) ;
  return (result);
}

relation relation::operator!=(relation x)
{
  relation result;
  result.i = (i != x.i);
  result.j = (j != x.j);
  return (result);
}
```

```
relation relation::operator>(relation x)
{
  relation result;
  result.i = (i > x.i);
  result.j = (j > x.j);
  return (result);
}

relation relation::operator>=(relation x)
{
  relation result;
  result.i = (i >= x.i);
  result.j = (j >= x.j);
  return (result);
}

relation relation::operator&&(relation x)
{
  relation result;
  result.i = (i && x.i);
  result.j = (j && x.j);
  return (result);
}

relation relation::operator||(relation x)
{
  relation result;
  result.i = (i || x.i);
  result.j = (j || x.j);
  return (result);
}

main()
{
  relation obj1(1, 2), obj2(3, 4);
  relation lt, loe, eq;
  relation ne, gt, goe;
  relation land, lor;

  cout << "Implicit operator function invocation\n";
  lt = obj1 < obj2; lt.display("<");
  loe = obj1 <= obj2; loe.display("<=");
```

```
        eq = obj1 == obj2; eq.display("==");
        ne = obj1 != obj2; ne.display("!=");
        gt = obj1 > obj2; gt.display(">");
        goe = obj1 >= obj2; goe.display(">=");
        land = obj1 && obj2; land.display("&&");
        lor = obj1 || obj2; lor.display("||");

        // The operation below is identical to the one above
        cout << "Explicit operator function invocation\n";
        lt = obj1.operator<(obj2); lt.display("<");
        loe = obj1.operator<=(obj2); loe.display("<=");
        eq = obj1.operator==(obj2); eq.display("==");
        ne = obj1.operator!=(obj2); ne.display("!=");
        gt = obj1.operator>(obj2); gt.display(">");
        goe = obj1.operator>=(obj2); goe.display(">=");
        land = obj1.operator&&(obj2); land.display("&&");
        lor = obj1.operator||(obj2); lor.display("||");
}
```

Output

```
Implicit operator function invocation
True: obj1 < obj2
True: obj1 <= obj2
False: obj1 == obj2
True: obj1 != obj2
False: obj1 > obj2
False: obj1 >= obj2
True: obj1 && obj2
True: obj1 || obj2

Explicit operator function invocation
True: obj1 < obj2
True: obj1 <= obj2
False: obj1 == obj2
True: obj1 != obj2
False: obj1 > obj2
False: obj1 >= obj2
True: obj1 && obj2
True: obj1 || obj2
```

```
// filename cpex61.c

#include <stdlib.h>
#include <stream.h>

// class declaration
class relation {
  private:
    int i, j;
  public:
    relation() { i = 0; j = 0; };
    relation(int ci, int cj) {
      i = ci; j = cj;
    };

    // overloaded binary relational operators < <= == != >
    // >= && || using class reference as an argument
    relation operator<(relation&);
    relation operator<=(relation&);
    relation operator==(relation&);
    relation operator!=(relation&);
    relation operator>(relation&);
    relation operator>=(relation&);
    relation operator&&(relation&);
    relation operator||(relation&);

    void display(char *str) {
      if (i && j)
        cout << "True: obj1 " << str << " obj2" << "\n";
      else
        cout << "False: obj1 " << str << " obj2" << "\n";
    }
};

relation relation::operator<(relation& x)
{
  relation result;
  result.i = (i < x.i);
  result.j = (j < x.j);
  return (result);
}
```

```
relation relation::operator<=(relation& x)
{
  relation result;
  result.i = (i <= x.i);
  result.j = (j <= x.j);
  return (result);
}

relation relation::operator==(relation& x)
{
  relation result;
  result.i = (i == x.i);
  result.j = (j == x.j) ;
  return (result);
}

relation relation::operator!=(relation& x)
{
  relation result;
  result.i = (i != x.i);
  result.j = (j != x.j);
  return (result);
}

relation relation::operator>(relation& x)
{
  relation result;
  result.i = (i > x.i);
  result.j = (j > x.j);
  return (result);
}

relation relation::operator>=(relation& x)
{
  relation result;
  result.i = (i >= x.i);
  result.j = (j >= x.j);
  return (result);
}
```

```
relation relation::operator&&(relation& x)
{
  relation result;
  result.i = (i && x.i);
  result.j = (j && x.j);
  return (result);
}

relation relation::operator||(relation& x)
{
  relation result;
  result.i = (i || x.i);
  result.j = (j || x.j);
  return (result);
}

main()
{
  relation obj1(1, 2), obj2(3, 4);
  relation lt, loe, eq;
  relation ne, gt, goe;
  relation land, lor;

  cout << "Implicit operator function invocation\n";
  lt = obj1 < obj2; lt.display("<");
  loe = obj1 <= obj2; loe.display("<=");
  eq = obj1 == obj2; eq.display("==");
  ne = obj1 != obj2; ne.display("!=");
  gt = obj1 > obj2; gt.display(">");
  goe = obj1 >= obj2; goe.display(">=");
  land = obj1 && obj2; land.display("&&");
  lor = obj1 || obj2; lor.display("||");

  // The operation below is identical to one above
  cout << "Explicit operator function invocation\n";
  lt = obj1.operator<(obj2); lt.display("<");
  loe = obj1.operator<=(obj2); loe.display("<=");
  eq = obj1.operator==(obj2); eq.display("==");
  ne = obj1.operator!=(obj2); ne.display("!=");
  gt = obj1.operator>(obj2); gt.display(">");
  goe = obj1.operator>=(obj2); goe.display(">=");
  land = obj1.operator&&(obj2); land.display("&&");
```

```
    lor = obj1.operator||(obj2); lor.display("||");
}
```

Output

```
Implicit operator function invocation
True: obj1 < obj2
True: obj1 <= obj2
False: obj1 == obj2
True: obj1 != obj2
False: obj1 > obj2
False: obj1 >= obj2
True: obj1 && obj2
True: obj1 || obj2
Explicit operator function invocation
True: obj1 < obj2
True: obj1 <= obj2
False: obj1 == obj2
True: obj1 != obj2
False: obj1 > obj2
False: obj1 >= obj2
True: obj1 && obj2
True: obj1 || obj2
```

// filename cpex62.c

```
#include <stdlib.h>
#include <stream.h>

// class declaration
class relation {
  private:
    int i, j;
  public:
    relation() { i = 0; j = 0; };
    relation(int ci, int cj) {
      i = ci; j = cj;
    };
    // friend functions can have two arguments
    // having one class or class reference argument
    friend relation operator<(relation x, relation y);
    friend relation operator<=(relation x, relation y);
```

```
      friend relation operator==(relation x, relation y);
      friend relation operator!=(relation x, relation y);
      friend relation operator>(relation x, relation y);
      friend relation operator>=(relation x, relation y);
      friend relation operator&&(relation x, relation y);
      friend relation operator||(relation x, relation y);
      void display(char *str) {
        if (i && j)
          cout << "True: obj1 " << str << " obj2" << "\n";
        else
          cout << "False: obj1 " << str << " obj2" << "\n";
      }
};

relation operator<(relation x, relation y)
{
   relation result;
   result.i = (x.i < y.i);
   result.j = (x.j < y.j);
   return (result);
}

relation operator<=(relation x, relation y)
{
   relation result;
   result.i = (x.i <= y.i);
   result.j = (x.j <= y.j);
   return (result);
}

relation operator==(relation x, relation y)
{
   relation result;
   result.i = (x.i == y.i);
   result.j = (x.j == y.j) ;
   return (result);
}

relation operator!=(relation x, relation y)
{
   relation result;
   result.i = (x.i != y.i);
```

```
  result.j = (x.j != y.j);
  return (result);
}

relation operator>(relation x, relation y)
{
  relation result;
  result.i = (x.i > y.i);
  result.j = (x.j > y.j);
  return (result);
}

relation operator>=(relation x, relation y)
{
  relation result;
  result.i = (x.i >= y.i);
  result.j = (x.j >= y.j);
  return (result);
}

relation operator&&(relation x, relation y)
{
  relation result;
  result.i = (x.i && y.i);
  result.j = (x.j && y.j);
  return (result);
}

relation operator||(relation x, relation y)
{
  relation result;
  result.i = (x.i || y.i);
  result.j = (x.j || y.j);
  return (result);
}

main()
{
  relation obj1(1, 2), obj2(3, 4);
  relation lt, loe, eq;
  relation ne, gt, goe;
  relation land, lor;
```

```
  lt = obj1 < obj2; lt.display("<");
  loe = obj1 <= obj2; loe.display("<=");
  eq = obj1 == obj2; eq.display("==");
  ne = obj1 != obj2; ne.display("!=");
  gt = obj1 > obj2; gt.display(">");
  goe = obj1 >= obj2; goe.display(">=");
  land = obj1 && obj2; land.display("&&");
  lor = obj1 || obj2; lor.display("||");
}
```

Output

```
True: obj1 < obj2
True: obj1 <= obj2
False: obj1 == obj2
True: obj1 != obj2
False: obj1 > obj2
False: obj1 >= obj2
True: obj1 && obj2
True: obj1 || obj2
```

6.7.3 Special Operators

The special operators ->, ->*, (), [], and comma (,) can all be overloaded.

- **Member Selector Operator ->**

The member select operator -> is considered a unary operator when overloading. The operator->() should return an object pointer or a reference to an object.

Example

// filename cpex63.c

```
#include <stdlib.h>
#include <stream.h>

class C {
  public:
```

```
    int i;
    char c;
    char *s;
    C(int ci, char cc, char *cs) {
      i = ci; c = cc; s = cs;
    };
    ~C() { i = c = 0; };
    // overloaded -> operator returns an object pointer
    C *operator->() { return (this); };
};

main()
{
  C object(1,'a',"hello");
  cout << "object->i=" << object->i << "\n";
  cout << "object->c=" << object->c << "\n";
  cout << "object->s=" << object->s << "\n";
}
```

Output

```
object->i=1
object->c=a
object->s=hello
```

• **Function Call Operator ()**

The operator () allows one to create an operator function that can be passed to an arbitrary number of arguments or operands.

Example

// filename cpex64.c

```
#include <stdlib.h>
#include <stream.h>

// arithmetic progression class declaration
class C {
  public:
    int a;
```

```
    int d;
    C(int ca, char cd) {
      a = ca; d = cd;
    };
    ~C() { a = d = 0; };
    // overloaded () operator allows arbitrary number of
    // arguments
    // calculate the nth term in a arithmetic progression
    int operator() (int n) { return (a + (n-1) * d); };
};

main()
{
  int t;
  C object(1,3);

  // invoke overloaded function operator()(12)
  t = object(12);
  cout << "arithmetic progression first term=1\n";
  cout << "difference=3\n";
  cout << "12th term is=" << t << "\n";
}
```

Output

```
arithmetic progression first term=1
difference=3
12th term is=34
```

- **Subscript or Array Index Operator []**

The operator [] is considered a binary operator when overloading. The operator[]() function is usually used for array subscripting.

Example

// filename cpex65.c

```
#include <stdlib.h>
#include <stream.h>
```

```
class C {
  private:
    char a[3];
  public:
    C(char ci, char cj, char ck) {
      a[0] = ci; a[1] = cj; a[2] = ck;
    };
    // overloaded [] operator used for array subscripting
    // & allows to use it on the left side of statement
    char &operator[] (int n) { return (a[n]); };
    // below is also syntatically correct but cannot
    // be used on the left side of assignment statement
    // char operator[] (int n) { return (a[n]); };
};

main()
{
  C object('a', 'b', 'z');

  cout << "object[1]=" << object[1] << "\n";
  // use of & allows to use
  // it on the left of assignment operator
  object[1] = 'z' ;
  cout << "object[1]=" << object[1] << "\n";
}
```

Output

```
object[1]=b
object[1]=z
```

- **Comma Operator ,**

Member operator, is considered a binary operator when overloading. The usual operation that should be used to perform when overloading is to discard the left-hand operand and assign the right-hand operand the value of the comma operation.

Example

// filename cpex66.c

```
#include <stdlib.h>
#include <stream.h>

class C {
  private:
    int a[2];
  public:
    C() {};
    C(int ci, int cj) {
      a[0] = ci; a[1] = cj;
    };
    // overload operator, used to return next object
    // values from the list
    C operator,(C Z) { return (Z); };
    void display() {
      cout << a[0] << " " << a[1] << "\n";
    }
};

main()
{
  C obj1(6,5), obj2(4,3), obj3(2,1);
  obj1.display();
  obj2.display();
  obj3.display();

  // return the last object values in the list
  cout << "assign last value in comma ";
  cout << "separated list\n";
  obj2 = (obj2, obj3, obj1);
  obj2.display();
}
```

Output

```
6 5
4 3
2 1
assign last value in comma separated list
6 5
```

6.7.4   new and delete Operators

The C++ reserved keywords new and `delete` can be overloaded. The new and `delete` are used in C++ for dynamic memory allocation and deletion. These operators can be overloaded to perform a particular type of user-defined allocation algorithm. They are equivalent to the C functions `malloc()` and `free()`, but have many advantages. The new creates an object of the given type to which it is applied and returns a pointer to it. The type must be an object type or pointer to a function. The functions cannot be allocated using new. Unlike function `malloc()`, the explicit type cast and `sizeof` operator is not needed when allocating memory using the operator new.

Example

```
// filename cpex67.c

#include <stdlib.h>
#include <stream.h>

main()
{
    int n, *p;
    int *pint; char *pchar;
    int *pi; char *pc; float *pf;

    // allocate space for an int using new
    p = new int;
    *p = 9;
    cout << "*p=" << *p << "\n";
    // deallocate p
    delete p;

    // allocate space for int using new and
    // initialize to a given value
    pint = new int(1);
    pchar = new char('a');
    cout << "*pint=" << *pint << "\n";
    cout << "*pchar=" << *pchar << "\n";

    // deallocate using delete
    delete pint; delete pchar;
    // allocate array of given data type
```

```
pi = new int[5];
pc = new char[10];
pf = new float[5];
pc = "hello";
for(n = 0; n < 5; n++) {
    pi[n] = n;
    pf[n] = n + (double)(n/9.0);
}

cout << "\ninteger array pi=";
for(n = 0; n < 5; n++)
    cout << pi[n] << ",";
cout << "\ncharacter array pc=";
for(n = 0; n < 5; n++)
    cout << pc[n] << ",";
cout << "\nfloat array pf=";
for(n = 0; n < 5; n++)
    cout << pf[n] << ",";
cout << "\n";

// deallocate arrays
delete [5] pi; delete [10] pc; delete [5] pf;
}
```

Output

```
*p=9
*pint=1
*pchar=a
integer array pi=0,1,2,3,4,
character array pc=h,e,l,l,o,
float array pf=0,1.11111,2.22222,3.33333,4.44444,
```

// filename cpex68.c

```
#include <stdlib.h>
#include <string.h>
#include <stream.h>

class bankacct {
  private:
    int sav_acct_no;
```

```
      int chk_acct_no;
   protected:
      char &acct_open_date;
   public:
      int sbalance;
      int cbalance;
      char name[20];
      // create account
      bankacct(char *cn, int cs, int csb, int cc, int ccb);
      // destroy account
      ~bankacct();

      // get account information using reference
      void getacctinfo(char *cn, int &cs, int &csb, int &cc,
                       int &ccb);
};

bankacct::bankacct(char *cn, int cs, int csb, int cc, int
ccb)
{
   cout << "Creating Bank Account\n";
   strcpy(name, cn);
   sav_acct_no = cs; sbalance = csb;
   chk_acct_no = cc; cbalance = ccb;
}

bankacct::~bankacct()
{
   cout << "Deleting Bank Account\n";
   strcpy(name, "\0");
   sav_acct_no = 0; sbalance = 0;
   chk_acct_no = 0; cbalance = 0;
}

void bankacct::getacctinfo(char *cn, int &cs, int &csb,
int &cc, int &ccb)
{
   strcpy(cn, name);
   cs = sav_acct_no; csb = sbalance;
   cc = chk_acct_no; ccb = cbalance;
}
```

```
main()
{
    bankacct *pa;
    char name[20];
    int sa, sb, ca, cb;

    // allocate and initialize an object bankacct using new
    pa = new bankacct("Jim", 9876, 87000, 5432, 1500);
    cout << "Account Information\n";
    pa->getacctinfo(name, sa, sb, ca, cb);
    cout << "customer name=" << name << "\n";
    cout << "savings account number #" << sa << "\n";
    cout << "savings balance=$" << sb << "\n";
    cout << "checking account number #" << ca << "\n";
    cout << "checking balance=$" << cb << "\n";
    // deallocate using delete
    delete pa;
}
```

Output

```
Creating Bank Account
Account Information
customer name=Jim
savings account number #9876
savings balance=$87000
checking account number #5432
checking balance=$1500
Deleting Bank Account
```

6.8   Function Overloading

Function overloading is one of the C++ polymorphism features that uses the same function name for two or more functions. Functions with the same name but different data type declarations for both functions and arguments can be overloaded. Functions having the same name and the same data type declaration for functions, but with different argument data type declaration or a different number of arguments, can also be overloaded.

6.8.1   Declaration Matching

Functions having the same name with a different data type declaration for the
return value and argument are overloaded. For example

```
/* valid overloading */
/* different data type declaration of function and */
/* different data type declaration of argument */
int func(int i);
double func(char i);
```

are overloaded but functions with the same name with a different data type
declaration for the return value but same data type declaration for the arguments are invalid as in

```
/* invalid overloading */
/* different data type declaration of function */
/* same data type declaration of arguments */
int func(int i);
double func(int i);
int func(int i, long j);
double func(int i, long j);
```

Example

```
// filename cpex69.c

#include <stdlib.h>
#include <stream.h>

float area(float l, int b)
{
  float a;
  a = l * b;
  cout << "Invoked function with return data type float,\n";
  cout << "argument data type of float and int.\n";
  return (a);
}

double area(double l, float b)
{
  double a;
```

```
   a = l * b;
   cout << "Invoked function with return data type double,\n";
   cout << "argument data type of double and float.\n";
   return (a);
}

main()
{
   float f;
   double d;

   // declaration matching: function's return data type
   // and argument data type are different
   f = area(2.2,3);
   cout << "Area of Rectangle(2.2x3)=" << f << "\n";
   d = area(1.5,2.5);
   cout << "Area of Rectangle(1.5x2.5)=" << d << "\n";
}
```

Output

```
Invoked function with return data type float,
argument data type of float and int.
Area of Rectangle(2.2x3)=6.6
Invoked function with return data type double,
argument data type of double and float.
Area of Rectangle(1.5x2.5)=3.75
```

6.8.2   Argument Matching

Functions that have the same name with the same declaration data type for a function but a different argument data type declaration or number of arguments are overloaded as in

```
/* overloaded function with different argument data type */
int func(int i);
int func(long i);

/* overloaded function with different argument numbers */
int func (int i);
int func (int i, int j);
```

Example

// filename cpex70.c

```
#include <stdlib.h>
#include <stream.h>

double area(float b, long h)
{
  double a;
  a = (b * h)/2;
  cout << "Invoked function with return data type double,\n";
  cout << "argument data type of float and long.\n";
  return (a);
}

double area(double b, float h)
{
  double a;
  a = (b * h)/2;
  cout << "Invoked function with return data type double,\n";
  cout << "argument data type of double and float.\n";
  return (a);
}

main()
{
  double a;

  // argument matching: different argument data type
  a = area(1.2,3);
  cout << "Area of Triangle=(2.2x3)/2=" << a << "\n";
  a = area(4.5,6.7);
  cout << "Area of Triangle=(1.5x2.5)/2=" << a << "\n";
}
```

Output

```
Invoked function with return data type double,
argument data type of float and long.
```

```
Area of Triangle=(2.2x3)/2=1.8
Invoked function with return data type double,
argument data type of double and float.
Area of Triangle=(1.5x2.5)/2=15.075
```

// filename cpex71.c

```c
#include <stdlib.h>
#include <values.h>
#include <math.h>
#include <stream.h>

double volume(double l, double b, double h)
{
  double v;
  v = l * b * h;
  cout << "Invoked function with return data type double,\n";
  cout << "3 arguments of data type double.\n";
  return (v);
}

double volume(double r, double h)
{
  double v;
  v = M_PI * pow(r,2.00) * h;
  cout << "Invoked function with return data type double,\n";
  cout << "2 arguments of data type double.\n";
  return (v);
}

double volume(double r)
{
  double v;
  v = (4 * M_PI * pow(r,3.00))/3;
  cout << "Invoked function with return data type double,\n";
  cout << "1 argument of data type double.\n";
  return (v);
}

main()
{
  double v;
```

```
// argument matching; different number of arguments

v = volume(1.1,2.2,3.3);
cout << "volume of cuboid=" << v << "\n";
v = volume(4.4,5.5);
cout << "volume of cylinder=" << v << "\n";
v = volume(6.6);
cout << "volume of sphere=" << v << "\n";
}
```

Output

```
Invoked function with return data type double,
3 arguments of data type double.
volume of cuboid=7.986
Invoked function with return data type double,
2 arguments of data type double.
volume of cylinder=334.517
Invoked function with return data type double,
1 argument of data type double.
volume of sphere=1204.26
```

6.8.3   Overloading Constructor Function

Constructor functions can also be easily overloaded. The overloaded constructor functions should have a different number of arguments and/or different argument data types. The overloading of constructor functions is useful when initializing the data members in different ways is necessary.

Example

```
// filename cpex72.c

#include <stdlib.h>
#include <stdio.h>
#include <string.h>
#include <stream.h>

class date {
  private:
    int day, month, year;
```

```
      char smonth[10];
   public:
      // overloaded constructor functions should have
      // different number of arguments and/or different
      // argument data type
      date (char *d);
      date (char *m, int d, int y);
      date (int d, int m, int y);

      void display();
      void sdisplay();
};

date::date(char *d)
{
   sscanf(d, "%d%*c%d%*c%d", &month, &day, &year);
}

date::date(char *m, int d, int y)
{
   strcpy(smonth,m);
   day = d; year = y;
}

date::date(int d, int m, int y)
{
   day = d; month = m; year = y;
}

void date::display()
{
   cout << month << "." << day;
   cout << "." << year << "\n";
}

void date::sdisplay()
{
   cout << smonth << " " << day;
   cout << " " << year << "\n";
}
```

```
main()
{
  date date1(01,01,94);
  date date2("01.01.95");
  date date3("January", 01, 96);

  date1.display();
  date2.display();
  date3.sdisplay();
}
```

Output

```
1.1.94
1.1.95
January 1 96
```

6.8.4   Address of Overloaded Function

The address of a function to be assigned to a pointer needs special care in C++. The pointer to a function should be declared in the proper manner to associate it with a given overloaded function to resolve ambiguity. The pointer should have the same return data type declarations, same number of arguments, and identical data type declarations for the arguments as that of the overloaded function to which it is to be assigned.

Example

// filename cpex73.c

```
#include <stdlib.h>
#include <stream.h>

float area(float l, int b)
{
  float a;
  a = l * b;
  return (a);
}
```

```
double area(double l, float b)
{
  double a;
  a = l * b;
  return (a);
}
main()
{
  float f;
  double d;
  float (*fp)(float, int);
  double (*dp)(double, float);

  fp = area; // points to area(float, int)
  dp = area; // points to area(double, float)
  f = fp(2.2,3);
  cout << "Area of Rectangle(2.2x3)=" << f << "\n";
  d = dp(1.5,2.5);
  cout << "Area of Rectangle(1.5x2.5)=" << d << "\n";
}
```

Output

```
Area of Rectangle(2.2x3)=6.6
Area of Rectangle(1.5x2.5)=3.75
```

6.9   Arrays, Pointers, and References

The arrays and pointers in C are important features that allow one to manipulate the given data type efficiently and elegantly. In C++ the array of objects and pointers to objects can be used to manipulate objects. Unlike a pointer, a reference is an implicit pointer that acts as another name for an object and cannot be changed.

6.9.1   Arrays of Objects

The arrays of object can be declared in the same way as any other variable. The array of objects can be initialized by specifying the initialization list like any other type of arrays. When an object is created, the value in the list is passed to the constructor function for initialization.

Example

```
// filename cpex74.c

#include <stdlib.h>
#include <stream.h>

class C {
  private:
    int i, j;
  public:
    C(int ci, int cj) { i = ci; j = cj; };

    int geti() { return i; };
    int getj() { return j; };
};

main()
{
  int k;

  // create array of objects
  // value in the list is passed to constructor
  C obj[3] =  { { 1, 2 }, { 3, 4 }, { 5, 6 }, };

  for(k=0; k < 3; k++ ) {
    cout << "object#" << k << "="
         << obj[k].geti() << " "
         << obj[k].getj() << "\n";
  }
}
```

Output

```
object#0=1 2
object#1=3 4
object#2=5 6
```

6.9.2 Pointers to Objects

A pointer is a C/C++ construct generally declared as

```
data_type *variable_name;
```

Pointers to objects and pointer arithmetic behave in the same way as pointers to any other variables. As in C, the class members should be accessed by arrow (->) for pointers and dot (.) with direct variables.

Example

```
// filename cpex75.c

#include <stdlib.h>
#include <string.h>
#include <stream.h>

class C {
  private:
    int i;
  protected:
    char c;
  public:
    int j;
    char str[10];
    C(int ci, char cc, char *cstr) {
        i = j = ci; c = cc; strcpy(str, cstr);
    };

    int geti() { return i; };
    char getch() { return c; };
};

main()
{
  int k;
  int *ip;
  char *sp;
  C obj(1, 'a', "hello");
  C *p;
```

```
    // pointer p points to obj
    // assign pointer to memory address using P rule
    p = &obj;
    cout << "p->geti()=" << p->geti() << "\n";
    cout << "p->getch()=" << p->getch() << "\n";
    cout << "p->str=" << p->str << "\n";
    ip = &obj.j;
    sp = obj.str;
    cout << "*ip=" << *ip << "\n";
    cout << "obj.str=" << obj.str << "\n";
}
```

Output

```
p->geti()=1
p->getch()=a
p->str=hello
*ip=1
obj.str=hello
```

// filename cpex76.c

```
#include <stdlib.h>
#include <string.h>
#include <stream.h>

class C {
  private:
    int i;
  protected:
    char c;
  public:
    int j;
    char str[10];
    C(int ci, char cc, char *cstr) {
        // implicit this pointer to object
        // can also be used to access members of class
        this->i = this->j = ci;
        this->c = cc;
        strcpy(this->str, cstr);
    };
```

```
        int geti() { return i; };
        char getch() { return c; };
    };

main()
{
    int k;
    C obj(1, 'a', "hello");
    C *p;

    p = &obj;

    cout << "p->geti()=" << p->geti() << "\n";
    cout << "p->getch()=" << p->getch() << "\n";
    cout << "p->str=" << p->str << "\n";
}
```

Output

```
p->geti()=1
p->getch()=a
p->str=hello
```

6.9.3 References

A reference is a C++ construct generally declared as

```
data_type &variable_name = initial_value ;
```

A reference is an alias or an alternative name for an object. A reference is an implicit pointer that acts as another name for an object and cannot be changed. Once a reference is bound to an object, it cannot point to another object.

References are usually preferred over pointers when a referred-to object is fixed. A reference must be initialized by giving it a preexisting object to refer to. Arguments can also be passed by reference rather than by value; this way the called function can manipulate the arguments. In C++ a function can return its argument by reference.

Example

```
// filename cex79.c

#include <stdlib.h>
#include <stream.h>

// swap values using pointers
void swap(int *a, int *b)
{
  register int tmp;
  tmp = *a; *a = *b; *b = tmp;
}

// swap values using reference
void swap(int &a, int &b)
{
  register int tmp;
  tmp = a; a = b; b = tmp;
}

main()
{
  int i, j;
  i = 1; j = 2;
  swap(&i, &j);

  cout << "swap using explicit pointers ";
  cout << "i=" << i << " j=" << j << "\n";

  i = 1; j = 2;
  swap(i, j);
  cout << "swap using reference i.e. implicit pointers ";
  cout << "i="<< i << " j=" << j << "\n";
}
```

Output

```
swap using explicit pointers i=2 j=1
swap using reference i.e implicit pointers i=2 j=1
```

```
// filename cpex78.c

#include <stdlib.h>
#include <iostream.h>

class C {
  private:
    int i, j;
  public:
    C(int ci, int cj) {
        i = ci; j = cj;
    };
    void swap(C &obj);
    int geti() { return i; };
    int getj() { return j; };
};

// swap values using class reference
void C::swap(C &obj)
{
  int tmp;
  tmp = obj.i;
  obj.i = obj.j;
  obj.j = tmp;
}

main()
{
  int k;
  C swapobj(1, 2);

  swapobj.swap(swapobj);
  cout << "swapobj.i=" << swapobj.geti() << "\n";
  cout << "swapobj.j=" << swapobj.getj() << "\n";
}
```

Output

```
swapobj.i=2
swapobj.j=1
```

6.10   Templates

A template means an object with a certain well-defined property. In C++, the keyword `template` allows declaration of classes and functions in terms of any type by providing a means of parameterization. Consider, for example, a flying kite template that specifies how to cut kites that all look pretty much the same; although they can be made of various materials such as paper, plastic, and colors, they all have the same basic shape. In the same way, a function or class `template` allows for the creation of similar looking functions or classes.

In C++, container classes are special kinds of classes. A container class is a class that holds an object of some other type. For example, lists, arrays, and sets are container classes. The type of objects contained is not important. Thus, the type of objecs contained can be an argument to a container class. The keyword `template` function or class declaration allows one to extend the notion of type of object contained by parameterizing it.

6.10.1 Function Templates

A function template is a global nonmember function that specifies how individual functions can be constructed. The general form of a function template declaration is

```
template<class T> data_type function_name(arg_list);
```

The function name declaration is prefixed by the keyword `template` followed by the parameter list enclosed in angle brackets < >. The angle brackets can contain more than one type of parameter. The type parameters are declared by the `class` keyword followed by an identifier T. The keyword `class` in the context of templates means identifier of any type T, not just that of a class. The expansion of the function definition is done by the compiler.

Example

```
// filename cpex79.c

#include <stdlib.h>
#include <stream.h>

// function template
// argument and return data of any type can be specified
```

```
template <class T>
T area(T l, T b)
{
  return (l * b);
}

main()
{
  int i; long l; float f; double d;

  i = area(1,2);
  cout << "area of rectangle=" << i << "\n";

  l = area(2,3);
  cout << "area of rectangle=" << l << "\n";

  f = area(3.4,4.5);
  cout << "area of rectangle=" << f << "\n";

  d = area(5.6,6.7);
  cout << "area of rectangle=" << d << "\n";
}
```

Output

```
area of rectangle=2
area of rectangle=6
area of rectangle=15.3
area of rectangle=37.52
```

6.10.2 Class Templates

A class template specifies how to construct individual classes. Unlike template functions, template classes need to be explicitly specified about the parameters over which they are instantiating. The general form of class template declaration is

```
template< class T> class class_name { private, public, pro-
tected members };
```

Like function declaration, the class name declaration is prefixed by the keyword `template` followed by a parameter list enclosed in angle brackets < >. The angle brackets can have more that one type or nontype parameters. The type parameters are declared by the `class` keyword followed by an identifier T. The keyword `class` in the context of templates means identifier of any type T, not just that of a class.

The class templates cannot be nested within other classes. The derived class template can have nontemplate base classes or base class templates. The class templates full expansion is done by the compiler.

Example

```
// filename cpex80.c

#include <stdlib.h>
#include <stream.h>

// template class declaration
template<class T>
class absolute {
  private:
    T i;
  public:
    absolute(const T&);
    T get_abs() const;
};

// template class constructor
// initialize i member
template<class T>
absolute<T>::absolute(const T& value)
:i(value)
{}

// template class member function
template<class T>
T absolute<T>::get_abs() const
{
  if(i > 0)
    return i;
  else
    return (-i);
```

```
}

main()
{
  absolute<int> x(-1);
  absolute<long> y(-100);
  absolute<float> z(-1.2);

  cout << x.get_abs() << "\n";
  cout << y.get_abs() << "\n";
  cout << z.get_abs() << "\n";
}
```

Output

```
1
100
1.2
```

6.10.3 Member Function Template

A member function of a class can be defined as a function template. The member function templates are defined outside their class declaration by prefixing them with a template declaration specification.

Example

```
// filename cpex81.c

#include <stdlib.h>
#include <stream.h>

// template class
template<class T>
class shape {
  private:
    T l, b;
  public:
    // constructor
    shape(T&, T&);
    T area();
```

```
};

// template constructor
template<class T>
shape<T>::shape(T& tl, T& tb)
{
  l = tl; b = tb;
}

// template member function
template<class T>
T shape<T>::area()
{
  return (l*b);
}

main()
{
  shape<int> r(2,3);

  cout << "area of rectangle(int)=" << r.area() << "\n";
  shape<float> s(2.5,2.5);
  cout << "area of rectangle(float)=" << s.area() << "\n";
}
```

Output

```
area of rectangle(int)=6
area of rectangle(float)=6.25
```

6.11 Exception Handling

Exception handling is a C++ feature which allows program to handle error conditions that are difficult to predict. The exception that could occur in a program are illegal integer divide, integer overflow exception, floating-point to integer conversion exception, floating-point divide by zero, floating point underflow, floating point overflow and so on.

Exception handling mechanism allows program encountering disastrous condition to continue execution of program gracefully.

Exception handling in C++ is achieved through C++ keywords `try`, `catch`, and `throw`. Statements that can generate exceptions are placed in `try` block. Immediately following the try block each exception handler beginning with the keyword `catch` is placed. Each handler has an argument of a different type. This allows different types to be handled and thrown in the try block.

Example

```
#include <stream.h>
#include <stream.h>

const OVERFLOW  0xffff
const UNDERFLOW 0x0001

/* class to print the exception message */
class exception {
  public:
    exception(char *string) {
      cout << "floating-point ";
      cout << string;
      cout << " exception occured";
      cout << endl;
    }
};

float divide(float numerator, float denominator) {
  if (denominator == 0)
    throw "floating-point divide by zero";
  if (numerator > OVERFLOW)
    throw exception("overflow");
  if (denominator < UNDERFLOW)
    throw execption("underflow");
  return (numerator/denominator);
}

main()
{
  try {
    divide(10, 0);
```

```
  }
  // catch handlers should immediately follow try
  catch(char *str) {
    cerr << str << endl;
  }
  catch(exception handler) {
    cout << "use proper values within valid range" << endl;
  }
}
```

6.12   The C++ Input/Output

C++, like C, has no built-in input or output facilities. The input and output in
C are via the stdio library and in C++ are handled via stream class libraries.
To use C++ stream class libraries for input and output, usually the header file
iostream.h or stream.h should be included. Since C++ is a superset of C,
all the input and output facilities provided by C can be used in C++ programs.
The stream classes are usually defined in iostream.h, stream.h,
fstream.h, and the like header files.

The iostream package allows a program to use any number of input or output
streams. Each stream has a source and sink, which can be standard input or
standard output or can be a file. The iostream library is implemented in two
layers. The lower layer is responsible for producing and consuming characters.
The upper layer performs formatting operations. These formatting operations
are implemented by the iostream class. The C++ iostream class library is as
specified in Table 6-4.

Table 6-4 C++ Input/Output Class Library

Class	Description
ios	Base stream class
istream	Input stream class
ostream	Output stream class
iostream	Input and output stream class
ifstream	Input file stream class
ofstream	Output file stream class
fstream	Input and output file stream class

The class hierarchy is as represented in Figure 6-6.

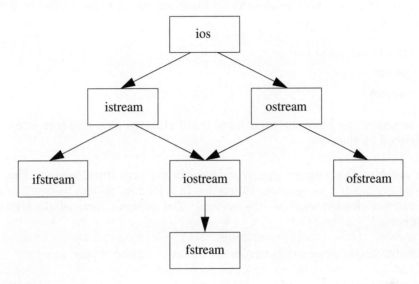

Figure 6-6
C++ iostream class library hierarchy

6.12.1 Stream Input/Output

When a C++ program is executed, four built-in classes are automatically opened, as shown in Table 6-5.

Table 6-5 Standard Input/Output Stream Classes

Stream	Description	Device
cin	Standard input stream	Keyboard
cout	Standard output stream	Screen
cerr	Standard error output stream	Screen
clog	Buffered standard error output stream	Screen

The stream input is via

- **istream**
- **iostream**

The program can have the predefined input stream cin or can also be defined by the user.

The stream output is via

- **ostream**
- **iostream**

The program can have the predefined input streams cout and cerr or can also be defined by the user.

The operators >> and << are overloaded to perform input/output. They can also be overloaded as operator functions. In addition, >> can be overloaded to the extract characters from the stream. The general form of the extractor function is

```
istream &operator>>(istream &stream, class_type &obj)
{
    statements
    return stream;
}
```

Similarly, << output operator can be overloaded as an insertion operator to insert characters into a stream. The general form of the inserter functions is

```
ostream &operator<<(ostream &stream, class_type obj)
{
    statements
    return stream
}
```

The operator functions are referred to as inserters and extractors, respectively.

The class istream has the member functions get(), getline(), ignore(), peek(), putback(), putback(), read(), seekg(), tellg(), and others that allow one to perform various operations on input stream.

Table 6-6 lists member functions and their actions.

Table 6-6 istream Member Function Actions

Member Function	Action
get()	Get a character from an input stream including white space
getline()	Read character until either limit or the delimiter is read
ignore()	Discard up to either number of characters or delimiter character
peek()	Return the next character from stream without actually reading it
putback()	Put a character back onto a stream
read()	Read a string of characters
seekg()	Move the position of get pointer in the stream
tellg()	Get the current position of the get pointer

The class ostream member functions are flush(), put(), seekp(), tellp(), write(), and others that allow one to perform various operations on the output stream. Table 6-7 lists these actions.

Table 6-7 ostream member function actions

Member Function	Action
flush()	Write buffered stream contents
put()	Write a single character to a stream
seekp()	Move the position of the put pointer in a stream
tellp()	Get the current position of the put pointer
write()	Write number of characters specified to a stream

Example

```
// filename cpex82.c

#include <stdlib.h>
#include <stream.h>
```

```
main()
{
  float anynum;
  char string[80];
  char character;
  int courseno; char grade;

  // i/o using stream cin, cout, cerr
  cout << "type a number\n";
  cin  >> anynum;  // "\n" is equivalent of endl
  cout << "input number is=" << anynum << endl;

  cout << "type a string\n";
  cin >> string;
  cout << "input string is=" << string << endl;

  cerr << "error: test error message\n";
  cerr << "error: test buffered error message\n";

  cout << "type in courseno and grade\n";
  cin >> courseno >> grade;
  cout << "courseno=" << courseno << " grade=" <<
          grade << "\n";
}
```

Output

```
type a number
input number is=10
type a string
input string is=hello
type in courseno and grade
courseno=101 grade=A
```

// filename cpex83.c

```
#include <stdlib.h>
#include <stream.h>

main()
{
  int i; float f; char c;
```

```
    cout << "type in an integer and a real number\n";
    cin >> i >> f;
    cout << "i=" << i << " f=" << f << endl;

    // flush the output buffer
    cout << flush;
    cout << "type in characters\n";
    cout << "type Ctrl-D when finished\n";

    // white spaces are not printed
    while(cin >> c)
        cout << c;
}
```

Output

```
type in an integer and a real number
99 1.21
i=99 f=1.21
type in characters
type Ctrl-D when finished
Good Morning
GoodMorning
```

// filename cpex84.c

```
#include <stdlib.h>
#include <stream.h>

main()
{
    unsigned char c;

    // white spaces are not printed
    // cin is object of type istream
    // cout is object of type ostream

    // get() is member function of class istream
    // put() is member function of class ostream
    // see iostream.h header file for other member functions
    cout << "type in characters\n";
```

```
    cout << "type Ctrl-D when finished\n";

  while((c = cin.get()) != EOF)
     cout.put(c);
}
```

Output

```
type in characters
type Ctrl-D when finished
This is a string
This is a string
```

// filename cpex85.c

```
#include <stdlib.h>
#include <string.h>
#include <stream.h>

main()
{
  char line1[80];
  char line2[80];

  // cin is object of type istream
  // cout is object of type ostream
  // getline(), read() are member functions of class istream
  // write() is a member function of class ostream
  // see iostream.h header file for member functions
  cout << "Enter a string" << endl;
  cin.getline(line1,80);
  cout << "standard output stream: " << line1 << endl;
  cout << "using member function write: ";
  cout.write(line1, strlen(line1));
  cout << endl;

  cout << "Enter a string" << endl;
  cin.read(line2,6);
  cout << "standard output stream: " << line2 << endl;
  cout << "using member function write: ";
  cout.write(line2, strlen(line2));
  cout << endl;
```

```
}
```

Output

```
Enter a string
This is line one
standard output stream: This is line one
using member function write: This is line one
Enter a string
This is line two
standard output stream: This i
using member function write: This i
```

// filename cpex86.c

```
#include <stdlib.h>
#include <string.h>
#include <stream.h>

class vehicle {
  private:
    int license;
  protected:
    int doors;
  public:
    char name[20];
    char color[20];
    vehicle() {};
    vehicle(char *n, char *c, int l){
      strcpy(name, n);
      strcpy(color, c);
      license = l;
    }
    // istream, ostream class are defined in iostream.h
    // overloaded >>(input), <<(output) operator
    // user defined extractor
    friend istream &operator>>(istream &stream,
          vehicle &obj);
    // user defined inserter
    friend ostream &operator<<(ostream &stream,
          vehicle obj);
};
```

```cpp
// input vehicle information
istream &operator>>(istream &stream, vehicle &obj)
{
  cout << "Enter name: ";
  stream >> obj.name;
  cout << "Enter color: ";
  stream >> obj.color;
  cout << "Enter license number: ";
  stream >> obj.license;
  return (stream);
}

// output vehicle information
ostream &operator<<(ostream &stream, vehicle obj)
{
  cout << "Name: ";
  stream << obj.name << endl;
  cout << "Color: ";
  stream << obj.color << endl;
  cout << "License: ";
  stream << obj.license << endl;
  return (stream);
}

main()
{
  vehicle car;

  // invoke overloaded << and >> operator functions
  cin >> car;
  cout << car;
}
```

Output

```
Enter name: RaceCar
Enter color: Red
Enter license number: 123456
Name: RaceCar
Color: Red
License: 123456
```

6.12.2 File Input/Output

The file input is achieved by binding a file name with an input stream using a variable of the class

*   **fstream**
*   **ifstream**

Since the ifstream class is derived from the istream class, it can also be used as regular stream input. The file should be open in appended mode unless the previously read data are to be discarded.

The file output is achieved by binding a file name with an output stream using a variable of the class

*   **fstream**
*   **ofstream**

Like file input since ofstream is derived from the fstream class, it can also be used as regular stream output.

The C++ language also allows file manipulation through close(), open(), read(), write(), and other member functions inherited from the istream and ostream classes. Table 6-8 lists member functions and actions.

Table 6-8 File Stream Class Member Function Actions

Member Function	Action
close()	Close the file linked to a stream
open()	Open a file and associate it with a stream
read()	Read specified number of characters from a stream
write()	Write specified number of characters to a stream

The open() function syntax is

```
void open(char *name, int mode, int prot_mode)
```

The possible values of the mode and actions are listed in Table 6-9.

Table 6-9 File Mode Value Actions

Mode	Action
ios::app	Append data to end of file
ios::ate	Seek to end of file and append data to end of file
ios::in	Open file for input only
ios::out	Open file for output only
ios::trunc	Discard previous contents of file
ios::nocreate	If file does not exists do not create new, open() fails
ios::noreplace	If file exists open() fails

Example

```
// filename cpex87.c

#include <stdlib.h>
#include <stream.h>

main()
{
   int i;
   char string[80];

   // file i/o
   // open file tdata1 for input
   ifstream infile("tdata1");
   if(!infile) {
      cerr << "Unable to open file tdata1 for input\n";
      exit(-1);
   }

   // read from input data file tdata1
   infile >> i >> string;
   cout << i << endl << string << endl;
   infile.close();

   // open file tdata for output
```

```
    ofstream outfile("tdata2");
    if(!outfile) {
       cerr << "Unable to open file tdata2 for output\n";
       exit(-1);
    }
    // write to data file tdata2
    outfile << "Introduction to C++ " << 'A' << endl;
    outfile << "Advanced C++ " << 'B' << endl;
    outfile.close();
}
```

Output

```
99
string
```

// filename cpex88.c

```
#include <stdlib.h>
#include <string.h>
#include <stream.h>

main()
{
  int i ;
  fstream datafile;
  char *string[] = { "one\n", "two\n", "three\n", };
  char buf[80] ;

  // file i/o
  // open file for input and output
  datafile.open("tdata3", ios::in | ios::out);
  if(!datafile) {
    cerr << "unable to open tdata3 for input and output"
            << endl;
    exit(-1);
  }

  // write to tdata3 using <<
  // and member function write
  datafile << "first\n";
  for(i=0; i<3; i++)
```

```
      datafile.write(string[i], strlen(string[i]));
   datafile << "last\n";
   // seek to beginning of tdata3

   datafile.seekg(0);
   // read tdata3 using >>
   // and member function read

   datafile >> buf;
   cout << buf;
   for(i=0; i<3; i++){
     datafile.read(buf, strlen(string[i]));
     cout << buf;
   }

   cout << endl;
   datafile >> buf;
   cout << buf << endl;
   datafile.close();
}
```

Output

```
first
one
two
three
last
```

// filename cpex89.c

```
#include <stdlib.h>
#include <string.h>
#include <stream.h>

class vehicle {
  private:
    int license;
  protected:
    int doors;
  public:
    char name[20];
```

```cpp
    char color[20];
    vehicle() {};
    vehicle(char *n, char *c, int l){
      strcpy(name, n);
      strcpy(color, c);
      license = l;
    }

    // istream, ostream class are defined in iostream.h
    // overloaded >>(input), <<(output) operator
    // user-defined extractor
    friend istream &operator>>(istream &stream,
          vehicle &obj);

    // user defined inserter
    friend ostream &operator<<(ostream &stream,
          vehicle obj);
};

// input vehicle information
istream &operator>>(istream &stream, vehicle &obj)
{
  cout << "Enter name: ";
  stream >> obj.name;
  cout << "Enter color: ";
  stream >> obj.color;
  cout << "Enter license number: ";
  stream >> obj.license;
  return (stream);
}

// output vehicle information
ostream &operator<<(ostream &stream, vehicle obj)
{
  stream << "Name: ";
  stream << obj.name << endl;
  stream << "Color: ";
  stream << obj.color << endl;
  stream << "License: ";
  stream << obj.license << endl;
  return (stream);
}
```

```
main()
{
  vehicle car;

  fstream fp("tdata4", ios::in | ios::out | ios::app);

  if(!fp) {
    cout << "unable to open data file\n";
    exit(-1);
  }

  cin >> car;
  cout << "The record entry is:\n";
  cout << car;

  // write the information to tdata4 file
  fp << car;
  fp.close();
}
```

Output

```
Enter name: RaceCar
Enter color: Yellow
Enter license number: 123456
The record entry is:
Name: RaceCar
Color: Yellow
License: 123456
```

6.12.3 Input/Ouput States

Every stream class has input/output states. They are also referred to as error states. The states can be examined via the member functions bad(), clear(), eof(), fail(), good(), and rdstate(). Table 6-10 lists the input/output states and their actions.

Table 6-10 Stream I/O State Functions and Their Actions

Member Function	Action
bad()	Returns true if some operation on stream failed
clear()	Sets the error state of stream
eof()	Returns true if the stream has reached end of file
fail()	Returns true if some operation like extraction on stream failed
good()	Returns true if eof(), bad(), and fail() are all false
rdstate()	Returns the current error state

Example

```
// filename cpex90.c

#include <stdlib.h>
#include <stream.h>

void state_err(int s)
{
  if(s&ios::eofbit)
    cout << "error eofbit:reached end of file\n";
  else if(s&ios::badbit)
    cout << "error badbit:stream i/o error\n";
  else if(s&ios::failbit)
    cout << "error failbit:stream operation on file
            failed\n";
}

main()
{
  int i, value ;
  ifstream infile("data");
  int state;

  int io_states[] ={ios::eofbit, ios::badbit, ios::failbit};
  if(!infile) {
    cerr << "error:unable to open file data\n";
```

```
    state = infile.rdstate();
    state_err(state);
  }

  // clear error state
  infile.clear(0);
  cout << "\nDirect State Access\n";
  value = infile.good();
  if(value)
    cout << "message: stream operation successful\n";
  cout << "\nError States\n";
  for(i=0; i<3; i++) {
    state_err(io_states[i]);
  }

  // set error state
  cout << "\nSet Error State\n";
  infile.clear(ios::eofbit);
  state = infile.rdstate();
  state_err(state);
  // directly access the state
  cout << "\nDirect State Access\n";
  value = infile.bad();
  if(!value)
    cerr << "error: stream bad error\n";
}
```

Output

```
error:unable to open file data
error badbit:stream i/o error
Direct State Access
message: stream operation successful
Error States
error eofbit:reached end of file
error badbit:stream i/o error
error failbit:stream operation on file failed
Set Error State
error eofbit:reached end of file
Direct State Access
error: stream bad error
```

6.12.4 Format States

The formatting in C++ is achieved through the flags that control the formatting states. The format can be changed via the member functions as listed in Table 6-11.

Table 6-11 Stream I/O Format Functions and Their Actions

Member Function	Action
fill()	Set the fill character and return previous character
flags()	Return the current flags
setprecision()	Set the number of significant digits to be printed and return the previous value
setf()	Set the specified flag on and return previous flags
setw()	Set the string buffer to specified width
unsetf()	Set the specified flag off and return previous flags
width()	Return the current minimum field width

The flags that control the output appearance can be changed by the setf() function. Table 6-12 lists the flags and their actions.

Table 6-12 Format Flags and Their Actions

Mode	Action
skipws	If set, skip white-space characters during input
left	If set, output is left justified
right	If set, output is right justified
internal	If set, add character between any leading sign or base indication and the value
dec, oct, hex	If set, display the output in decimal, octal, hexadecimal
showbase	if set, causes base of numeric value to be shown like a leading 0 for octal, a 0x or 0X for hexadecimal setting depending on the uppercase flag
showpoint	If set, decimal point and trailing zeros to be displayed for all floating-point output
showpos	If set, causes a leading + sign to be displayed before positive values
scientific	If set, causes scientific notation to be used for floating-point insertion
fixed	If set, by default size decimal places are displayed; If precision field is set, it uses number of digits equal to value set by function precision()

Table 6-12 Format Flags and Their Actions (continued)

Mode	Action
uppercase	If set, causes hexadecimal x and floating point e to be displayed in uppercase as X and E
unitbuf	If set, buffer the output, flush the buffer after each insertion operation
stdio	If set, flush stream after each output and write to the physical disk

Example

```
// filename cpex91.c

#include <stdlib.h>
#include <stream.h>

void display_flags()
{
  int i, j;
  long flag;
  char *flags[] = {
    "skipws",
    "left",
    "right",
    "internal",
    "dec",
    "oct",
    "hex",
    "showbase",
    "showpoint",
    "uppercase",
    "showpos",
    "scientific",
    "unitbuf",
    "stdio",
  };

  // print current flag format
  flag = cout.flags();
  cout << "flag" << " state" << endl;
```

```
    cout << "----" << " -----" << endl;
    for(i=1, j=0; i<ios::stdio; i=i<<1, j++) {
      if(i&flag)
        cout << flags[j] << " on" << endl;
      else
        cout << flags[j] << " off" << endl;
    }
}

main()
{
  int n = 10;
  float f = -1.21;
  char *str = "happy birthday";

  // set flags
  cout.setf(ios::left | ios::showpos | ios::scientific);

  // unset flags
  cout.unsetf(ios::internal | ios::showpoint | ios::stdio);
  display_flags();
  cout << endl;
  cout << "n=" << n << " f=" << f;
  cout << " str=" << str << endl;
}
```

Output

```
flag state
---- -----
skipws on
left on
right off
internal off
dec off
oct off
hex off
showbase off
showpoint off
uppercase off
showpos on
scientific on
```

```
unitbuf off
stdio off
n=+10 f=-1.210000e+00 str=happy birthday
```

// filename cpex92.c

```
#include <stdlib.h>
#include <stream.h>

main()
{
  int num = 100;
  cout << "octal=" << oct << num << endl;
  cout << "decimal=" << dec << num << endl;
  cout << "hex=" << hex << num << endl;
  // set to octal base
  cout << setbase(8);
  cout << "octal=" << num << endl;
  // set precision to 4 digits
  cout.precision(4);
  // minimum width
  cout.width(9);
  cout << 1.23456789 << endl;
  cout << 123.456789 << endl;
  // fill space by character #
  cout.fill('#');
  cout << 1.23 << endl;
  cout << "Good Bye!" << endl;
}
```

Output

```
octal=144
decimal=100
hex=64
octal=144
    1.235
123.5
1.23
Good Bye!
```

6.13 Exercises

6.1   Enter the following text lines into a file called cptest.c; then execute
      make cptest to create the cptest binary file. Run cptest. What output do
      you see on the terminal?

```
#include <stdlib.h>
#include <stream.h>

main()
{
  cout << "Introduction to C++ programming language\n";
  cout << "Course number 200\n";
}
```

6.2   Write a program that prints the following text on the standard output.
      a) C++ is a high level programming language.
      b) Object oriented applications can be written using C++.

6.3   List 10 C++ reserved keywords. What are the restrictions on the use of
      these variables?

6.4   What is the general form of a C++ program?

6.5   What is a class?

6.6   What is an object?

6.7   What is object encapsulation, polymorphism, and inheritance?

6.8   Write a program to implement a class person. The class should contain
      at least one member in each private, protected, and public part. From
      class person, create an object student which should contain student,
      name, ID, grade, and year. Print this information on standard output.

6.9   Can static data members be referred by the qualification to the class?

6.10 How are the const data members initialized? Write a program to initial-
      ize const data members i and j to the value of -1 and 49. Print this value
      on standard output.

6.11 Can a class member function access private, protected, or public data
      members of a class?

6.12 Write a program using class that has the data member function add(),
      which performs addition of all the integer data members and prints the

result on the terminal.

6.13   What are constructors and destructors? Do constructors have return types? Do destructors have arguments and return types?

6.14   What is a friend? What are some advantages and disadvantages of using friends?

6.15   Implement the member function add() from Exercise 6.12 as a friend function.

6.16   What are the differences between a class and a struct?

6.17   What is a derived class? Write a program containing a general-purpose class called shape. Create a derived class called circle with the member function area() to calculate the area of a circle.

6.18   Graphically illustrate the derived class member access inheritance from the base class.

6.19   What is the order of invocation of the constructor in a derived class? How about the destructor?

6.20   What is the general form of a derived class constructor?

6.21   Write a program with a general-purpose class called shape having the virtual member function area(). Create a derived class called rectangle with the member function area() that overrides base class functionality. Print the area of the rectangle.

6.22   What is an abstract class? What is a virtual constructor and destructor?

6.23   Convert the base class shape of Exercise 6.21 into an abstract class.

6.24   What is operator overloading? What operators cannot be overloaded?

6.25   Write a program containing one unary and binary overloaded operator function.

6.26   Implement a program with the overloaded ->* operator function.

6.27   What are the functions of the new and delete C++ operators? What is the difference between the operator new and the malloc() function?

6.28   What are the different conditions under which a given function can be overloaded?

6.29   What is a reference? How does it differ from a pointer? Write a program that swaps two values a and b only if a > b using references and pointers. Display these values on the terminal.

6.30 What is the syntax for function and class templates?

6.31 Implement a template version of the function hypot() with arguments base(b) and perpendicular (p) that returns hypotenuse (h). Calculate the value of the hypotenuse for the arguments of data type int, long, and float. Display these values on the terminal. *Hint*: Use h = sqrt($b^2 + p^2$).

6.32 Write a program that reads a line width of 80 characters from a file and prints it on the terminal.

Appendix

ASCII Character Set

Table A-1 Octal Equivalent of Each Character

000 nul	001 soh	002 stx	003 etx	004 eot	005 enq	006 ack	007 bel
010 bs	011 ht	012 nl	013 vt	014 np	015 cr	016 so	017 si
020 dle	021 dc1	022 dc2	023 dc3	024 dc4	025 nak	026 syn	027 etb
030 can	031 em	032 sub	033 esc	034 fs	035 gs	036 rs	037 us
040 sp	041 !	042 "	043 #	044 $	045 %	046 &	047 '
050 (	051)	052 *	053 +	054 ,	055 -	056 .	057 /
060 0	061 1	062 2	063 3	064 4	065 5	066 6	067 7
070 8	071 9	072 :	073 ;	074 <	075 =	076 >	077 ?
100 @	101 A	102 B	103 C	104 D	105 E	106 F	107 G
110 H	111 I	112 J	113 K	114 L	115 M	116 N	117 O
120 P	121 Q	122 R	123 S	124 T	125 U	126 V	127 W
130 X	131 Y	132 Z	133 [	134 \	135]	136 ^	137 _
140 '	141 a	142 b	143 c	144 d	145 e	146 f	147 g
150 h	151 i	152 j	153 k	154 l	155 m	156 n	157 o
160 p	161 q	162 r	163 s	164 t	165 u	166 v	167 w
170 x	171 y	172 z	173 {	174		175 }	176 ~	177 del

Table A-2 Hexadecimal Equivalent of Each Character

00 nul	01 soh	02 stx	03 etx	04 eot	05 enq	06 ack	07 bel
08 bs	09 ht	0a nl	0b vt	0c np	0d cr	0e so	0f si
10 dle	11 dc1	12 dc2	13 dc3	14 dc4	15 nak	16 syn	17 etb
18 can	19 em	1a sub	1b esc	1c fs	1d gs	1e rs	1f us
20 sp	21 !	22 "	23 #	24 $	25 %	26 &	27 '
28 (	29)	2a *	2b +	2c ,	2d -	2e .	2f /
30 0	31 1	32 2	33 3	34 4	35 5	36 6	37 7
38 8	39 9	3a :	3b ;	3c <	3d =	3e >	3f ?
40 @	41 A	42 B	43 C	44 D	45 E	46 F	47 G
48 H	49 I	4a J	4b K	4c L	4d M	4e N	4f O
50 P	51 Q	52 R	53 S	54 T	55 U	56 V	57 W
58 X	59 Y	5a Z	5b [	5c \	5d]	5e ^	5f _
60 '	61 a	62 b	63 c	64 d	65 e	66 f	67 g
68 h	69 i	6a j	6b k	6c l	6d m	6e n	6f o
70 p	71 q	72 r	73 s	74 t	75 u	76 v	77 w
78 x	79 y	7a z	7b {	7c		7d }	7e ~	7f del

Index